T0074587

Supervised Machine Learning for Text Analysis in R

Supervised Machine Learning for Text Analysis in R

Emil Hvitfeldt
Julia Silge

CRC Press

Taylor & Francis Group
Boca Raton London New York

CRC Press is an imprint of the
Taylor & Francis Group, an **informa** business
A CHAPMAN & HALL BOOK

First edition published 2022
by CRC Press
6000 Broken Sound Parkway NW, Suite 300, Boca Raton, FL 33487-2742

and by CRC Press
2 Park Square, Milton Park, Abingdon, Oxon, OX14 4RN

© 2022 Taylor & Francis Group, LLC

CRC Press is an imprint of Taylor & Francis Group, LLC

Reasonable efforts have been made to publish reliable data and information, but the author and publisher cannot assume responsibility for the validity of all materials or the consequences of their use. The authors and publishers have attempted to trace the copyright holders of all material reproduced in this publication and apologize to copyright holders if permission to publish in this form has not been obtained. If any copyright material has not been acknowledged please write and let us know so we may rectify in any future reprint.

Except as permitted under U.S. Copyright Law, no part of this book may be reprinted, reproduced, transmitted, or utilized in any form by any electronic, mechanical, or other means, now known or hereafter invented, including photocopying, microfilming, and recording, or in any information storage or retrieval system, without written permission from the publishers.

For permission to photocopy or use material electronically from this work, access www.copyright. com or contact the Copyright Clearance Center, Inc. (CCC), 222 Rosewood Drive, Danvers, MA 01923, 978-750-8400. For works that are not available on CCC please contact mpkbookspermissions@tandf.co.uk

Trademark notice: Product or corporate names may be trademarks or registered trademarks and are used only for identification and explanation without intent to infringe.

ISBN: 978-0-367-55418-7 (hbk)
ISBN: 978-0-367-55419-4 (pbk)
ISBN: 978-1-003-09345-9 (ebk)

DOI: 10.1201/9781003093459

Typeset in LMR10 font
by KnowledgeWorks Global Ltd.

In loving memory of my mother-in-law Lisa, who was the first soul to hear about and fully encourage the idea that eventually became this book —E.H.

For Grace, Violet, and Lewis, who (thanks to the pandemic and remote school) had a front row seat to most of my work on this book —J.S.

Contents

Preface   xiii

I Natural Language Features   1

1 Language and modeling   3
  1.1 Linguistics for text analysis   3
  1.2 A glimpse into one area: morphology   5
  1.3 Different languages   6
  1.4 Other ways text can vary   7
  1.5 Summary   8
    1.5.1 In this chapter, you learned: 8

2 Tokenization   9
  2.1 What is a token?   9
  2.2 Types of tokens 13
    2.2.1 Character tokens 16
    2.2.2 Word tokens 18
    2.2.3 Tokenizing by n-grams 19
    2.2.4 Lines, sentence, and paragraph tokens 22
  2.3 Where does tokenization break down? 25
  2.4 Building your own tokenizer 26
    2.4.1 Tokenize to characters, only keeping letters 27
    2.4.2 Allow for hyphenated words 29
    2.4.3 Wrapping it in a function 32
  2.5 Tokenization for non-Latin alphabets 33
  2.6 Tokenization benchmark 34
  2.7 Summary 35
    2.7.1 In this chapter, you learned: 35

3 Stop words   37
  3.1 Using premade stop word lists 38
    3.1.1 Stop word removal in R 41
  3.2 Creating your own stop words list 43
  3.3 All stop word lists are context-specific 48
  3.4 What happens when you remove stop words 49
  3.5 Stop words in languages other than English 50
  3.6 Summary 52

     3.6.1   In this chapter, you learned: 52

4 Stemming   **53**
  4.1   How to stem text in R   54
  4.2   Should you use stemming at all?   58
  4.3   Understand a stemming algorithm   61
  4.4   Handling punctuation when stemming   63
  4.5   Compare some stemming options   65
  4.6   Lemmatization and stemming   68
  4.7   Stemming and stop words   70
  4.8   Summary   71
     4.8.1   In this chapter, you learned: 72

5 Word Embeddings   **73**
  5.1   Motivating embeddings for sparse, high-dimensional data . .   73
  5.2   Understand word embeddings by finding them yourself . . .   77
  5.3   Exploring CFPB word embeddings   81
  5.4   Use pre-trained word embeddings   88
  5.5   Fairness and word embeddings   93
  5.6   Using word embeddings in the real world   95
  5.7   Summary   96
     5.7.1   In this chapter, you learned: 97

II   Machine Learning Methods   **99**

Overview   **101**

6 Regression   **105**
  6.1   A first regression model   106
     6.1.1   Building our first regression model   107
     6.1.2   Evaluation   112
  6.2   Compare to the null model   117
  6.3   Compare to a random forest model   119
  6.4   Case study: removing stop words   122
  6.5   Case study: varying n-grams   126
  6.6   Case study: lemmatization   129
  6.7   Case study: feature hashing   133
     6.7.1   Text normalization   137
  6.8   What evaluation metrics are appropriate?   139
  6.9   The full game: regression   142
     6.9.1   Preprocess the data   142
     6.9.2   Specify the model   143
     6.9.3   Tune the model   144
     6.9.4   Evaluate the modeling   146
  6.10 Summary   153
     6.10.1 In this chapter, you learned: 153

7 Classification **155**
  7.1 A first classification model 156
      7.1.1 Building our first classification model 158
      7.1.2 Evaluation 161
  7.2 Compare to the null model 166
  7.3 Compare to a lasso classification model 167
  7.4 Tuning lasso hyperparameters 170
  7.5 Case study: sparse encoding 179
  7.6 Two-class or multiclass? 183
  7.7 Case study: including non-text data 191
  7.8 Case study: data censoring 195
  7.9 Case study: custom features 201
      7.9.1 Detect credit cards 202
      7.9.2 Calculate percentage censoring 204
      7.9.3 Detect monetary amounts 205
  7.10 What evaluation metrics are appropriate? 206
  7.11 The full game: classification 208
      7.11.1 Feature selection 209
      7.11.2 Specify the model 210
      7.11.3 Evaluate the modeling 212
  7.12 Summary 220
      7.12.1 In this chapter, you learned: 221

III Deep Learning Methods **223**

Overview **225**

8 Dense neural networks **231**
  8.1 Kickstarter data 232
  8.2 A first deep learning model 237
      8.2.1 Preprocessing for deep learning 237
      8.2.2 One-hot sequence embedding of text 240
      8.2.3 Simple flattened dense network 244
      8.2.4 Evaluation 248
  8.3 Using bag-of-words features 253
  8.4 Using pre-trained word embeddings 257
  8.5 Cross-validation for deep learning models 263
  8.6 Compare and evaluate DNN models 267
  8.7 Limitations of deep learning 271
  8.8 Summary 272
      8.8.1 In this chapter, you learned: 272

9 Long short-term memory (LSTM) networks **273**
  9.1 A first LSTM model 273
      9.1.1 Building an LSTM 275
      9.1.2 Evaluation 279

9.2   Compare to a recurrent neural network 283
9.3   Case study: bidirectional LSTM 286
9.4   Case study: stacking LSTM layers 288
9.5   Case study: padding 289
9.6   Case study: training a regression model 292
9.7   Case study: vocabulary size 295
9.8   The full game: LSTM 297
    9.8.1   Preprocess the data 297
    9.8.2   Specify the model 298
9.9   Summary 301
    9.9.1   In this chapter, you learned: 302

10 Convolutional neural networks   **303**
10.1 What are CNNs? 303
    10.1.1 Kernel 304
    10.1.2 Kernel size 304
10.2 A first CNN model 305
10.3 Case study: adding more layers 309
10.4 Case study: byte pair encoding 317
10.5 Case study: explainability with LIME 324
10.6 Case study: hyperparameter search 330
10.7 Cross-validation for evaluation 334
10.8 The full game: CNN 337
    10.8.1 Preprocess the data 337
    10.8.2 Specify the model 338
10.9 Summary 341
    10.9.1 In this chapter, you learned: 342

IV   Conclusion   **343**

Text models in the real world   **345**

Appendix   **347**

A Regular expressions   **347**
A.1 Literal characters 347
    A.1.1 Meta characters 349
A.2 Full stop, the wildcard 349
A.3 Character classes 350
    A.3.1 Shorthand character classes 352
A.4 Quantifiers 353
A.5 Anchors 355
A.6 Additional resources 355

B Data   **357**
B.1 Hans Christian Andersen fairy tales 357

B.2 Opinions of the Supreme Court of the United States 358
B.3 Consumer Financial Protection Bureau (CFPB) complaints . 359
B.4 Kickstarter campaign blurbs 359

C Baseline linear classifier **361**
C.1 Read in the data 361
C.2 Split into test/train and create resampling folds 362
C.3 Recipe for data preprocessing 363
C.4 Lasso regularized classification model 363
C.5 A model workflow 364
C.6 Tune the workflow 366

References **369**

Index **379**

Preface

Modeling as a statistical practice can encompass a wide variety of activities. This book focuses on *supervised or predictive modeling for text*, using text data to make predictions about the world around us. We use the tidymodels[1] framework for modeling, a consistent and flexible collection of R packages developed to encourage good statistical practice.

Supervised machine learning using text data involves building a statistical model to estimate some output from input that includes language. The two types of models we train in this book are regression and classification. Think of regression models as predicting numeric or continuous outputs, such as predicting the year of a United States Supreme Court opinion from the text of that opinion. Think of classification models as predicting outputs that are discrete quantities or class labels, such as predicting whether a GitHub issue is about documentation or not from the text of the issue. Models like these can be used to make predictions for new observations, to understand what features or characteristics contribute to differences in the output, and more. We can evaluate our models using performance metrics to determine which are best, which are acceptable for our specific context, and even which are fair.

> Text data is important for many domains, from healthcare to marketing to the digital humanities, but specialized approaches are necessary to create features (predictors) for machine learning from language.

Natural language that we as speakers and/or writers use must be dramatically transformed to a machine-readable, numeric representation to be ready for computation. In this book, we explore typical text preprocessing steps from the ground up and consider the effects of these steps. We also show how to fluently use the **textrecipes** R package (Hvitfeldt 2020a) to prepare text data within a modeling pipeline.

---

[1] https://www.tidymodels.org/

Silge and Robinson (2017) provides a practical introduction to text mining with R using tidy data principles, based on the **tidytext** package. If you have already started on the path of gaining insight from your text data, a next step is using that text directly in predictive modeling. Text data contains within it latent information that can be used for insight, understanding, and better decision-making, and predictive modeling with text can bring that information and insight to light. If you have already explored how to analyze text as demonstrated in Silge and Robinson (2017), this book will move one step further to show you how to *learn and make predictions* from that text data with supervised models. If you are unfamiliar with this previous work, this book will still provide a robust introduction to how text can be represented in useful ways for modeling and a diverse set of supervised modeling approaches for text.

Outline

The book is divided into three sections. We make a (perhaps arbitrary) distinction between *machine learning methods* and *deep learning methods* by defining deep learning as any kind of multilayer neural network (LSTM, bi-LSTM, CNN) and machine learning as anything else (regularized regression, naive Bayes, SVM, random forest). We make this distinction both because these different methods use separate software packages and modeling infrastructure, and from a pragmatic point of view, it is helpful to split up the chapters this way.

- **Natural language features:** How do we transform text data into a representation useful for modeling? In these chapters, we explore the most common preprocessing steps for text, when they are helpful, and when they are not.

- **Machine learning methods:** We investigate the power of some of the simpler and more lightweight models in our toolbox.

- **Deep learning methods:** Given more time and resources, we see what is possible once we turn to neural networks.

Some of the topics in the second and third sections overlap as they provide different approaches to the same tasks.

Throughout the book, we will demonstrate with examples and build models using a selection of text data sets. A description of these data sets can be found in Appendix B.

We use three kinds of info boxes throughout the book to invite attention to notes and other ideas.

Some boxes call out warnings or possible problems to watch out for.

Boxes marked with hexagons highlight information about specific R packages and how they are used. We use **bold** for the names of R packages.

Topics this book will not cover

This book serves as a thorough introduction to prediction and modeling with text, along with detailed practical examples, but there are many areas of natural language processing we do not cover. The *CRAN Task View on Natural Language Processing*[2] provides details on other ways to use R for computational linguistics. Specific topics we do not cover include:

- **Reading text data into memory:** Text data may come to a data practitioner in any of a long list of heterogeneous formats. Text data exists in PDFs, databases, plain text files (single or multiple for a given project), websites, APIs, literal paper, and more. The skills needed to access and sometimes wrangle text data sets so that they are in memory and ready for analysis are so varied and extensive that we cannot hope to cover them in this book. We point readers to R packages such as **readr** (Wickham and Hester 2020), **pdftools** (Ooms 2020a), and **httr** (Wickham 2020), which we have found helpful in these tasks.

---

[2] https://cran.r-project.org/web/views/NaturalLanguageProcessing.html

- **Unsupervised machine learning for text:** Silge and Robinson (2017) provide an introduction to one method of unsupervised text modeling, and Chapter 5 does dive deep into word embeddings, which learn from the latent structure in text data. However, many more unsupervised machine learning algorithms can be used for the goal of learning about the structure or distribution of text data when there are no outcome or output variables to predict.

- **Text generation:** The deep learning model architectures we discuss in Chapters 8, 9, and 10 can be used to generate new text, as well as to model existing text. Chollet and Allaire (2018) provide details on how to use neural network architectures and training data for text generation.

- **Speech processing:** Models that detect words in audio recordings of speech are typically based on many of the principles outlined in this book, but the training data is *audio* rather than written text. R users can access pre-trained speech-to-text models via large cloud providers, such as Google Cloud's Speech-to-Text API accessible in R through the **google-LanguageR** package (Edmondson 2020).

- **Machine translation:** Machine translation of text between languages, based on either older statistical methods or newer neural network methods, is a complex, involved topic. Today, the most successful and well-known implementations of machine translation are proprietary, because large tech companies have access to both the right expertise and enough data in multiple languages to train successful models for general machine translation. Google is one such example, and Google Cloud's Translation API is again available in R through the **googleLanguageR** package.

Who is this book for?

This book is designed to provide practical guidance and directly applicable knowledge for data scientists and analysts who want to integrate text into their modeling pipelines.

We assume that the reader is somewhat familiar with R, predictive modeling concepts for non-text data, and the **tidyverse**[3] family of packages (Wickham et al. 2019). For users who don't have this background with tidyverse code, we recommend *R for Data Science*[4] (Wickham and Grolemund 2017). Helpful

---

[3] https://www.tidyverse.org/
[4] http://r4ds.had.co.nz/

resources for getting started with modeling and machine learning include a free interactive course[5] developed by one of the authors (JS) and *Hands-On Machine Learning with R*[6] (Boehmke and Greenwell 2019), as well as *An Introduction to Statistical Learning*[7] (James et al. 2013).

We don't assume an extensive background in text analysis, but *Text Mining with R*[8] (Silge and Robinson 2017), by one of the authors (JS) and David Robinson, provides helpful skills in exploratory data analysis for text that will promote successful text modeling. This book is more advanced than *Text Mining with R* and will help practitioners use their text data in ways not covered in that book.

Acknowledgments

We are so thankful for the contributions, help, and perspectives of people who have supported us in this project. There are several we would like to thank in particular.

We would like to thank Max Kuhn and Davis Vaughan for their investment in the **tidymodels** packages, David Robinson for his collaboration on the **tidytext** package, and Yihui Xie for his work on **knitr**, **bookdown**, and the R Markdown ecosystem. Thank you to Desirée De Leon for the site design of the online work and to Sarah Lin for the expert creation of the published work's index. We would also like to thank Carol Haney, Kasia Kulma, David Mimno, Kanishka Misra, and an additional anonymous technical reviewer for their detailed, insightful feedback that substantively improved this book, as well as our editor John Kimmel for his perspective and guidance during the process of writing and publishing.

This book was written in the open, and multiple people contributed via pull requests or issues. Special thanks goes to the four people who contributed via GitHub pull requests (in alphabetical order by username): @fellennert, Riva Quiroga (@rivaquiroga), Darrin Speegle (@speegled), Tanner Stauss (@tmstauss).

Note box icons by Smashicons from flaticon.com.

---

[5] https://supervised-ml-course.netlify.com/

[6] https://bradleyboehmke.github.io/HOML/

[7] http://faculty.marshall.usc.edu/gareth-james/ISL/

[8] https://www.tidytextmining.com/

Colophon

This book was written in RStudio[9] using **bookdown**[10]. The website[11] is hosted via GitHub Pages[12], and the complete source is available on GitHub[13]. We generated all plots in this book using **ggplot2**[14] and its light theme (`theme_light()`). The `autoplot()` method for `conf_mat()`[15] has been modified slightly to allow colors; modified code can be found online[16].

This version of the book was built with R version 4.1.0 (2021-05-18) and the following packages:

package	version	source
bench	1.1.1	CRAN (R 4.1.0)
bookdown	0.23	CRAN (R 4.1.0)
broom	0.7.9	CRAN (R 4.1.0)
corpus	0.10.2	CRAN (R 4.1.0)
dials	0.0.9	CRAN (R 4.1.0)
discrim	0.1.1	CRAN (R 4.1.0)
doParallel	1.0.16	CRAN (R 4.1.0)
glmnet	4.1-1	CRAN (R 4.1.0)
gt	0.3.1	CRAN (R 4.1.0)
hcandersenr	0.2.0	CRAN (R 4.1.0)
htmltools	0.5.1.1	CRAN (R 4.1.0)
htmlwidgets	1.5.3	CRAN (R 4.1.0)
hunspell	3.0.1	CRAN (R 4.1.0)
irlba	2.3.3	CRAN (R 4.1.0)
jiebaR	0.11	CRAN (R 4.1.0)
jsonlite	1.7.2	CRAN (R 4.1.0)
kableExtra	1.3.4	CRAN (R 4.1.0)
keras	2.4.0	CRAN (R 4.1.0)
klaR	0.6-15	CRAN (R 4.1.0)
LiblineaR	2.10-12	CRAN (R 4.1.0)
lime	0.5.2	CRAN (R 4.1.0)
lobstr	1.1.1	CRAN (R 4.1.0)
naivebayes	0.9.7	CRAN (R 4.1.0)

---

[9] https://www.rstudio.com/ide/
[10] https://bookdown.org
[11] https://smltar.com
[12] https://pages.github.com
[13] https://github.com/EmilHvitfeldt/smltar
[14] https://ggplot2.tidyverse.org
[15] https://yardstick.tidymodels.org/reference/conf_mat.html
[16] https://github.com/EmilHvitfeldt/smltar/blob/master/_common.R

package	version	source
parsnip	0.1.6	CRAN (R 4.1.0)
prismatic	1.0.0	CRAN (R 4.1.0)
quanteda	3.1.0	CRAN (R 4.1.0)
ranger	0.13.1	CRAN (R 4.1.0)
recipes	0.1.16	CRAN (R 4.1.0)
remotes	2.4.0	CRAN (R 4.1.0)
reticulate	1.20	CRAN (R 4.1.0)
rsample	0.1.0	CRAN (R 4.1.0)
rsparse	0.4.0	CRAN (R 4.1.0)
scico	1.2.0	CRAN (R 4.1.0)
scotus	1.0.0	Github (EmilHvitfeldt/scotus)
servr	0.23	CRAN (R 4.1.0)
sessioninfo	1.1.1	CRAN (R 4.1.0)
slider	0.2.2	CRAN (R 4.1.0)
SnowballC	0.7.0	CRAN (R 4.1.0)
spacyr	1.2.1	CRAN (R 4.1.0)
stopwords	2.2	CRAN (R 4.1.0)
styler	1.5.1	CRAN (R 4.1.0)
text2vec	0.6	CRAN (R 4.1.0)
textdata	0.4.1	CRAN (R 4.1.0)
textfeatures	0.3.3	CRAN (R 4.1.0)
textrecipes	0.4.1	CRAN (R 4.1.0)
tfruns	1.5.0	CRAN (R 4.1.0)
themis	0.1.4	CRAN (R 4.1.0)
tidymodels	0.1.3	CRAN (R 4.1.0)
tidytext	0.3.1	CRAN (R 4.1.0)
tidyverse	1.3.1	CRAN (R 4.1.0)
tokenizers	0.2.1	CRAN (R 4.1.0)
tokenizers.bpe	0.1.0	CRAN (R 4.1.0)
tufte	0.10	CRAN (R 4.1.0)
tune	0.1.5	CRAN (R 4.1.0)
UpSetR	1.4.0	CRAN (R 4.1.0)
vip	0.3.2	CRAN (R 4.1.0)
widyr	0.1.4	CRAN (R 4.1.0)
workflows	0.2.3	CRAN (R 4.1.0)
yardstick	0.0.8	CRAN (R 4.1.0)

Part I

Natural Language Features

1

Language and modeling

Machine learning and deep learning models for text are executed by computers, but they are designed and created by human beings using language generated by human beings. As natural language processing (NLP) practitioners, we bring our assumptions about what language is and how language works into the task of creating modeling features from natural language and using those features as inputs to statistical models. This is true *even when* we don't think about how language works very deeply or when our understanding is unsophisticated or inaccurate; speaking a language is not the same as having an explicit knowledge of how that language works. We can improve our machine learning models for text by heightening that knowledge.

Throughout the course of this book, we will discuss creating predictors or features from text data, fitting statistical models to those features, and how these tasks are related to language. Data scientists involved in the everyday work of text analysis and text modeling typically don't have formal training in how language works, but there is an entire field focused on exactly that, *linguistics*.

1.1 Linguistics for text analysis

Briscoe (2013) provides helpful introductions to what linguistics is and how it intersects with the practical computational field of natural language processing. The broad field of linguistics includes subfields focusing on different aspects of language, which are somewhat hierarchical, as shown in Table 1.1.

These fields each study a different level at which language exhibits organization. When we build supervised machine learning models for text data, we use these levels of organization to create *natural language features*, i.e., predictors or inputs for our models. These features often depend on the morphological characteristics of language, such as when text is broken into sequences of characters for a recurrent neural network deep learning model. Sometimes these features depend on the syntactic characteristics of language, such as when models use part-of-speech information. These roughly hierarchical levels of

TABLE 1.1: Some subfields of linguistics, moving from smaller structures to broader structures

Linguistics subfield	What does it focus on?
Phonetics	Sounds that people use in language
Phonology	Systems of sounds in particular languages
Morphology	How words are formed
Syntax	How sentences are formed from words
Semantics	What sentences mean
Pragmatics	How language is used in context

organization are key to the process of transforming unstructured language to a mathematical representation that can be used in modeling.

At the same time, this organization and the rules of language can be ambiguous; our ability to create text features for machine learning is constrained by the very nature of language. Beatrice Santorini, a linguist at the University of Pennsylvania, compiles examples of linguistic ambiguity from news headlines[1]:

- Include Your Children When Baking Cookies

- March Planned For Next August

- Enraged Cow Injures Farmer with Ax

- Wives Kill Most Spouses In Chicago

If you don't have knowledge about what linguists study and what they know about language, these news headlines are just hilarious. To linguists, these are hilarious because they exhibit certain kinds of semantic ambiguity.

Notice also that the first two subfields on this list are about sounds, i.e., speech. Most linguists view speech as primary, and writing down language as text as a technological step.

Remember that some language is signed, not spoken, so the description laid out here is itself limited.

---

[1] https://www.ling.upenn.edu/~beatrice/humor/headlines.html

Written text is typically less creative and further from the primary language than we would wish. This points out how fundamentally limited modeling from written text is. Imagine that the abstract language data we want exists in some high-dimensional latent space; we would like to extract that information using the text somehow, but it just isn't completely possible. Any features we create or model we build are inherently limited.

1.2 A glimpse into one area: morphology

How can a deeper knowledge of how language works inform text modeling? Let's focus on **morphology**, the study of words' internal structures and how they are formed, to illustrate this. Words are medium to small in length in English; English has a moderately low ratio of morphemes (the smallest unit of language with meaning) to words while other languages like Turkish and Russian have a higher ratio of morphemes to words (Bender 2013). Related to this, languages can be either more analytic (like Mandarin or modern English, breaking up concepts into separate words) or synthetic (like Hungarian or Swahili, combining concepts into one word).

Morphology focuses on how morphemes such as prefixes, suffixes, and root words come together to form words. Some languages, like Danish, use many compound words. Danish words such as "brandbil" (fire truck), "politibil" (police car), and "lastbil" (truck) all contain the morpheme "bil" (car) and start with prefixes denoting the type of car. Because of these compound words, some nouns seem more descriptive than their English counterpart; "vaskebjørn" (raccoon) splits into the morphemes "vaske" and "bjørn," literally meaning "washing bear"[2]. When working with Danish and other languages with compound words, such as German, compound splitting to extract more information can be beneficial (**Sugisaki and Tuggener 2018**). However, even the very question of what a word is turns out to be difficult, and not only for languages other than English. Compound words in English like "real estate" and "dining room" represent one concept but contain whitespace.

The morphological characteristics of a text data set are deeply connected to preprocessing steps like tokenization (Chapter 2), removing stop words (Chapter 3), and even stemming (Chapter 4). These preprocessing steps for creating natural language features, in turn, can have significant effects on model predictions or interpretation.

---

[2]The English word "raccoon" derives from an Algonquin word meaning, "scratches with his hands!"

1.3 Different languages

We believe that most of the readers of this book are probably native English speakers, and certainly most of the text used in training machine learning models is English. However, English is by no means a dominant language globally, especially as a native or first language. As an example close to home for us, of the two authors of this book, one is a native English speaker and one is not. According to the comprehensive and detailed Ethnologue project[3], less than 20% of the world's population speaks English at all.

Bender (2011) provides guidance to computational linguists building models for text, for any language. One specific point she makes is to name the language being studied.

> **Do** state the name of the language that is being studied, even if it's English. Acknowledging that we are working on a particular language foregrounds the possibility that the techniques may in fact be language-specific. Conversely, neglecting to state that the particular data used were in, say, English, gives [a] false veneer of language-independence to the work.

This idea is simple (acknowledge that the models we build are typically language-specific) but the #BenderRule[4] has led to increased awareness of the limitations of the current state of this field. Our book is not geared toward academic NLP researchers developing new methods, but toward data scientists and analysts working with everyday data sets; this issue is relevant even for us. Name the languages used in training models (Bender 2019), and think through what that means for their generalizability. We will practice what we preach and tell you that most of the text used for modeling in this book is English, with some text in Danish and a few other languages.

---

[3] https://www.ethnologue.com/language/eng

[4] https://twitter.com/search?q=%23BenderRule

1.4 Other ways text can vary

The concept of differences in language is relevant for modeling beyond only the broadest language level (for example, English vs. Danish vs. German vs. Farsi). Language from a specific dialect often cannot be handled well with a model trained on data from the same language but not inclusive of that dialect. One dialect used in the United States is African American Vernacular English (AAVE). Models trained to detect toxic or hate speech are more likely to falsely identify AAVE as hate speech (Sap et al. 2019); this is deeply troubling not only because the model is less accurate than it should be, but because it amplifies harm against an already marginalized group.

Language is also changing over time. This is a known characteristic of language; if you notice the evolution of your own language, don't be depressed or angry, because it means that people are using it! Teenage girls are especially effective at language innovation and have been for centuries (McCulloch 2015); innovations spread from groups such as young women to other parts of society. This is another difference that impacts modeling.

Differences in language relevant for models also include the use of slang, and even the context or medium of that text.

Consider two bodies of text, both mostly standard written English, but one made up of tweets and one made up of medical documents. If an NLP practitioner trains a model on the data set of tweets to predict some characteristics of the text, it is very possible (in fact, likely, in our experience) that the model will perform poorly if applied to the data set of medical documents[5]. Like machine learning in general, text modeling is exquisitely sensitive to the data used for training. This is why we are somewhat skeptical of AI products such as sentiment analysis APIs, not because they *never* work well, but because they work well only when the text you need to predict from is a good match to the text such a product was trained on.

---

[5]Practitioners have built specialized computational resources for medical text (Johnson 1999).

1.5   Summary

Linguistics is the study of how language works, and while we don't believe
real-world NLP practitioners must be experts in linguistics, learning from such
domain experts can improve both the accuracy of our models and our understanding of why they do (or don't!) perform well. Predictive models for text
reflect the characteristics of their training data, so differences in language over
time, between dialects, and in various cultural contexts can prevent a model
trained on one data set from being appropriate for application in another. A
large amount of the text modeling literature focuses on English, but English
is not a dominant language around the world.

1.5.1   In this chapter, you learned:

- that areas of linguistics focus on topics from sounds to how language is
  used

- how a topic like morphology is connected to text modeling steps

- to identify the language you are modeling, even if it is English

- about many ways language can vary and how this can impact model results

2

Tokenization

To build features for supervised machine learning from natural language, we need some way of representing raw text as numbers so we can perform computation on them. Typically, one of the first steps in this transformation from natural language to feature, or any of kind of text analysis, is *tokenization*. Knowing what tokenization and tokens are, along with the related concept of an n-gram, is important for almost any natural language processing task.

2.1 What is a token?

In R, text is typically represented with the *character* data type, similar to strings in other languages. Let's explore text from fairy tales written by Hans Christian Andersen, available in the **hcandersenr** package (Hvitfeldt 2019a). This package stores text as lines such as those you would read in a book; this is just one way that you may find text data in the wild and does allow us to more easily read the text when doing analysis. If we look at the first paragraph of one story titled "The Fir-Tree," we find the text of the story is in a character vector: a series of letters, spaces, and punctuation stored as a vector.

> The **tidyverse** is a collection of packages for data manipulation, exploration, and visualization.

```
library(tokenizers)
library(tidyverse)
library(tidytext)
library(hcandersenr)
```

```
the_fir_tree <- hcandersen_en %>%
  filter(book == "The fir tree") %>%
  pull(text)

head(the_fir_tree, 9)
```

```
#> [1] "Far down in the forest, where the warm sun and the fresh air made a
sweet"
#> [2] "resting-place, grew a pretty little fir-tree; and yet it was not happy,
it"
#> [3] "wished so much to be tall like its companions— the pines and firs which
grew"
#> [4] "around it. The sun shone, and the soft air fluttered its leaves, and
the"
#> [5] "little peasant children passed by, prattling merrily, but the fir-tree
heeded"
#> [6] "them not. Sometimes the children would bring a large basket of
raspberries or"
#> [7] "strawberries, wreathed on a straw, and seat themselves near the
fir-tree, and"
#> [8] "say, \"Is it not a pretty little tree?\" which made it feel more
unhappy than"
#> [9] "before."
```

The first nine lines stores the first paragraph of the story, each line consisting of a series of character symbols. These elements don't contain any metadata or information to tell us which characters are words and which aren't. Identifying these kinds of boundaries between words is where the process of tokenization comes in.

In tokenization, we take an input (a string) and a token type (a meaningful unit of text, such as a word) and split the input into pieces (tokens) that correspond to the type (Manning, Raghavan, and Schütze 2008). Figure 2.1 outlines this process.

Most commonly, the meaningful unit or type of token that we want to split text into units of is a **word**. However, it is difficult to clearly define what a word is, for many or even most languages. Many languages, such as Chinese, do not use white space between words at all. Even languages that do use white space, including English, often have particular examples that are ambiguous (Bender 2013). Romance languages like Italian and French use pronouns and negation words that may better be considered prefixes with a space, and English contractions like "didn't" may more accurately be considered two words with no space.

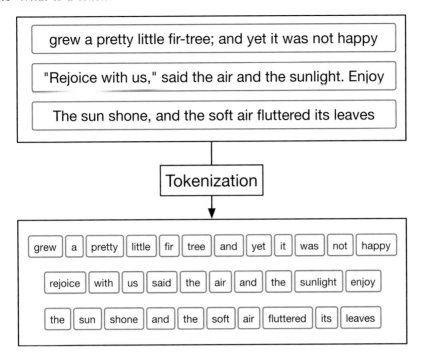

FIGURE 2.1: A black box representation of a tokenizer. The text of these three example text fragments has been converted to lowercase and punctuation has been removed before the text is split.

To understand the process of tokenization, let's start with a overly simple definition for a word: any selection of alphanumeric (letters and numbers) symbols. Let's use some regular expressions (or regex for short, see Appendix A) with `strsplit()` to split the first two lines of "The Fir-Tree" by any characters that are not alphanumeric.

```
strsplit(the_fir_tree[1:2], "[^a-zA-Z0-9]+")
```

```
#> [[1]]
#>  [1] "Far"     "down"    "in"      "the"     "forest" "where"  "the"     "warm"
#>  [9] "sun"     "and"     "the"     "fresh"  "air"     "made"   "a"       "sweet"
#>
#> [[2]]
#>  [1] "resting" "place"   "grew"    "a"       "pretty" "little" "fir"
#>  [8] "tree"    "and"     "yet"     "it"      "was"     "not"    "happy"
#> [15] "it"
```

At first sight, this result looks pretty decent. However, we have lost all punctuation, which may or may not be helpful for our modeling goal, and the hero of this story (`"fir-tree"`) was split in half. Already it is clear that tokenization is going to be quite complicated. Luckily for us, a lot of work has been invested in this process, and typically it is best to use these existing tools. For example, **tokenizers** (Mullen et al. 2018) and **spaCy** (Honnibal et al. 2020) implement fast, consistent tokenizers we can use. Let's demonstrate with the **tokenizers** package.

```
library(tokenizers)
tokenize_words(the_fir_tree[1:2])
```

```
#> [[1]]
#>  [1] "far"     "down"   "in"     "the"    "forest" "where"  "the"    "warm"
#>  [9] "sun"     "and"    "the"    "fresh"  "air"    "made"   "a"      "sweet"
#>
#> [[2]]
#>  [1] "resting" "place"  "grew"   "a"      "pretty" "little" "fir"
#>  [8] "tree"    "and"    "yet"    "it"     "was"    "not"    "happy"
#> [15] "it"
```

We see sensible single-word results here; the `tokenize_words()` function uses the **stringi** package (Gagolewski 2020) and C++ under the hood, making it very fast. Word-level tokenization is done by finding word boundaries according to the specification from the International Components for Unicode (ICU). How does this word boundary algorithm[1] work? It can be outlined as follows:

- Break at the start and end of text, unless the text is empty.

- Do not break within CRLF (new line characters).

- Otherwise, break before and after new lines (including CR and LF).

- Do not break within emoji zwj sequences.

- Keep horizontal whitespace together.

- Ignore Format and Extend characters, except after sot, CR, LF, and new lines.

- Do not break between most letters.

---

[1] https://www.unicode.org/reports/tr29/tr29-35.html#Default_Word_Boundaries

- Do not break letters across certain punctuation.

- Do not break within sequences of digits, or digits adjacent to letters ("3a," or "A3").

- Do not break within sequences, such as "3.2" or "3,456.789."

- Do not break between Katakana.

- Do not break from extenders.

- Do not break within emoji flag sequences.

- Otherwise, break everywhere (including around ideographs).

While we might not understand what each and every step in this algorithm is doing, we can appreciate that it is many times more sophisticated than our initial approach of splitting on non-alphanumeric characters. In most of this book, we will use the **tokenizers** package as a baseline tokenizer for reference. Your choice of tokenizer will influence your results, so don't be afraid to experiment with different tokenizers or, if necessary, to write your own to fit your problem.

2.2 Types of tokens

Thinking of a token as a word is a useful way to start understanding tokenization, even if it is hard to implement concretely in software. We can generalize the idea of a token beyond only a single word to other units of text. We can tokenize text at a variety of units including:

- characters,

- words,

- sentences,

- lines,

- paragraphs, and

- n-grams

In the following sections, we will explore how to tokenize text using the **tokenizers** package. These functions take a character vector as the input and return lists of character vectors as output. This same tokenization can also be done using the **tidytext** (Silge and Robinson 2016) package, for workflows using tidy data principles where the input and output are both in a dataframe.

```
sample_vector <- c("Far down in the forest",
                   "grew a pretty little fir-tree")
sample_tibble <- tibble(text = sample_vector)
```

 The **tokenizers** package offers fast, consistent tokenization in R for tokens such as words, letters, n-grams, lines, paragraphs, and more.

The tokenization achieved by using `tokenize_words()` on `sample_vector`:

```
tokenize_words(sample_vector)
```

```
#> [[1]]
#> [1] "far"    "down"    "in"    "the"    "forest"
#>
#> [[2]]
#> [1] "grew"    "a"      "pretty" "little" "fir"    "tree"
```

will yield the same results as using `unnest_tokens()` on `sample_tibble`; the only difference is the data structure, and thus how we might use the result moving forward in our analysis.

```
sample_tibble %>%
  unnest_tokens(word, text, token = "words")
```

```
#> # A tibble: 11 x 1
#>     word
#>     <chr>
#>  1 far
#>  2 down
#>  3 in
#>  4 the
#>  5 forest
#>  6 grew
#>  7 a
#>  8 pretty
#>  9 little
#> 10 fir
#> 11 tree
```

The **tidytext** package provides functions to transform text to and from
tidy formats, allowing us to work seamlessly with other **tidyverse** tools.

Arguments used in `tokenize_words()` can be passed through `unnest_tokens()` using the "the dots"[2], ...

```
sample_tibble %>%
  unnest_tokens(word, text, token = "words", strip_punct = FALSE)
```

```
#> # A tibble: 12 x 1
#>     word
#>     <chr>
#>  1 far
#>  2 down
#>  3 in
#>  4 the
#>  5 forest
#>  6 grew
```

---

[2] https://adv-r.hadley.nz/functions.html#fun-dot-dot-dot

```
#>  7 a
#>  8 pretty
#>  9 little
#> 10 fir
#> 11 -
#> 12 tree
```

2.2.1   Character tokens

Perhaps the simplest tokenization is character tokenization, which splits texts into characters. Let's use `tokenize_characters()` with its default parameters; this function has arguments to convert to lowercase and to strip all non-alphanumeric characters. These defaults will reduce the number of different tokens that are returned. The `tokenize_*()` functions by default return a list of character vectors, one character vector for each string in the input.

```
tft_token_characters <- tokenize_characters(x = the_fir_tree,
                                             lowercase = TRUE,
                                             strip_non_alphanum = TRUE,
                                             simplify = FALSE)
```

What do we see if we take a look?

```
head(tft_token_characters) %>%
  glimpse()
```

```
#> List of 6
#>  $ : chr [1:57] "f" "a" "r" "d" ...
#>  $ : chr [1:57] "r" "e" "s" "t" ...
#>  $ : chr [1:61] "w" "i" "s" "h" ...
#>  $ : chr [1:56] "a" "r" "o" "u" ...
#>  $ : chr [1:64] "l" "i" "t" "t" ...
#>  $ : chr [1:64] "t" "h" "e" "m" ...
```

We don't have to stick with the defaults. We can keep the punctuation and spaces by setting `strip_non_alphanum = FALSE`, and now we see that spaces and punctuation are included in the results too.

```
tokenize_characters(x = the_fir_tree,
                    strip_non_alphanum = FALSE) %>%
  head() %>%
  glimpse()
```

```
#> List of 6
#>  $ : chr [1:73] "f" "a" "r" " " ...
#>  $ : chr [1:74] "r" "e" "s" "t" ...
#>  $ : chr [1:76] "w" "i" "s" "h" ...
#>  $ : chr [1:72] "a" "r" "o" "u" ...
#>  $ : chr [1:77] "l" "i" "t" "t" ...
#>  $ : chr [1:77] "t" "h" "e" "m" ...
```

The results have more elements because the spaces and punctuation have not been removed.

Depending on the format you have your text data in, it might contain ligatures. Ligatures are when multiple graphemes or letters are combined as a single character The graphemes "f" and "l" are combined into "fl," or "f" and "f" into "ff." When we apply normal tokenization rules the ligatures will not be split up.

```
tokenize_characters("flowers")
```

```
#> [[1]]
#> [1] "fl" "o" "w" "e" "r" "s"
```

We might want to have these ligatures separated back into separate characters, but first, we need to consider a couple of things. First, we need to consider if the presence of ligatures is a meaningful feature to the question we are trying to answer. Second, there are two main types of ligatures: stylistic and functional. Stylistic ligatures are when two characters are combined because the spacing between the characters has been deemed unpleasant. Functional ligatures like the German Eszett (also called the scharfes S, meaning sharp s) ß, is an official letter of the German alphabet. It is described as a long S and Z and historically has never gotten an uppercase character. This has led the typesetters to use SZ or SS as a replacement when writing a word in uppercase. Additionally, ß is omitted entirely in German writing in Switzerland and is replaced with ss. Other examples include the "W" in the Latin alphabet (two "v" or two "u" joined together), and æ, ø, and å in the Nordic languages. Some place names for historical reasons use the old spelling "aa" instead of å. In Section 6.7.1 we will discuss text normalization approaches to deal with ligatures.

2.2.2   Word tokens

Tokenizing at the word level is perhaps the most common and widely used tokenization. We started our discussion in this chapter with this kind of tokenization, and as we described before, this is the procedure of splitting text into words. To do this, let's use the `tokenize_words()` function.

```
tft_token_words <- tokenize_words(x = the_fir_tree,
                                  lowercase = TRUE,
                                  stopwords = NULL,
                                  strip_punct = TRUE,
                                  strip_numeric = FALSE)
```

The results show us the input text split into individual words.

```
head(tft_token_words) %>%
  glimpse()
```

```
#> List of 6
#>  $ : chr [1:16] "far" "down" "in" "the" ...
#>  $ : chr [1:15] "resting" "place" "grew" "a" ...
#>  $ : chr [1:15] "wished" "so" "much" "to" ...
#>  $ : chr [1:14] "around" "it" "the" "sun" ...
#>  $ : chr [1:12] "little" "peasant" "children" "passed" ...
#>  $ : chr [1:13] "them" "not" "sometimes" "the" ...
```

We have already seen `lowercase = TRUE`, and `strip_punct = TRUE` and `strip_numeric = FALSE` control whether we remove punctuation and numeric characters, respectively. We also have `stopwords = NULL`, which we will talk about in more depth in Chapter 3.

Let's create a tibble with two fairy tales, "The Fir-Tree" and "The Little Mermaid." Then we can use `unnest_tokens()` together with some **dplyr** verbs to find the most commonly used words in each.

```
hcandersen_en %>%
  filter(book %in% c("The fir tree", "The little mermaid")) %>%
  unnest_tokens(word, text) %>%
  count(book, word) %>%
  group_by(book) %>%
  arrange(desc(n)) %>%
  slice(1:5)
```

```
#> # A tibble: 10 x 3
#> # Groups:   book [2]
#>    book                word      n
#>    <chr>               <chr> <int>
#>  1 The fir tree        the     278
#>  2 The fir tree        and     161
#>  3 The fir tree        tree     76
#>  4 The fir tree        it       66
#>  5 The fir tree        a        56
#>  6 The little mermaid  the     817
#>  7 The little mermaid  and     398
#>  8 The little mermaid  of      252
#>  9 The little mermaid  she     240
#> 10 The little mermaid  to      199
```

The five most common words in each fairy tale are fairly uninformative, with the exception being "tree" in the "The Fir-Tree."

These uninformative words are called **stop words** and will be explored in-depth in Chapter 3.

2.2.3   Tokenizing by n-grams

An n-gram (sometimes written "ngram") is a term in linguistics for a contiguous sequence of n items from a given sequence of text or speech. The item can be phonemes, syllables, letters, or words depending on the application, but when most people talk about n-grams, they mean a group of n words. In this book, we will use n-gram to denote word n-grams unless otherwise stated.

We use Latin prefixes so that a 1-gram is called a unigram, a 2-gram is called a bigram, a 3-gram called a trigram, and so on.

Some example n-grams are:

- **unigram:** "Hello," "day," "my," "little"

- **bigram:** "fir tree," "fresh air," "to be," "Robin Hood"

- **trigram:** "You and I," "please let go," "no time like," "the little mermaid"

The benefit of using n-grams compared to words is that n-grams capture word order that would otherwise be lost. Similarly, when we use character n-grams, we can model the beginning and end of words, because a space will be located at the end of an n-gram for the end of a word and at the beginning of an n-gram of the beginning of a word.

To split text into word n-grams, we can use the function tokenize_ngrams(). It has a few more arguments, so let's go over them one by one.

```
tft_token_ngram <- tokenize_ngrams(x = the_fir_tree,
                                   lowercase = TRUE,
                                   n = 3L,
                                   n_min = 3L,
                                   stopwords = character(),
                                   ngram_delim = " ",
                                   simplify = FALSE)
```

We have seen the arguments lowercase, stopwords, and simplify before; they work the same as for the other tokenizers. We also have n, the argument to determine which degree of n-gram to return. Using n = 1 returns unigrams, n = 2 bigrams, n = 3 gives trigrams, and so on. Related to n is the n_min argument, which specifies the minimum number of n-grams to include. By default both n and n_min are set to 3 making tokenize_ngrams() return only trigrams. By setting n = 3 and n_min = 1, we will get all unigrams, bigrams, and trigrams of a text. Lastly, we have the ngram_delim argument, which specifies the separator between words in the n-grams; notice that this defaults to a space.

Let's look at the result of n-gram tokenization for the first line of "The Fir-Tree."

```
tft_token_ngram[[1]]
```

```
#>  [1] "far down in"       "down in the"        "in the forest"      "the forest where"
#>  [5] "forest where the"  "where the warm"     "the warm sun"       "warm sun and"
#>  [9] "sun and the"       "and the fresh"      "the fresh air"      "fresh air made"
#> [13] "air made a"        "made a sweet"
```

Notice how the words in the trigrams overlap so that the word "down" appears in the middle of the first trigram and beginning of the second trigram. N-gram tokenization slides along the text to create overlapping sets of tokens.

It is important to choose the right value for n when using n-grams for the question we want to answer. Using unigrams is faster and more efficient, but we don't capture information about word order. Using a higher value for n keeps more information, but the vector space of tokens increases dramatically, corresponding to a reduction in token counts. A sensible starting point in most cases is three. However, if you don't have a large vocabulary in your data set, consider starting at two instead of three and experimenting from there. Figure 2.2 demonstrates how token frequency starts to decrease dramatically for trigrams and higher-order n-grams.

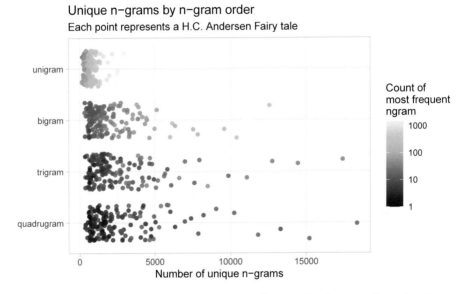

FIGURE 2.2: Using longer n-grams results in a higher number of unique tokens with fewer counts. Note that the color maps to counts on a logarithmic scale.

We are not limited to use only one degree of n-grams. We can, for example, combine unigrams and bigrams in an analysis or model. Getting multiple degrees of n-grams is a little different depending on what package you are using; using `tokenize_ngrams()` you can specify n and n_min.

```
tft_token_ngram <- tokenize_ngrams(x = the_fir_tree,
                                   n = 2L,
                                   n_min = 1L)
tft_token_ngram[[1]]
```

```
#>  [1] "far"          "far down"      "down"          "down in"      "in"
#>  [6] "in the"       "the"           "the forest"    "forest"       "forest where"
#> [11] "where"        "where the"     "the"           "the warm"     "warm"
#> [16] "warm sun"     "sun"           "sun and"       "and"          "and the"
#> [21] "the"          "the fresh"     "fresh"         "fresh air"    "air"
#> [26] "air made"     "made"          "made a"        "a"            "a sweet"
#> [31] "sweet"
```

Combining different degrees of n-grams can allow you to extract different levels of detail from text data. Unigrams tell you which individual words have been used a lot of times; some of these words could be overlooked in bigram or trigram counts if they don't co-appear with other words often. Consider a scenario where every time the word "dog" was used it came after an adjective: "happy dog," "sad dog," "brown dog," "white dog," "playful dog," etc. If this is fairly consistent and the adjectives varied enough, then bigrams would not be able to detect that this story is about dogs. Similarly "very happy" and "not happy" will be recognized as different from bigrams and not with unigrams alone.

2.2.4 Lines, sentence, and paragraph tokens

Tokenizers to split text into larger units of text like lines, sentences, and paragraphs are rarely used directly for modeling purposes, as the tokens produced tend to be fairly unique. It is very uncommon for multiple sentences in a text to be identical! However, these tokenizers are useful for preprocessing and labeling.

For example, Jane Austen's novel *Northanger Abbey* (as available in the **janeaustenr** package) is already preprocessed with each line being at most 80 characters long. However, it might be useful to split the data into chapters and paragraphs instead.

Let's create a function that takes a dataframe containing a variable called `text` and turns it into a dataframe where the text is transformed into paragraphs. First, we can collapse the text into one long string using `collapse = "\n"` to denote line breaks, and then next we can use `tokenize_paragraphs()` to identify the paragraphs and put them back into a dataframe. We can add a paragraph count with `row_number()`.

```
add_paragraphs <- function(data) {
  pull(data, text) %>%
    paste(collapse = "\n") %>%
    tokenize_paragraphs() %>%
    unlist() %>%
    tibble(text = .) %>%
    mutate(paragraph = row_number())
}
```

Now we take the raw text data and add the chapter count by detecting when the characters "CHAPTER" appears at the beginning of a line. Then we nest() the text column, apply our add_paragraphs() function, and then unnest() again.

```
library(janeaustenr)
```

```
northangerabbey_paragraphed <- tibble(text = northangerabbey) %>%
  mutate(chapter = cumsum(str_detect(text, "^CHAPTER "))) %>%
  filter(chapter > 0,
         !str_detect(text, "^CHAPTER ")) %>%
  nest(data = text) %>%
  mutate(data = map(data, add_paragraphs)) %>%
  unnest(cols = c(data))
```

```
glimpse(northangerabbey_paragraphed)
```

```
#> Rows: 1,020
#> Columns: 3
#> $ chapter   <int> 1, 1, 1, 1, 1, 1, 1, 1, 1, 1, 1, 1, 1, 1, 1, 1, 1, 1, 2, 2, ~
#> $ text      <chr> "No one who had ever seen Catherine Morland in her infancy w~
#> $ paragraph <int> 1, 2, 3, 4, 5, 6, 7, 8, 9, 10, 11, 12, 13, 14, 15, 16, 17, 1~
```

Now we have 1020 separate paragraphs we can analyze. Similarly, we could go a step further to split these chapters into sentences, lines, or words.

It can be useful to be able to reshape text data to get a different observational unit. As an example, if you wanted to build a sentiment classifier that would classify sentences as hostile or not, then you need to work with and train your model on sentences of text. Turning pages or paragraphs into sentences is a necessary step in your workflow.

Let us look at how we can turn the_fir_tree from a "one line per element" vector to a "one sentence per element." the_fir_tree comes as a vector so we start by using paste() to combine the lines back together. We use a space as the separator, and then we pass it to the `tokenize_sentences()` function from the **tokenizers** package, which will perform sentence splitting.

```
the_fir_tree_sentences <- the_fir_tree %>%
  paste(collapse = " ") %>%
  tokenize_sentences()

head(the_fir_tree_sentences[[1]])
```

```
#> [1] "Far down in the forest, where the warm sun and the fresh air made a
sweet resting-place, grew a pretty little fir-tree; and yet it was not happy,
it wished so much to be tall like its companions— the pines and firs which grew
around it."
#> [2] "The sun shone, and the soft air fluttered its leaves, and the little
peasant children passed by, prattling merrily, but the fir-tree heeded them
not."
#> [3] "Sometimes the children would bring a large basket of raspberries or
strawberries, wreathed on a straw, and seat themselves near the fir-tree, and
say, \"Is it not a pretty little tree?\""
#> [4] "which made it feel more unhappy than before."
#> [5] "And yet all this while the tree grew a notch or joint taller every
year; for by the number of joints in the stem of a fir-tree we can discover its
age."
#> [6] "Still, as it grew, it complained."
```

If you have lines from different categories as we have in the `hcandersen_en` dataframe, which contains all the lines of the fairy tales in English, then we would like to be able to turn these lines into sentences while preserving the `book` column in the data set. To do this we use `nest()` and `map_chr()` to create a dataframe where each fairy tale is its own element and then we use the `unnest_sentences()` function from the tidytext package to split the text into sentences.

```
hcandersen_sentences <- hcandersen_en %>%
  nest(data = c(text)) %>%
  mutate(data = map_chr(data, ~ paste(.x$text, collapse = " "))) %>%
  unnest_sentences(sentences, data)
```

Now that we have turned the text into "one sentence per element," we can analyze on the sentence level.

2.3 Where does tokenization break down?

Tokenization will generally be one of the first steps when building a model or any kind of text analysis, so it is important to consider carefully what happens in this step of data preprocessing. As with most software, there is a trade-off between speed and customizability, as demonstrated in Section 2.6. The fastest tokenization methods give us less control over how it is done.

While the defaults work well in many cases, we encounter situations where we want to impose stricter rules to get better or different tokenized results. Consider the following sentence.

Don't forget you owe the bank $1 million for the house.

This sentence has several interesting aspects that we need to decide whether to keep or to ignore when tokenizing. The first issue is the contraction in `"Don't"`, which presents us with several possible options. The fastest option is to keep this as one word, but it could also be split up into `"do"` and `"n't"`.

The next issue at hand is how to deal with `"$1"`; the dollar sign is an important part of this sentence as it denotes a kind of currency. We could either remove or keep this punctuation symbol, and if we keep the dollar sign, we can choose between keeping one or two tokens, `"$1"` or `"$"` and `"1"`. If we look at the default for `tokenize_words()`, we notice that it defaults to removing most punctuation including $.

```
tokenize_words("$1")
```

```
#> [[1]]
#> [1] "1"
```

We can keep the dollar sign if we don't strip punctuation.

```
tokenize_words("$1", strip_punct = FALSE)
```

```
#> [[1]]
#> [1] "$" "1"
```

When dealing with this sentence, we also need to decide whether to keep the final period as a token or not. If we remove it, we will not be able to locate the last word in a sentence using n-grams.

Information lost to tokenization (especially default tokenization) occurs more frequently in online and more casual text. Multiple spaces, extreme use of exclamation characters, and deliberate use of capitalization can be completely lost depending on our choice of tokenizer and tokenization parameters. At the same time, it is not always worth keeping that kind of information about how text is being used. If we are studying trends in disease epidemics using Twitter data, the style the tweets are written in is likely not nearly as important as what words are used. However, if we are trying to model social groupings, language style and how individuals use language toward each other becomes much more important.

Another thing to consider is the degree of compression each type of tokenization provides. The choice of tokenization results in a different pool of possible tokens and can influence performance. By choosing a method that gives fewer possible tokens you allow later computational tasks to be performed faster. However, that comes with the risk of collapsing together categories of a different meaning. It is also worth noting that the spread of the number of different tokens varies with your choice of tokenizer.

Figure 2.3 illustrates these points. Each of the fairy tales from **hcandersenr** has been tokenized in five different ways and the number of distinct tokens has been plotted along the x-axis (note that the x-axis is logarithmic). We see that the number of distinct tokens decreases if we convert words to lowercase or extract word stems (see Chapter 4 for more on stemming). Second, notice that the distributions of distinct tokens for character tokenizers are quite narrow; these texts use all or most of the letters in the English alphabet.

2.4   Building your own tokenizer

Sometimes the out-of-the-box tokenizers won't be able to do what you need them to do. In this case, we will have to wield **stringi/stringr** and regular expressions (see Appendix A).

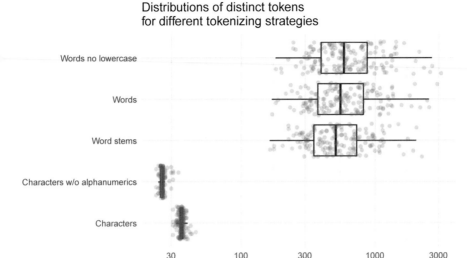

FIGURE 2.3: The number of distinct tokens can vary enormously for different tokenizers

There are two main approaches to tokenization.

1. *Split* the string up according to some rule.
2. *Extract* tokens based on some rule.

The number and complexity of our rules are determined by our desired outcome. We can reach complex outcomes by chaining together many smaller rules. In this section, we will implement a couple of specialty tokenizers to showcase these techniques.

2.4.1 Tokenize to characters, only keeping letters

Here we want to modify what `tokenize_characters()` does, such that we only keep letters. There are two main options. We can use `tokenize_characters()` and remove anything that is not a letter, or we can extract the letters one by one. Let's try the latter option. This is an **extract** task, and we will use `str_extract_all()` as each string has the possibility of including more than one token. Since we want to extract letters we can use the letters character class `[:alpha:]` to match letters and the quantifier `{1}` to only extract the first one.

In this example, leaving out the quantifier yields the same result as including it. However, for more complex regular expressions, specifying the
quantifier allows the string handling to run faster.

```
letter_tokens <- str_extract_all(
  string = "This sentence include 2 numbers and 1 period.",
  pattern = "[:alpha:]{1}"
)
letter_tokens
```

```
#> [[1]]
#>  [1] "T" "h" "i" "s" "s" "e" "n" "t" "e" "n" "c" "e" "i" "n" "c" "l" "u" "d" "e"
#> [20] "n" "u" "m" "b" "e" "r" "s" "a" "n" "d" "p" "e" "r" "i" "o" "d"
```

We may be tempted to specify the character class as something like [a-zA-Z]{1}.
This option would run faster, but we would lose non-English letter characters.
This is a design choice we have to make depending on the goals of our specific
problem.

```
danish_sentence <- "Så mødte han en gammel heks på landevejen"
```

```
str_extract_all(danish_sentence, "[:alpha:]")
```

```
#> [[1]]
#>  [1] "S" "å" "m" "ø" "d" "t" "e" "h" "a" "n" "e" "n" "g" "a" "m" "m" "e" "l" "h"
#> [20] "e" "k" "s" "p" "å" "l" "a" "n" "d" "e" "v" "e" "j" "e" "n"
```

```
str_extract_all(danish_sentence, "[a-zA-Z]")
```

```
#> [[1]]
#>  [1] "S" "m" "d" "t" "e" "h" "a" "n" "e" "n" "g" "a" "m" "m" "e" "l" "h" "e" "k"
#> [20] "s" "p" "l" "a" "n" "d" "e" "v" "e" "j" "e" "n"
```

Choosing between [:alpha:] and [a-zA-Z] may seem quite similar, but the resulting differences can have a big impact on your analysis.

2.4.2 Allow for hyphenated words

In our examples so far, we have noticed that the string "fir-tree" is typically split into two tokens. Let's explore two different approaches for how to handle this hyphenated word as one token. First, let's split on white space; this is a decent way to identify words in English and some other languages, and it does not split hyphenated words as the hyphen character isn't considered a white-space. Second, let's find a regex to match words with a hyphen and extract those.

Splitting by white space is not too difficult because we can use character classes, as shown in Table A.2. We will use the white space character class [:space:] to split our sentence.

```
str_split("This isn't a sentence with hyphenated-words.", "[:space:]")
```

```
#> [[1]]
#> [1] "This"          "isn't"          "a"
#> [4] "sentence"      "with"           "hyphenated-words."
```

This worked pretty well. This version doesn't drop punctuation, but we can achieve this by removing punctuation characters at the beginning and end of words.

```
str_split("This isn't a sentence with hyphenated-words.", "[:space:]") %>%
  map(~ str_remove_all(.x, "^[:punct:]+|[:punct:]+$"))
```

```
#> [[1]]
#> [1] "This"          "isn't"          "a"              "sentence"
#> [5] "with"          "hyphenated-words"
```

This regex used to remove the punctuation is a little complicated, so let's discuss it piece by piece.

- The regex ^[:punct:]+ will look at the beginning of the string (^) to match any punctuation characters ([:punct:]), where it will select one or more (+).

- The other regex [:punct:]+$ will look for punctuation characters ([:punct:]) that appear one or more times (+) at the end of the string ($).

- These will alternate (|) so that we get matches from both sides of the words.

- The reason we use the quantifier + is that there are cases where a word is followed by multiple characters we don't want, such as "okay..." and "Really?!!!".

We are using map() since str_split() returns a list, and we want str_remove_all() to be applied to each element in the list. (The example here only has one element.)

Now let's see if we can get the same result using extraction. We will start by constructing a regular expression that will capture hyphenated words; our definition here is a word with one hyphen located inside it. Since we want the hyphen to be inside the word, we will need to have a non-zero number of characters on either side of the hyphen.

```
str_extract_all(
  string = "This isn't a sentence with hyphenated-words.",
  pattern = "[:alpha:]+-[:alpha:]+"
)
```

```
#> [[1]]
#> [1] "hyphenated-words"
```

Wait, this only matched the hyphenated word! This happened because we are only matching words with hyphens. If we add the quantifier ? then we can match 0 or 1 occurrences.

```
str_extract_all(
  string = "This isn't a sentence with hyphenated-words.",
  pattern = "[:alpha:]+-?[:alpha:]+"
)
```

```
#> [[1]]
#> [1] "This"            "isn"              "sentence"        "with"
#> [5] "hyphenated-words"
```

Now we are getting more words, but the ending of `"isn't"` is not there anymore and we lost the word `"a"`. We can get matches for the whole contraction by expanding the character class `[:alpha:]` to include the character `'`. We do that by using `[[:alpha:]']`.

```
str_extract_all(
  string = "This isn't a sentence with hyphenated-words.",
  pattern = "[[:alpha:]']+-?[[:alpha:]']+"
)
```

```
#> [[1]]
#> [1] "This"            "isn't"            "sentence"        "with"
#> [5] "hyphenated-words"
```

Next, we need to find out why `"a"` wasn't matched. If we look at the regular expression, we remember that we imposed the restriction that a non-zero number of characters needed to surround the hyphen to avoid matching words that start or end with a hyphen. This means that the smallest possible pattern matched is two characters long. We can fix this by using an alternation with `|`. We will keep our previous match on the left-hand side, and include `[:alpha:]{1}` on the right-hand side to match the single length words that won't be picked up by the left-hand side. Notice how we aren't using `[[:alpha:]']` since we are not interested in matching single `'` characters.

```
str_extract_all(
  string = "This isn't a sentence with hyphenated-words.",
  pattern = "[[:alpha:]']+-?[[:alpha:]']+|[:alpha:]{1}"
)
```

```
#> [[1]]
#> [1] "This"            "isn't"            "a"              "sentence"
#> [5] "with"            "hyphenated-words"
```

That is getting to be quite a complex regex, but we are now getting the same answer as before.

2.4.3   Wrapping it in a function

We have shown how we can use regular expressions to extract the tokens we want, perhaps to use in modeling. So far, the code has been rather unstructured. We would ideally wrap these tasks into functions that can be used the same way `tokenize_words()` is used.

Let's start with the example with hyphenated words. To make the function a little more flexible, let's add an option to transform all the output to lowercase.

```r
tokenize_hyphenated_words <- function(x, lowercase = TRUE) {
  if (lowercase)
    x <- str_to_lower(x)

  str_split(x, "[:space:]") %>%
    map(~ str_remove_all(.x, "^[:punct:]+|[:punct:]+$"))
}


tokenize_hyphenated_words(the_fir_tree[1:3])
```

```
#> [[1]]
#>  [1] "far"    "down"    "in"     "the"    "forest" "where" "the"    "warm"
#>  [9] "sun"    "and"     "the"    "fresh"  "air"    "made"  "a"      "sweet"
#>
#> [[2]]
#>  [1] "resting-place" "grew"          "a"              "pretty"
#>  [5] "little"        "fir-tree"      "and"            "yet"
#>  [9] "it"            "was"           "not"            "happy"
#> [13] "it"
#>
#> [[3]]
#>  [1] "wished"  "so"      "much"    "to"          "be"
#>  [6] "tall"    "like"    "its"     "companions"  "the"
#> [11] "pines"   "and"     "firs"    "which"       "grew"
```

Notice how we transformed to lowercase first because the rest of the operations are case insensitive.

Next let's turn our character n-gram tokenizer into a function, with a variable `n` argument.

```r
tokenize_character_ngram <- function(x, n) {
  ngram_loc <- str_locate_all(x, paste0("(?=(\\w{", n, "}))"))

  map2(ngram_loc, x, ~str_sub(.y, .x[, 1], .x[, 1] + n - 1))
}

tokenize_character_ngram(the_fir_tree[1:3], n = 3)
```

```
#> [[1]]
#>  [1] "Far" "dow" "own" "the" "for" "ore" "res" "est" "whe" "her" "ere" "the"
#> [13] "war" "arm" "sun" "and" "the" "fre" "res" "esh" "air" "mad" "ade" "swe"
#> [25] "wee" "eet"
#>
#> [[2]]
#>  [1] "res" "est" "sti" "tin" "ing" "pla" "lac" "ace" "gre" "rew" "pre" "ret"
#> [13] "ett" "tty" "lit" "itt" "ttl" "tle" "fir" "tre" "ree" "and" "yet" "was"
#> [25] "not" "hap" "app" "ppy"
#>
#> [[3]]
#>  [1] "wis" "ish" "she" "hed" "muc" "uch" "tal" "all" "lik" "ike" "its" "com"
#> [13] "omp" "mpa" "pan" "ani" "nio" "ion" "ons" "the" "pin" "ine" "nes" "and"
#> [25] "fir" "irs" "whi" "hic" "ich" "gre" "rew"
```

We can use `paste0()` in this function to construct an actual regex.

2.5 Tokenization for non-Latin alphabets

Our discussion of tokenization so far has focused on text where words are separated by white space and punctuation. For such text, even a quite basic tokenizer can give decent results. However, many written languages don't separate words in this way.

One of these languages is Chinese where each "word" can be represented by one or more consecutive characters. Splitting Chinese text into words is called "word segmentation" and is still an active area of research (Ma, Ganchev, and Weiss 2018; Huang et al. 2020).

We are not going to go into depth in this area, but we want to showcase that word segmentation is indeed possible with R as well. We use the **jiebaR** package (Wenfeng and Yanyi 2019). It is conceptually similar to the **tokenizers**

package, but we need to create a worker that is passed into `segment()` along
with the string we want to segment.

```
library(jiebaR)
words <- c("下面是不分行输出的结果", "下面是不输出的结果")

engine1 <- worker(bylines = TRUE)

segment(words, engine1)
```

```
#> [[1]]
#> [1] "下面" "是"   "不"    "分行" "输出" "的"    "结果"
#>
#> [[2]]
#> [1] "下面" "是"   "不"    "输出" "的"    "结果"
```

2.6   Tokenization benchmark

Not all tokenization packages are the same. Most open-source tokenizers in R
are well-designed, but they are designed to serve different purposes. Some have
a multitude of arguments to allow you to customize your tokenizer for greater
flexibility, but this flexibility comes at a price; they tend to have relatively
slower performance.

While we can't easily quantify flexibility, it is straightforward to benchmark
some of the tokenizers available in R so you can pick the one that best suits
your needs.

```
bench::mark(check = FALSE, iterations = 10,
  `corpus` = corpus::text_tokens(hcandersen_en$text),
  `tokenizers` = tokenizers::tokenize_words(hcandersen_en$text),
  `text2vec` = text2vec::word_tokenizer(hcandersen_en$text),
  `quanteda` = quanteda::tokenize_word(hcandersen_en$text),
  `base R` = strsplit(hcandersen_en$text, "\\s")
)
```

```
#> # A tibble: 5 x 6
#>   expression       min   median `itr/sec` mem_alloc `gc/sec`
#>   <bch:expr> <bch:tm> <bch:tm>     <dbl> <bch:byt>    <dbl>
#> 1 corpus       89.5ms   91.6ms      10.4   12.21MB     2.61
#> 2 tokenizers  121.1ms  124.5ms      7.83    1.08MB     1.96
#> 3 text2vec      101ms    103ms      9.60   21.06MB     2.40
#> 4 quanteda    196.1ms  201.2ms      4.94    8.71MB     1.24
#> 5 base R      361.8ms  371.9ms      2.66   10.51MB    0.664
```

The corpus package (Perry 2020) offers excellent performance for tokenization, and other options are not much worse. One exception is using a base R function as a tokenizer; you will see significant performance gains by instead using a package built specifically for text tokenization.

2.7   Summary

To build a predictive model, text data needs to be split into meaningful units, called tokens. These tokens range from individual characters to words to n-grams and even more complex structures, and the particular procedure used to identify tokens from text can be important to your results. Fast and consistent tokenizers are available, but understanding how they behave and in what circumstances they work best will set you up for success. It's also possible to build custom tokenizers when necessary. Once text data is tokenized, a common next preprocessing step is to consider how to handle very common words that are not very informative— stop words. Chapter 3 examines this in detail.

2.7.1   In this chapter, you learned:

- that tokens are meaningful units of text, such as words or n-grams

- to implement different kinds of tokenization, the process of splitting text into tokens

- how different kinds of tokenization affect the distribution of tokens

- how to build your own tokenizer when the fast, consistent tokenizers that are available are not flexible enough

3

Stop words

Once we have split text into tokens, it often becomes clear that not all words carry the same amount of information, if any information at all, for a predictive modeling task. Common words that carry little (or perhaps no) meaningful information are called *stop words*. It is common advice and practice to remove stop words for various NLP tasks, but the task of stop word removal is more nuanced than many resources may lead you to believe. In this chapter, we will investigate what a stop word list is, the differences between them, and the effects of using them in your preprocessing workflow.

The concept of stop words has a long history with Hans Peter Luhn credited with coining the term in 1960 (Luhn 1960). Examples of these words in English are "a," "the," "of," and "didn't." These words are very common and typically don't add much to the meaning of a text but instead ensure the structure of a sentence is sound.

> Categorizing words as either informative or non-informative is limiting, and we prefer to consider words as having a more fluid or continuous amount of information associated with them. This informativeness is context-specific as well. In fact, stop words themselves are often important in genre or authorship identification.

Historically, one of the main reasons for removing stop words was to decrease the computational time for text mining; it can be regarded as a dimensionality reduction of text data and was commonly-used in search engines to give better results (Huston and Croft 2010).

Stop words can have different roles in a corpus. We generally categorize stop words into three groups: global, subject, and document stop words.

Global stop words are words that are almost always low in meaning in a given language; these are words such as "of" and "and" in English that are needed to glue text together. These words are likely a safe bet for removal, but they are low in number. You can find some global stop words in pre-made stop word lists (Section 3.1).

DOI: 10.1201/9781003093459-3

Next up are subject-specific stop words. These words are uninformative for a given subject area. Subjects can be broad like finance and medicine or can be more specific like obituaries, health code violations, and job listings for librarians in Kansas. Words like "bath," "bedroom," and "entryway" are generally not considered stop words in English, but they may not provide much information for differentiating suburban house listings and could be subject stop words for certain analysis. You will likely need to manually construct such a stop word list (Section 3.2). These kinds of stop words may improve your performance if you have the domain expertise to create a good list.

Lastly, we have document-level stop words. These words do not provide any or much information for a given document. These are difficult to classify and won't be worth the trouble to identify. Even if you can find document stop words, it is not obvious how to incorporate this kind of information in a regression or classification task.

3.1   Using premade stop word lists

A quick option for using stop words is to get a list that has already been created. This is appealing because it is not difficult, but be aware that not all lists are created equal. Nothman, Qin, and Yurchak (2018) found some alarming results in a study of 52 stop word lists available in open-source software packages. Among some of the more grave issues were misspellings ("fify" instead of "fifty"), the inclusion of clearly informative words such as "computer" and "cry," and internal inconsistencies, such as including the word "has" but not the word "does." This is not to say that you should never use a stop word list that has been included in an open-source software project. However, you should always inspect and verify the list you are using, both to make sure it hasn't changed since you used it last, and also to check that it is appropriate for your use case.

There is a broad selection of stop word lists available today. For the purpose of this chapter, we will focus on three of the lists of English stop words provided by the **stopwords** package (Benoit, Muhr, and Watanabe 2021). The first is from the SMART (System for the Mechanical Analysis and Retrieval of Text) Information Retrieval System, an information retrieval system developed at Cornell University in the 1960s (Lewis et al. 2004). The second is the English Snowball stop word list (Porter 2001), and the last is the English list from the Stopwords ISO[1] collection. These stop word lists are all considered general purpose and not domain-specific.

---

[1] https://github.com/stopwords-iso/stopwords-iso

The **stopwords** package contains a comprehensive collection of stop word lists in one place for ease of use in analysis and other packages.

Before we start delving into the content inside the lists, let's take a look at how many words are included in each.

```
library(stopwords)
length(stopwords(source = "smart"))
length(stopwords(source = "snowball"))
length(stopwords(source = "stopwords-iso"))
```

```
#> [1] 571
#> [1] 175
#> [1] 1298
```

The lengths of these lists are quite different, with the longest list being over seven times longer than the shortest! Let's examine the overlap of the words that appear in the three lists in an UpSet plot in Figure 3.1. An UpSet plot (Lex et al. 2014) visualizes intersections and aggregates of intersections of sets using a matrix layout, presenting the number of elements as well as summary statistics.

The UpSet plot in Figure 3.1 shows us that these three lists are almost true subsets of each other. The only exception is a set of 10 words that appear in Snowball and ISO but not in the SMART list. What are those words?

```
setdiff(stopwords(source = "snowball"),
        stopwords(source = "smart"))
```

```
#>  [1] "she's"   "he'd"    "she'd"   "he'll"   "she'll"  "shan't"  "mustn't"
#>  [8] "when's"  "why's"   "how's"
```

All these words are contractions. This is *not* because the SMART lexicon doesn't include contractions; if we look, there are almost 50 of them.

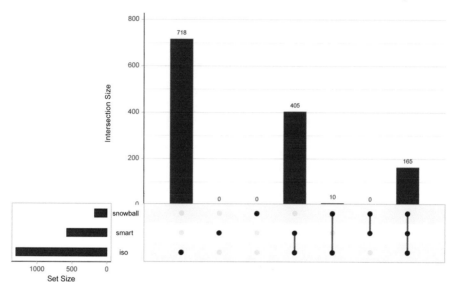

FIGURE 3.1: Set intersections for three common stop word lists visualized as an UpSet plot

```
str_subset(stopwords(source = "smart"), "'")
```

```
#>  [1] "a's"       "ain't"     "aren't"    "c'mon"     "c's"       "can't"
#>  [7] "couldn't"  "didn't"    "doesn't"   "don't"     "hadn't"    "hasn't"
#> [13] "haven't"   "he's"      "here's"    "i'd"       "i'll"      "i'm"
#> [19] "i've"      "isn't"     "it'd"      "it'll"     "it's"      "let's"
#> [25] "shouldn't" "t's"       "that's"    "there's"   "they'd"    "they'll"
#> [31] "they're"   "they've"   "wasn't"    "we'd"      "we'll"     "we're"
#> [37] "we've"     "weren't"   "what's"    "where's"   "who's"     "won't"
#> [43] "wouldn't"  "you'd"     "you'll"    "you're"    "you've"
```

We seem to have stumbled upon an inconsistency: why does SMART include "he's" but not "she's"? It is hard to say, but this could be worth rectifying before applying these stop word lists to an analysis or model preprocessing. This stop word list was likely generated by selecting the most frequent words across a large corpus of text that had more representation for text about men than women. This is once again a reminder that we should always look carefully at any pre-made word list or another artifact we use to make sure it works well with our needs[2].

---

[2]This advice applies to any kind of pre-made lexicon or word list, not just stop words. For instance, the same concerns apply to sentiment lexicons. The NRC sentiment lexicon of

It is perfectly acceptable to start with a premade word list and remove or append additional words according to your particular use case.

When you select a stop word list, it is important that you consider its size and breadth. Having a small and concise list of words can moderately reduce your token count while not having too great of an influence on your models, assuming that you picked appropriate words. As the size of your stop word list grows, each word added will have a diminishing positive effect with the increasing risk that a meaningful word has been placed on the list by mistake. In Section 6.4, we show the effects of different stop word lists on model training.

3.1.1 Stop word removal in R

Now that we have seen stop word lists, we can move forward with removing these words. The particular way we remove stop words depends on the shape of our data. If you have your text in a tidy format with one word per row, you can use `filter()` from **dplyr** with a negated `%in%` if you have the stop words as a vector, or you can use `anti_join()` from **dplyr** if the stop words are in a `tibble()`. Like in our previous chapter, let's examine the text of "The Fir-Tree" by Hans Christian Andersen, and use **tidytext** to tokenize the text into words.

```
library(hcandersenr)
library(tidyverse)
library(tidytext)

fir_tree <- hca_fairytales() %>%
  filter(book == "The fir tree",
         language == "English")

tidy_fir_tree <- fir_tree %>%
  unnest_tokens(word, text)
```

Let's use the Snowball stop word list as an example. Since the stop words return from this function as a vector, we will use `filter()`.

Mohammad and Turney (2013) associates the word "white" with trust and the word "black" with sadness, which could have unintended consequences when analyzing text about racial groups.

```
tidy_fir_tree %>%
  filter(!(word %in% stopwords(source = "snowball")))
```

```
#> # A tibble: 1,547 x 3
#>    book          language word
#>    <chr>         <chr>    <chr>
#>  1 The fir tree  English  far
#>  2 The fir tree  English  forest
#>  3 The fir tree  English  warm
#>  4 The fir tree  English  sun
#>  5 The fir tree  English  fresh
#>  6 The fir tree  English  air
#>  7 The fir tree  English  made
#>  8 The fir tree  English  sweet
#>  9 The fir tree  English  resting
#> 10 The fir tree  English  place
#> # ... with 1,537 more rows
```

If we use the `get_stopwords()` function from **tidytext** instead, then we can use
the `anti_join()` function.

```
tidy_fir_tree %>%
  anti_join(get_stopwords(source = "snowball"))
```

```
#> # A tibble: 1,547 x 3
#>    book          language word
#>    <chr>         <chr>    <chr>
#>  1 The fir tree  English  far
#>  2 The fir tree  English  forest
#>  3 The fir tree  English  warm
#>  4 The fir tree  English  sun
#>  5 The fir tree  English  fresh
#>  6 The fir tree  English  air
#>  7 The fir tree  English  made
#>  8 The fir tree  English  sweet
#>  9 The fir tree  English  resting
#> 10 The fir tree  English  place
#> # ... with 1,537 more rows
```

The result of these two stop word removals is the same since we used the same
stop word list in both cases.

3.2 Creating your own stop words list

Another way to get a stop word list is to create one yourself. Let's explore a few different ways to find appropriate words to use. We will use the tokenized data from "The Fir-Tree" as a first example. Let's take the words and rank them by their count or frequency.

Most frequent tokens in "The Fir-Tree"

1: the	25: said	49: trees	73: their	97: asked
2: and	26: what	50: we	74: which	98: can
3: tree	27: as	51: been	75: again	99: could
4: it	28: that	52: down	76: am	100: cried
5: a	29: he	53: oh	77: are	101: going
6: in	30: you	54: very	78: beautiful	102: grew
7: of	31: its	55: when	79: evening	103: if
8: to	32: out	56: where	80: him	104: large
9: i	33: be	57: who	81: like	105: looked
10: was	34: them	58: children	82: me	106: made
11: they	35: this	59: dumpty	83: more	107: many
12: fir	36: branches	60: humpty	84: about	108: seen
13: were	37: came	61: or	85: christmas	109: stairs
14: all	38: for	62: shall	86: do	110: think
15: with	39: now	63: there	87: fell	111: too
16: but	40: one	64: while	88: fresh	112: up
17: on	41: story	65: will	89: from	113: yes
18: then	42: would	66: after	90: here	114: air
19: had	43: forest	67: by	91: last	115: also
20: is	44: have	68: come	92: much	116: away
21: at	45: how	69: happy	93: no	117: birds
22: little	46: know	70: my	94: princess	118: corner
23: so	47: thought	71: old	95: tall	119: cut
24: not	48: mice	72: only	96: young	120: did

FIGURE 3.2: Words from "The Fir Tree" ordered by count or frequency

We recognize many of what we would consider stop words in the first column here, with three big exceptions. We see `tree` at 3, `fir` at 12, and `little` at 22. These words appear high on our list, but they do provide valuable information as they all reference the main character. What went wrong with this approach? Creating a stop word list using high-frequency words works best when it is created on a **corpus** of documents, not an individual document. This is because the words found in a single document will be document-specific and the overall pattern of words will not generalize that well.

In NLP, a corpus is a set of texts or documents. The set of Hans Christian Andersen's fairy tales can be considered a corpus, with each fairy tale a document within that corpus. The set of United States Supreme Court opinions can be considered a different corpus, with each written opinion being a document within *that* corpus. Both data sets are described in more detail in Appendix B.

The word "tree" does seem important as it is about the main character, but it could also be appearing so often that it stops providing any information. Let's try a different approach, extracting high-frequency words from the corpus of *all* English fairy tales by H.C. Andersen.

120 most frequent tokens in H.C. Andersen's English fairy tales

1: the	25: not	49: their	73: good	97: too
2: and	26: were	50: by	74: do	98: went
3: of	27: so	51: we	75: more	99: come
4: a	28: all	52: will	76: here	100: never
5: to	29: be	53: like	77: its	101: much
6: in	30: at	54: are	78: did	102: house
7: was	31: one	55: what	79: man	103: know
8: it	32: there	56: if	80: see	104: every
9: he	33: him	57: me	81: can	105: looked
10: that	34: from	58: up	82: through	106: many
11: i	35: have	59: very	83: beautiful	107: again
12: she	36: little	60: would	84: must	108: eyes
13: had	37: then	61: no	85: has	109: our
14: his	38: which	62: been	86: away	110: quite
15: they	39: them	63: about	87: thought	111: young
16: but	40: this	64: over	88: still	112: even
17: as	41: old	65: where	89: than	113: shall
18: her	42: out	66: an	90: well	114: tree
19: with	43: could	67: how	91: people	115: go
20: for	44: when	68: only	92: time	116: your
21: is	45: into	69: came	93: before	117: long
22: on	46: now	70: or	94: day	118: upon
23: said	47: who	71: down	95: other	119: two
24: you	48: my	72: great	96: stood	120: water

FIGURE 3.3: Words in all English fairy tales by Hans Christian Andersen ordered by count or frequency

This list is more appropriate for our concept of stop words, and now it is time for us to make some choices. How many do we want to include in our stop word list? Which words should we add and/or remove based on prior information? Selecting the number of words to remove is best done by a case-by-case basis as it can be difficult to determine a priori how many different "meaningless" words appear in a corpus. Our suggestion is to start with a low number like 20 and increase by 10 words until you get to words that are not appropriate as stop words for your analytical purpose.

It is worth keeping in mind that such a list is not perfect. Depending on how your text was generated or processed, strange tokens can surface as possible stop words due to encoding or optical character recognition errors. Further, these results are based on the corpus of documents we have available, which is potentially biased. In our example here, all the fairy tales were written by the same European white man from the early 1800s.

This bias can be minimized by removing words we would expect to be over-represented or to add words we expect to be under-represented.

Easy examples are to include the complements to the words in the list if they are not already present. Include "big" if "small" is present, "old" if "young" is present. This example list has words associated with women often listed lower in rank than words associated with men. With "man" being at rank 79 but "woman" at rank 179, choosing a threshold of 100 would lead to only one of these words being included. Depending on how important you think such nouns are going to be in your texts, consider either adding "woman" or deleting "man".[3]

Figure 3.4 shows how the words associated with men have a higher rank than the words associated with women. By using a single threshold to create a stop word list, you would likely only include one form of such words.

Imagine now we would like to create a stop word list that spans multiple different genres, in such a way that the subject-specific stop words don't overlap. For this case, we would like words to be denoted as a stop word only if it is a stop word in all the genres. You could find the words individually in each genre and use the right intersections. However, that approach might take a substantial amount of time.

Below is a bad approach where we try to create a multi-language list of stop words. To accomplish this we calculate the *inverse document frequency*[4] (IDF) of each word. The IDF of a word is a quantity that is low for commonly-used words in a collection of documents and high for words not used often in a collection of documents. It is typically defined as

$$idf(\text{term}) = \ln\left(\frac{n_{\text{documents}}}{n_{\text{documents containing term}}}\right)$$

---

[3]On the other hand, the more biased stop word list may be helpful when modeling a corpus with gender imbalance, depending on your goal; words like "she" and "her" can identify where women are mentioned.

[4]https://www.tidytextmining.com/tfidf.html

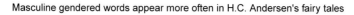

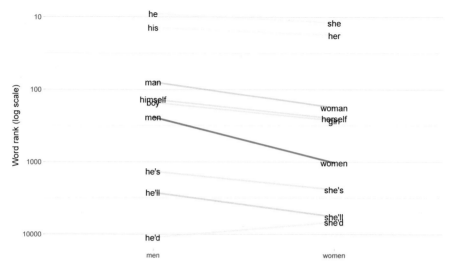

FIGURE 3.4: Tokens ranked according to total occurrences, with rank 1 having the most occurrences

If the word "dog" appears in 4 out of 100 documents then it would have an `idf("dog")` = `log(100/4)` = `3.22`, and if the word "cat" appears in 99 out of 100 documents then it would have an `idf("cat")` = `log(100/99)` = `0.01`. Notice how the idf values goes to zero (as a matter of fact when a term appears in all the documents then the idf of that word is 0 `log(100/100)` = `log(1)` = `0`), the more documents it is contained in. What happens if we create a stop word list based on words with the lowest IDF? The following function takes a tokenized dataframe and returns a dataframe with a column for each word and a column for the IDF.

```
library(rlang)
calc_idf <- function(df, word, document) {
  words <- df %>% pull({{word}}) %>% unique()
  n_docs <- length(unique(pull(df, {{document}})))
  n_words <- df %>%
    nest(data = c({{word}})) %>%
    pull(data) %>%
    map_dfc(~ words %in% unique(pull(.x, {{word}}))) %>%
    rowSums()

  tibble(word = words,
```

```
idf = log(n_docs / n_words))
}
```

Here is the result when we try to create a cross-language list of stop words, by taking each fairy tale as a document. It is not very good!

The overlap between words that appear in each language is very small, but these words are what we mostly see in this list.

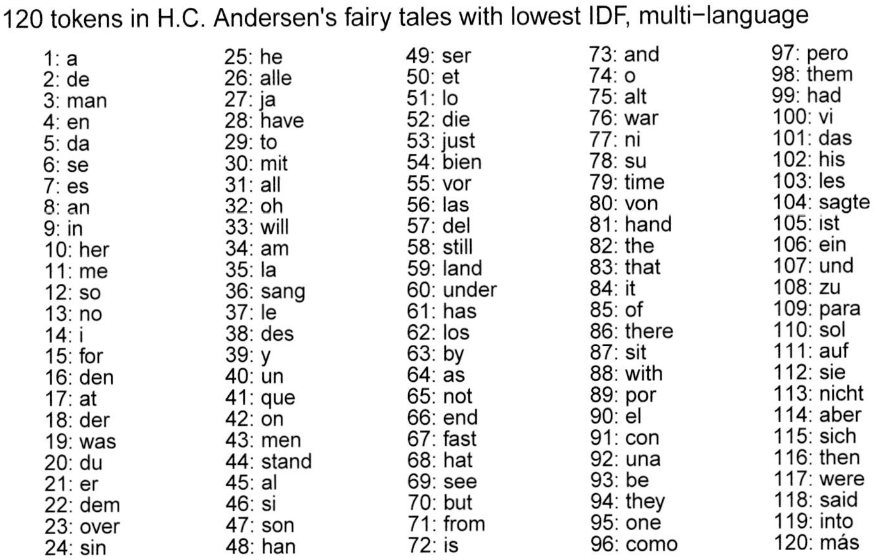

120 tokens in H.C. Andersen's fairy tales with lowest IDF, multi−language

1: a	25: he	49: ser	73: and	97: pero
2: de	26: alle	50: et	74: o	98: them
3: man	27: ja	51: lo	75: alt	99: had
4: en	28: have	52: die	76: war	100: vi
5: da	29: to	53: just	77: ni	101: das
6: se	30: mit	54: bien	78: su	102: his
7: es	31: all	55: vor	79: time	103: les
8: an	32: oh	56: las	80: von	104: sagte
9: in	33: will	57: del	81: hand	105: ist
10: her	34: am	58: still	82: the	106: ein
11: me	35: la	59: land	83: that	107: und
12: so	36: sang	60: under	84: it	108: zu
13: no	37: le	61: has	85: of	109: para
14: i	38: des	62: los	86: there	110: sol
15: for	39: y	63: by	87: sit	111: auf
16: den	40: un	64: as	88: with	112: sie
17: at	41: que	65: not	89: por	113: nicht
18: der	42: on	66: end	90: el	114: aber
19: was	43: men	67: fast	91: con	115: sich
20: du	44: stand	68: hat	92: una	116: then
21: er	45: al	69: see	93: be	117: were
22: dem	46: si	70: but	94: they	118: said
23: over	47: son	71: from	95: one	119: into
24: sin	48: han	72: is	96: como	120: más

FIGURE 3.5: Words from all of H.C. Andersen's fairy tales in Danish, English, French, German, and Spanish, counted and ordered by IDF

This didn't work very well because there is very little overlap between common words. Instead, let us limit the calculation to only one language and calculate the IDF of each word we can find compared to words that appear in a lot of documents.

120 tokens in H.C. Andersen's fairy tales with lowest IDF, English only

1: a	25: them	49: if	73: good	97: own
2: the	26: be	50: little	74: must	98: come
3: and	27: from	51: over	75: my	99: its
4: to	28: had	52: are	76: than	100: whole
5: in	29: then	53: very	77: away	101: just
6: that	30: were	54: you	78: more	102: many
7: it	31: said	55: him	79: has	103: never
8: but	32: into	56: we	80: thought	104: made
9: of	33: by	57: great	81: did	105: stood
10: was	34: have	58: how	82: other	106: yet
11: as	35: which	59: their	83: still	107: looked
12: there	36: this	60: came	84: do	108: again
13: on	37: up	61: been	85: even	109: say
14: at	38: out	62: down	86: before	110: may
15: is	39: what	63: would	87: me	111: yes
16: for	40: who	64: where	88: know	112: went
17: with	41: no	65: or	89: much	113: every
18: all	42: an	66: she	90: see	114: each
19: not	43: now	67: can	91: here	115: such
20: they	44: i	68: could	92: well	116: world
21: one	45: only	69: about	93: through	117: some
22: he	46: old	70: her	94: day	118: long
23: his	47: like	71: will	95: too	119: eyes
24: so	48: when	72: time	96: people	120: go

FIGURE 3.6: Words from all of H.C. Andersen's fairy tales in English, counted and ordered by IDF

This time we get better results. The list starts with "a," "the," "and," and "to" and continues with many more reasonable choices of stop words. We need to look at these results manually to turn this into a list. We need to go as far down in rank as we are comfortable with. You as a data practitioner are in full control of how you want to create the list. If you don't want to include "little" you are still able to add "are" to your list even though it is lower on the list.

3.3 All stop word lists are context-specific

Context is important in text modeling, so it is important to ensure that the stop word lexicon you use reflects the word space that you are planning on using it in. One common concern to consider is how pronouns bring information to your text. Pronouns are included in many different stop word lists (although inconsistently), but they will often *not* be noise in text data. Similarly, Bender et al. (2021) discuss how a list of about 400 "Dirty, Naughty, Obscene or Otherwise Bad Words" were used to filter and remove text before training a trillion parameter large language model, to protect it from learning offensive language, but the authors point out that in some community contexts, such words are reclaimed or used to describe marginalized identities.

On the other hand, sometimes you will have to add in words yourself, depending on the domain. If you are working with texts for dessert recipes, certain ingredients (sugar, eggs, water) and actions (whisking, baking, stirring) may be frequent enough to pass your stop word threshold, but you may want to keep them as they may be informative. Throwing away "eggs" as a common word would make it harder or downright impossible to determine if certain recipes are vegan or not while whisking and stirring may be fine to remove as distinguishing between recipes that do and don't require a whisk might not be that big of a deal.

3.4 What happens when you remove stop words

We have discussed different ways of finding and removing stop words; now let's see what happens once you do remove them. First, let's explore the impact of the number of words that are included in the list. Figure 3.7 shows what percentage of words are removed as a function of the number of words in a text. The different colors represent the three different stop word lists we have considered in this chapter.

We notice, as we would predict, that larger stop word lists remove more words than shorter stop word lists. In this example with fairy tales, over half of the words have been removed, with the largest list removing over 80% of the words. We observe that shorter texts have a lower percentage of stop words. Since we are looking at fairy tales, this could be explained by the fact that a story has to be told regardless of the length of the fairy tale, so shorter texts are going to be denser with more informative words.

Another problem you may face is dealing with misspellings.

Most premade stop word lists assume that all the words are spelled correctly.

Handling misspellings when using premade lists can be done by manually adding common misspellings. You could imagine creating all words that are a certain string distance away from the stop words, but we do not recommend this as you would quickly include informative words this way.

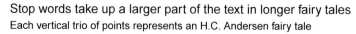

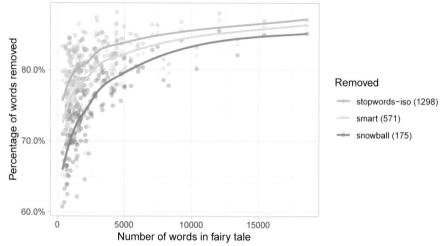

FIGURE 3.7: Proportion of words removed for different stop word lists and different document lengths

One of the downsides of creating your own stop word lists using frequencies is that you are limited to using words that you have already observed. It could happen that "she'd" is included in your training corpus but the word "he'd" did not reach the threshold. This is a case where you need to look at your words and adjust accordingly. Here the large premade stop word lists can serve as inspiration for missing words.

In Section 6.4, we investigate the influence of removing stop words in the context of modeling. Given the right list of words, we see no harm to the model performance, and sometimes find improvement due to noise reduction (Feldman, and Sanger 2007).

3.5   Stop words in languages other than English

So far in this chapter, we have focused on English stop words, but English is not representative of every language. The notion of "short" and "long" lists we have used so far are specific to English as a language. You should expect different languages to have a different number of "uninformative" words, and for this number to depend on the morphological richness of a language; lists that contain all possible morphological variants of each stop word could become quite large.

Different languages have different numbers of words in each class of words. An example is how the grammatical case influences the articles used in German. The following tables show the use of definite and indefinite articles in German[5]. Notice how German nouns have three genders (masculine, feminine, and neuter), which are not uncommon in languages around the world. Articles are almost always considered to be stop words in English as they carry very little information. However, German articles give some indication of the case, which can be used when selecting a list of stop words in German.

German Definite Articles (the)

	Masculine	Feminine	Neuter	Plural
Nominative	der	die	das	die
Accusative	den	die	das	die
Dative	dem	der	dem	den
Genitive	des	der	des	der

German Indefinite Articles (a/an)

	Masculine	Feminine	Neuter
Nominative	ein	eine	ein
Accusative	einen	eine	ein
Dative	einem	einer	einem
Genitive	eines	einer	eines

Building lists of stop words in Chinese has been done both manually and automatically (Zou, Wang, Deng, Han, and Wang 2006) but so far none has been accepted as a standard (Zou, Wang, Deng, and Han 2006). A full discussion of stop word identification in Chinese text would be out of scope for this book, so we will just highlight some of the challenges that differentiate it from English.

Chinese text is much more complex than portrayed here. With different systems and billions of users, there is much we won't be able to touch on here.

---

[5] https://deutsch.lingolia.com/en/grammar/nouns-and-articles/articles-noun-markers

The main difference from English is the use of logograms instead of letters to convey information. However, Chinese characters should not be confused with Chinese words. The majority of words in modern Chinese are composed of multiple characters. This means that inferring the presence of words is more complicated, and the notion of stop words will affect how this segmentation of characters is done.

3.6   Summary

In many standard NLP workflows, the removal of stop words is presented as a default or the correct choice without comment. Although removing stop words can improve the accuracy of your machine learning using text data, choices around such a step are complex. The content of existing stop word lists varies tremendously, and the available strategies for building your own can have subtle to not-so-subtle effects on your model results.

3.6.1   In this chapter, you learned:

- what a stop word is and how to remove stop words from text data

- how different stop word lists can vary

- that the impact of stop word removal is different for different kinds of texts

- about the bias built in to stop word lists and strategies for building such lists

4

Stemming

When we deal with text, often documents contain different versions of one base word, often called a *stem*. "The Fir-Tree," for example, contains more than one version (i.e., inflected form) of the word `"tree"`.

```
library(hcandersenr)
library(tidyverse)
library(tidytext)

fir_tree <- hca_fairytales() %>%
  filter(book == "The fir tree",
         language == "English")

tidy_fir_tree <- fir_tree %>%
  unnest_tokens(word, text) %>%
  anti_join(get_stopwords())

tidy_fir_tree %>%
  count(word, sort = TRUE) %>%
  filter(str_detect(word, "^tree"))
```

```
#> # A tibble: 3 x 2
#>   word         n
#>   <chr>    <int>
#> 1 tree        76
#> 2 trees       12
#> 3 tree's       1
```

Trees, we see once again, are important in this story; the singular form appears 76 times and the plural form appears 12 times. (We'll come back to how we might handle the apostrophe in `"tree's"` later in this chapter.)

What if we aren't interested in the difference between `"trees"` and `"tree"` and we want to treat both together? That idea is at the heart of *stemming*, the process of identifying the base word (or stem) for a data set of words. Stemming is concerned with the linguistics subfield of morphology, how words are formed. In this example, `"trees"` would lose its letter `"s"` while `"tree"` stays the same. If we counted word frequencies again after stemming, we would find that there are 88 occurrences of the stem `"tree"` (89, if we also find the stem for `"tree's"`).

4.1   How to stem text in R

There have been many algorithms built for stemming words over the past half century or so; we'll focus on two approaches. The first is the stemming algorithm of Porter (1980), probably the most widely used stemmer for English. Porter himself released the algorithm implemented in the framework Snowball[1] with an open-source license; you can use it from R via the **SnowballC** package (Bouchet-Valat 2020). (It has been extended to languages other than English as well.)

```
library(SnowballC)
```

```
tidy_fir_tree %>%
  mutate(stem = wordStem(word)) %>%
  count(stem, sort = TRUE)
```

```
#> # A tibble: 570 x 2
#>    stem        n
#>    <chr>   <int>
#>  1 tree       88
#>  2 fir        34
#>  3 littl      23
#>  4 said       22
#>  5 stori      16
#>  6 thought    16
#>  7 branch     15
#>  8 on         15
#>  9 came       14
#> 10 know       14
#> # ... with 560 more rows
```

---

[1] https://snowballstem.org/

Take a look at those stems. Notice that we do now have 88 incidences of
`"tree"`. Also notice that some words don't look like they are spelled as real
words; this is normal and expected with this stemming algorithm. The Porter
algorithm identifies the stem of both `"story"` and `"stories"` as `"stori"`, not a
regular English word but instead a special stem object.

If you want to tokenize *and* stem your text data, you can try out the
function `tokenize_word_stems()` from the **tokenizers** package, which implements Porter stemming just as we demonstrated here. For more on
tokenization, see Chapter 2.

Does Porter stemming only work for English? Far from it! We can use the
`language` argument to implement Porter stemming in multiple languages. First
we can tokenize the text and `nest()` into list-columns.

```
stopword_df <- tribble(~language, ~two_letter,
                       "danish",  "da",
                       "english", "en",
                       "french",  "fr",
                       "german",  "de",
                       "spanish", "es")

tidy_by_lang <- hca_fairytales() %>%
  filter(book == "The fir tree") %>%
  select(text, language) %>%
  mutate(language = str_to_lower(language)) %>%
  unnest_tokens(word, text) %>%
  nest(data = word)
```

Then we can remove stop words (using `get_stopwords(language = "da")` and similar for each language) and stem with the language-specific Porter algorithm.
What are the top-20 stems for "The Fir-Tree" in each of these five languages,
after removing the Snowball stop words for that language?

```
tidy_by_lang %>%
  inner_join(stopword_df) %>%
  mutate(data = map2(
    data, two_letter, ~ anti_join(.x, get_stopwords(language = .y)))
  ) %>%
```

```
unnest(data) %>%
mutate(stem = wordStem(word, language = language)) %>%
group_by(language) %>%
count(stem) %>%
top_n(20, n) %>%
ungroup %>%
ggplot(aes(n, fct_reorder(stem, n), fill = language)) +
geom_col(show.legend = FALSE) +
facet_wrap(~language, scales = "free_y", ncol = 2) +
labs(x = "Frequency", y = NULL)
```

Figure 4.1 demonstrates some of the challenges in working with languages other than English; the stop word lists may not be even from language to language, and tokenization strategies that work for a language like English may struggle for a language like French with more stop word contractions. Given that, we see here words about little fir trees at the top for all languages, in their stemmed forms.

The Porter stemmer is an algorithm that starts with a word and ends up with a single stem, but that's not the only kind of stemmer out there. Another class of stemmer are dictionary-based stemmers. One such stemmer is the stemming algorithm of the Hunspell[2] library. The "Hun" in Hunspell stands for Hungarian; this set of NLP algorithms was originally written to handle Hungarian but has since been extended to handle many languages with compound words and complicated morphology. The Hunspell library is used mostly as a spell checker, but as part of identifying correct spellings, this library identifies word stems as well. You can use the Hunspell library from R via the **hunspell** (Ooms 2020b) package.

```
library(hunspell)
```

```
tidy_fir_tree %>%
  mutate(stem = hunspell_stem(word)) %>%
  unnest(stem) %>%
  count(stem, sort = TRUE)
```

---

[2] http://hunspell.github.io/

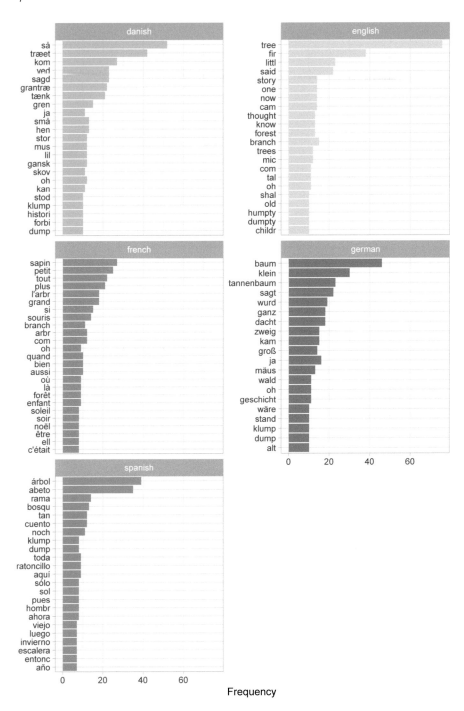

FIGURE 4.1: Porter stemming results in five languages

```
#> # A tibble: 595 x 2
#>    stem        n
#>    <chr>   <int>
#>  1 tree       89
#>  2 fir        34
#>  3 little     23
#>  4 said       22
#>  5 story      16
#>  6 branch     15
#>  7 one        15
#>  8 came       14
#>  9 know       14
#> 10 now        14
#> # ... with 585 more rows
```

Notice that the code here is a little different (we had to use unnest()) and that the results are a little different. We have only real English words, and we have more total rows in the result. What happened?

```
hunspell_stem("discontented")
```

```
#> [[1]]
#> [1] "contented" "content"
```

We have *two* stems! This stemmer works differently; it uses both morphological analysis of a word and existing dictionaries to find possible stems. It's possible to end up with more than one, and it's possible for a stem to be a word that is not related by meaning to the original word. For example, one of the stems of "number" is "numb" with this library. The Hunspell library was built to be a spell checker, so depending on your analytical purposes, it may not be an appropriate choice.

4.2 Should you use stemming at all?

You will often see stemming as part of NLP pipelines, sometimes without much comment about when it is helpful or not. We encourage you to think of stemming as a preprocessing step in text modeling, one that must be thought through and chosen (or not) with good judgment.

Why does stemming often help, if you are training a machine learning model for text? Stemming *reduces the feature space* of text data. Let's see this in action, with a data set of United States Supreme Court opinions available in the **scotus** package, discussed in more detail in Section B.2. How many words are there, after removing a standard data set of stopwords?

```
library(scotus)

tidy_scotus <- scotus_filtered %>%
  unnest_tokens(word, text) %>%
  anti_join(get_stopwords())

tidy_scotus %>%
  count(word, sort = TRUE)
```

```
#> # A tibble: 167,879 x 2
#>    word        n
#>    <chr>    <int>
#>  1 court   286448
#>  2 v       204176
#>  3 state   148320
#>  4 states  128160
#>  5 case    121439
#>  6 act     111033
#>  7 s.ct    108168
#>  8 u.s     106413
#>  9 upon    105069
#> 10 united  103267
#> # ... with 167,869 more rows
```

There are 167,879 distinct words in this data set we have created (after removing stopwords) but notice that even in the most common words we see a pair like `"state"` and `"states"`. A common data structure for modeling, and a helpful mental model for thinking about the sparsity of text data, is a matrix. Let's `cast()` this tidy data to a sparse matrix, technically, a document-feature matrix object from the **quanteda** (Benoit et al. 2018) package.

```
tidy_scotus %>%
  count(case_name, word) %>%
  cast_dfm(case_name, word, n)
```

```
#> Document-feature matrix of: 9,642 documents, 167,879
features (99.49% sparse) and 0 docvars.
```

Look at the sparsity of this matrix. It's high! Think of this sparsity as the sparsity of data that we will want to use to build a supervised machine learning model.

What if instead we use stemming as a preprocessing step here?

```
tidy_scotus %>%
  mutate(stem = wordStem(word)) %>%
  count(case_name, stem) %>%
  cast_dfm(case_name, stem, n)
```

```
#> Document-feature matrix of: 9,642 documents, 135,570
features (99.48% sparse) and 0 docvars.
```

We reduced the number of word features by many thousands, although the sparsity did not change much. Why is it possibly helpful to reduce the number of features? Common sense says that reducing the number of word features in our data set so dramatically will improve the performance of any machine learning model we train with it, *assuming that we haven't lost any important information by stemming.*

There is a growing body of academic research demonstrating that stemming can be counterproductive for text modeling. For example, Schofield and Mimno (2016) and related work explore how choices around stemming and other preprocessing steps don't help and can actually hurt performance when training topic models for text. From Schofield and Mimno (2016) specifically,

---

> Despite their frequent use in topic modeling, we find that stemmers produce no meaningful improvement in likelihood and coherence and in fact can degrade topic stability.

Topic modeling is an example of unsupervised machine learning for text and is not the same as the predictive modeling approaches we'll be focusing on in this book, but the lesson remains that stemming may or may not be beneficial for any specific context. As we work through the rest of this chapter and learn more about stemming, consider what information we lose when we stem text in exchange for reducing the number of word features. Stemming can be helpful in some contexts, but typical stemming algorithms are somewhat aggressive and have been built to favor sensitivity (or recall, or the true positive rate) at the expense of specificity (or precision, or the true negative rate).

Most common stemming algorithms you are likely to encounter will success-fully reduce words to stems (i.e., not leave extraneous word endings on the words) but at the expense of collapsing some words with dramatic differences in meaning, semantics, use, etc. to the same stems. Examples of the latter are numerous, but some include:

- meaning and mean

- likely, like, liking

- university and universe

In a supervised machine learning context, this affects a model's positive pre-dictive value (precision), or ability to not incorrectly label true negatives as positive. In Chapter 7, we will train models to predict whether a complaint to the United States Consumer Financial Protection Bureau was about a mort-gage or not. Stemming can increase a model's ability to find the positive ex-amples, i.e., the complaints about mortgages. However, if the complaint text is over-stemmed, the resulting model loses its ability to label the negative examples, the complaints *not* about mortgages, correctly.

4.3 Understand a stemming algorithm

If stemming is going to be in our NLP toolbox, it's worth sitting down with one approach in detail to understand how it works under the hood. The Porter stemming algorithm is so approachable that we can walk through its outline in less than a page or so. It involves five steps, and the idea of a word **measure**.

Think of any word as made up alternating groups of vowels V and consonants C. One or more vowels together are one instance of V, and one or more consonants togther are one instance of C. We can write any word as

$$[C](VC)^m[V]$$

where m is called the "measure" of the word. The first C and the last V in brackets are optional. In this framework, we could write out the word `tree` as

$$CV$$

with C being "tr" and V being "ee"; it's an `m = 0` word. We would write out the word `algorithms` as

$$VCVCVC$$

and it is an m = 3 word.

- The first step of the Porter stemmer is (perhaps this seems like cheating) actually made of three substeps working with plural and past participle word endings. In the first substep (1a), "sses" is replaced with "ss," "ies" is replaced with "i," and final single "s" letters are removed. The second substep (1b) depends on the measure of the word m but works with endings like "eed," "ed," "ing," adding "e" back on to make endings like "ate," "ble," and "ize" when appropriate. The third substep (1c) replaces "y" with "i" for words of a certain m.

- The second step of the Porter stemmer takes the output of the first step and regularizes a set of 20 endings. In this step, "ization" goes to "ize," "alism" goes to "al," "aliti" goes to "al" (notice that the ending "i" there came from the first step), and so on for the other 17 endings.

- The third step again processes the output, using a list of seven endings. Here, "ical" and "iciti" both go to "ic," "ful" and "ness" are both removed, and so forth for the three other endings in this step.

- The fourth step involves a longer list of endings to deal with again (19), and they are all removed. Endings like "ent," "ism," "ment," and more are removed in this step.

- The fifth and final step has two substeps, both which depend on the measure m of the word. In this step, depending on m, final "e" letters are sometimes removed and final double letters are sometimes removed.

How would this work for a few example words? The word "supervised" loses its "ed" in step 1b and is not touched by the rest of the algorithm, ending at "supervis". The word "relational" changes "ational" to "ate" in step 2 and loses its final "e" in step 5, ending at "relat". Notice that neither of these results are regular English words, but instead special stem objects. This is expected.

This algorithm was first published in Porter (1980) and is still broadly used; read Willett (2006) for background on how and why it has become a stemming standard. We can reach even *further* back and examine what is considered the first ever published stemming algorithm in Lovins (1968). The domain Lovins worked in was engineering, so her approach was particularly suited to technical terms. This algorithm uses much larger lists of word endings, conditions, and rules than the Porter algorithm and, although considered old-fashioned, is actually faster!

Check out the steps of a Snowball stemming algorithm for German[3].

4.4 Handling punctuation when stemming

Punctuation contains information that can be used in text analysis. Punctuation *is* typically less information-dense than the words themselves, and thus it is often removed early in a text mining analysis project, but it's worth thinking through the impact of punctuation specifically on stemming. Think about words like `"they're"` and `"child's"`.

We've already seen how punctuation and stemming can interact with our small example of "The Fir-Tree"; none of the stemming strategies we've discussed so far have recognized `"tree's"` as belonging to the same stem as `"trees"` and `"tree"`.

```
tidy_fir_tree %>%
  count(word, sort = TRUE) %>%
  filter(str_detect(word, "^tree"))
```

```
#> # A tibble: 3 x 2
#>   word       n
#>   <chr>  <int>
#> 1 tree      76
#> 2 trees     12
#> 3 tree's     1
```

It is possible to split tokens not only on white space but **also** on punctuation, using a regular expression (see Appendix A).

---

[3] https://snowballstem.org/algorithms/german/stemmer.html

```
fir_tree_counts <- fir_tree %>%
  unnest_tokens(word, text, token = "regex", pattern = "\\s+|[[:punct:]]+") %>%
  anti_join(get_stopwords()) %>%
  mutate(stem = wordStem(word)) %>%
  count(stem, sort = TRUE)

fir_tree_counts
```

```
#> # A tibble: 572 x 2
#>     stem         n
#>     <chr>    <int>
#>  1 tree        89
#>  2 fir         34
#>  3 littl       23
#>  4 said        22
#>  5 stori       16
#>  6 thought     16
#>  7 branch      15
#>  8 on          15
#>  9 came        14
#> 10 know        14
#> # ... with 562 more rows
```

Now we are able to put all these related words together, having identified them with the same stem.

```
fir_tree_counts %>%
  filter(str_detect(stem, "^tree"))
```

```
#> # A tibble: 1 x 2
#>   stem       n
#>   <chr> <int>
#> 1 tree     89
```

Handling punctuation in this way further reduces sparsity in word features. Whether this kind of tokenization and stemming strategy is a good choice in any particular data analysis situation depends on the particulars of the text characteristics.

4.5 Compare some stemming options

Let's compare a few simple stemming algorithms and see what results we end with. Let's look at "The Fir-Tree," specifically the tidied data set from which we have removed stop words. Let's compare three very straightforward stemming approaches.

- **Only remove final instances of the letter "s."** This probably strikes you as not a great idea after our discussion in this chapter, but it is something that people try in real life, so let's see what the impact is.

- **Handle plural endings with slightly more complex rules in the "S" stemmer.** The S-removal stemmer or "S" stemmer of Harman (1991) is a simple algorithm with only three rules.[4]

- **Implement actual Porter stemming.** We can now compare to the most commonly-used stemming algorithm in English.

```
stemming <- tidy_fir_tree %>%
  select(-book, -language) %>%
  mutate(`Remove S` = str_remove(word, "s$"),
         `Plural endings` = case_when(str_detect(word, "[^e|aies$]ies$") ~
                              str_replace(word, "ies$", "y"),
                            str_detect(word, "[^e|a|oes$]es$") ~
                              str_replace(word, "es$", "e"),
                            str_detect(word, "[^ss$|us$]s$") ~
                              str_remove(word, "s$"),
                            TRUE ~ word),
         `Porter stemming` = wordStem(word)) %>%
  rename(`Original word` = word)
```

Figure 4.2 shows the results of these stemming strategies. All successfully handled the transition from "trees" to "tree" in the same way, but we have different results for "stories" to "story" or "stori", different handling of "branches", and more. There are subtle differences in the output of even these straightforward stemming approaches that can effect the transformation of text features for modeling.

---

[4]This simple, "weak" stemmer is handy to have in your toolkit for many applications. Notice how we implement it here using `dplyr::case_when()`.

```
stemming %>%
  gather(Type, Result, `Remove S`:`Porter stemming`) %>%
  mutate(Type = fct_inorder(Type)) %>%
  count(Type, Result) %>%
  group_by(Type) %>%
  top_n(20, n) %>%
  ungroup %>%
  ggplot(aes(fct_reorder(Result, n),
             n, fill = Type)) +
  geom_col(show.legend = FALSE) +
  facet_wrap(~Type, scales = "free_y") +
  coord_flip() +
  labs(x = NULL, y = "Frequency")
```

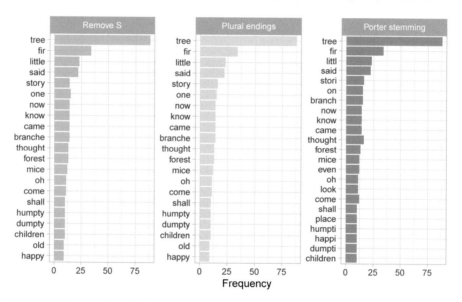

FIGURE 4.2: Results for three different stemming strategies

Porter stemming is the most different from the other two approaches. In the top-20 words here, we don't see a difference between removing only the letter "s" and taking the slightly more sophisticated "S" stemmer approach to plural endings. In what situations *do* we see a difference?

```
stemming %>%
  filter(`Remove S` != `Plural endings`) %>%
  distinct(`Remove S`, `Plural endings`, .keep_all = TRUE)
```

```
#> # A tibble: 13 x 4
#>    `Original word` `Remove S`   `Plural endings` `Porter stemming`
#>    <chr>           <chr>        <chr>            <chr>
#>  1 raspberries     raspberrie   raspberry        raspberri
#>  2 strawberries    strawberrie  strawberry       strawberri
#>  3 less            les          less             less
#>  4 us              u            us               u
#>  5 brightness      brightnes    brightness       bright
#>  6 conscious       consciou     conscious        consciou
#>  7 faintness       faintnes     faintness        faint
#>  8 happiness       happines     happiness        happi
#>  9 ladies          ladie        lady             ladi
#> 10 babies          babie        baby             babi
#> 11 anxious         anxiou       anxious          anxiou
#> 12 princess        princes      princess         princess
#> 13 stories         storie       story            stori
```

We also see situations where the same sets of original words are bucketed differently (not just with different stem labels) under different stemming strategies. In the following very small example, two of the strategies bucket these words into two stems while one strategy buckets them into one stem.

```
stemming %>%
  gather(Type, Result, `Remove S`:`Porter stemming`) %>%
  filter(Result %in% c("come", "coming")) %>%
  distinct(`Original word`, Type, Result)
```

```
#> # A tibble: 9 x 3
#>   `Original word` Type            Result
#>   <chr>           <chr>           <chr>
#> 1 come            Remove S        come
#> 2 comes           Remove S        come
#> 3 coming          Remove S        coming
#> 4 come            Plural endings  come
#> 5 comes           Plural endings  come
#> 6 coming          Plural endings  coming
#> 7 come            Porter stemming come
#> 8 comes           Porter stemming come
#> 9 coming          Porter stemming come
```

These different characteristics can either be positive or negative, depending on the nature of the text being modeled and the analytical question being pursued.

Language use is connected to culture and identity. How might the results of stemming strategies be different for text created with the same language (like English) but in different social or cultural contexts, or by people with different identities? With what kind of text do you think stemming algorithms behave most consistently, or most as expected? What impact might that have on text modeling?

4.6   Lemmatization and stemming

When people use the word "stemming" in natural language processing, they typically mean a system like the one we've been describing in this chapter, with rules, conditions, heuristics, and lists of word endings. Think of stemming as typically implemented in NLP as **rule-based**, operating on the word by itself. There is another option for normalizing words to a root that takes a different approach. Instead of using rules to cut words down to their stems, lemmatization uses knowledge about a language's structure to reduce words down to their lemmas, the canonical or dictionary forms of words. Think of lemmatization as typically implemented in NLP as **linguistics-based**, operating on the word in its context.

Lemmatization requires more information than the rule-based stemmers we've discussed so far. We need to know what part of speech a word is to correctly identify its lemma,[5] and we also need more information about what words mean in their contexts. Often lemmatizers use a rich lexical database like WordNet[6] as a way to look up word meanings for a given part-of-speech use (Miller 1995). Notice that lemmatization involves more linguistic knowledge of a language than stemming.

How does lemmatization work in languages other than English? Lookup dictionaries connecting words, lemmas, and parts of speech for languages other than English have been developed as well.

---

[5]Part-of-speech information is also sometimes used directly in machine learning
[6]https://wordnet.princeton.edu/

A modern, efficient implementation for lemmatization is available in the excellent spaCy[7] library (Honnibal et al. 2020), which is written in Python.

NLP practitioners who work with R can use this library via the **spacyr** package (Benoit and Matsuo 2020), the **cleanNLP**[8] package (Arnold 2017), or as an "engine" in the **textrecipes**[9] package (Hvitfeldt 2020a).

Section 6.6 demonstrates how to use textrecipes with spaCy as an engine and include lemmas as features for modeling. You might also consider using spaCy directly in R Markdown via its Python engine[10].

Let's briefly walk through how to use spacyr.

```
library(spacyr)
spacy_initialize(entity = FALSE)

fir_tree %>%
  mutate(doc_id = paste0("doc", row_number())) %>%
  select(doc_id, everything()) %>%
  spacy_parse() %>%
  anti_join(get_stopwords(), by = c("lemma" = "word")) %>%
  count(lemma, sort = TRUE) %>%
  top_n(20, n) %>%
  ggplot(aes(n, fct_reorder(lemma, n))) +
  geom_col() +
  labs(x = "Frequency", y = NULL)
```

Figure 4.3 demonstrates how different lemmatization is from stemming, especially if we compare to Figure 4.2. Punctuation characters are treated as tokens (these punctuation tokens can have predictive power for some modeling questions!), and all pronouns are lemmatized to -PRON-. We see our familiar friends "tree" and "fir," but notice that we see the normalized version "say" instead of "said," "come" instead of "came," and similar. This transformation to the canonical or dictionary form of words is the goal of lemmatization.

---

[7] https://spacy.io/
[8] https://statsmaths.github.io/cleanNLP/
[9] https://textrecipes.tidymodels.org/
[10] https://rstudio.github.io/reticulate/articles/r_markdown.html

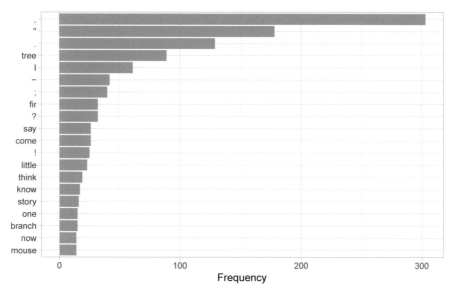

FIGURE 4.3: Results for lemmatization, rather than stemming

Why did we need to initialize the spaCy library? You may not need to, but spaCy is a full-featured NLP pipeline that not only tokenizes and identifies lemmas but also performs entity recognition. We will not use entity recognition in modeling or analysis in this book, and it takes a lot of computational power. Initializing with entity = FALSE will allow lemmatization to run much faster.

Implementing lemmatization is slower and more complex than stemming. Just like with stemming, lemmatization often improves the true positive rate (or recall) but at the expense of the true negative rate (or precision) compared to not using lemmatization, but typically less so than stemming.

4.7 Stemming and stop words

Our deep dive into stemming came *after* our chapters on tokenization (Chapter 2) and stop words (Chapter 3) because this is typically when you will want to implement stemming, if appropriate to your analytical question. Stop word lists are usually unstemmed, so you need to remove stop words before stemming text data. For example, the Porter stemming algorithm transforms words like `"themselves"` to `"themselv"`, so stemming first would leave you without the ability to match up to the commonly-used stop word lexicons.

A handy trick is to use the following function on your stop word list to return the words that don't have a stemmed version in the list. If the function returns a length 0 vector then you can stem and remove stop words in any order.

```
library(stopwords)
not_stemmed_in <- function(x) {
  x[!SnowballC::wordStem(x) %in% x]
}

not_stemmed_in(stopwords(source = "snowball"))
```

```
#>  [1] "ourselves"   "yourselves" "his"       "they"     "themselves"
#>  [6] "this"        "are"        "was"       "has"      "does"
#> [11] "you're"      "he's"       "she's"     "it's"     "we're"
#> [16] "they're"     "i've"       "you've"    "we've"    "they've"
#> [21] "let's"       "that's"     "who's"     "what's"   "here's"
#> [26] "there's"     "when's"     "where's"   "why's"    "how's"
#> [31] "because"     "during"     "before"    "above"    "once"
#> [36] "any"         "only"       "very"
```

Here we see that many of the words that are lost are the contractions.

In Section 3.2, we explored whether to include "tree" as a stop word for "The Fir-Tree." Now we can understand that this is more complicated than we first discussed, because there are different versions of the base word ("trees," "tree's") in our data set. Interactions between preprocessing steps can have a major impact on your analysis.

4.8 Summary

In this chapter, we explored stemming, the practice of identifying and extracting the base or stem for a word using rules and heuristics. Stemming reduces

the sparsity of text data, which can be helpful when training models, but at
the cost of throwing information away. Lemmatization is another way to normalize words to a root, based on language structure and how words are used
in their context.

4.8.1   In this chapter, you learned:

- about the most broadly-used stemming algorithms

- how to implement stemming

- that stemming changes the sparsity or feature space of text data

- the differences between stemming and lemmatization

5

Word Embeddings

> You shall know a word by the company it keeps.
> — John Rupert Firth[1]

So far in our discussion of natural language features, we have discussed preprocessing steps such as tokenization, removing stop words, and stemming in detail. We implement these types of preprocessing steps to be able to represent our text data in some data structure that is a good fit for modeling.

5.1 Motivating embeddings for sparse, high-dimensional data

What kind of data structure might work well for typical text data? Perhaps, if we wanted to analyze or build a model for consumer complaints to the United States Consumer Financial Protection Bureau (CFPB)[2], described in Section B.3, we would start with straightforward word counts. Let's create a sparse matrix, where the matrix elements are the counts of words in each document.

```
library(tidyverse)
library(tidytext)
library(SnowballC)

complaints <- read_csv("data/complaints.csv.gz")
```

---

[1] https://en.wikiquote.org/wiki/John_Rupert_Firth
[2] https://www.consumerfinance.gov/data-research/consumer-complaints/

```
complaints %>%
  unnest_tokens(word, consumer_complaint_narrative) %>%
  anti_join(get_stopwords(), by = "word") %>%
  mutate(stem = wordStem(word)) %>%
  count(complaint_id, stem) %>%
  cast_dfm(complaint_id, stem, n)
```

```
#> Document-feature matrix of: 117,214 documents, 46,099
features (99.88% sparse) and 0 docvars.
```

 A *sparse matrix* is a matrix where most of the elements are zero. When working with text data, we say our data is "sparse" because most documents do not contain most words, resulting in a representation of mostly zeroes. There are special data structures and algorithms for dealing with sparse data that can take advantage of their structure. For example, an array can more efficiently store the locations and values of only the non-zero elements instead of all elements.

The data set of consumer complaints used in this book has been filtered to those submitted to the CFPB since January 1, 2019 that include a consumer complaint narrative (i.e., some submitted text).

Another way to represent our text data is to create a sparse matrix where the elements are weighted, rather than straightforward counts only. The *term frequency* of a word is how frequently a word occurs in a document, and the *inverse document frequency* of a word decreases the weight for commonly-used words and increases the weight for words that are not used often in a collection of documents. It is typically defined as:

$$idf(\text{term}) = \ln \left(\frac{n_{\text{documents}}}{n_{\text{documents containing term}}} \right)$$

These two quantities can be combined to calculate a term's tf-idf (the two quantities multiplied together). This statistic measures the frequency of a term adjusted for how rarely it is used, and it is an example of a weighting scheme that can often work better than counts for predictive modeling with text features.

```
complaints %>%
  unnest_tokens(word, consumer_complaint_narrative) %>%
  anti_join(get_stopwords(), by = "word") %>%
  mutate(stem = wordStem(word)) %>%
  count(complaint_id, stem) %>%
  bind_tf_idf(stem, complaint_id, n) %>%
  cast_dfm(complaint_id, stem, tf_idf)
```

```
#> Document-feature matrix of: 117,214 documents, 46,099
features (99.88% sparse) and 0 docvars.
```

Notice that, in either case, our final data structure is incredibly sparse and of high dimensionality with a huge number of features. Some modeling algorithms and the libraries that implement them can take advantage of the memory characteristics of sparse matrices for better performance; an example of this is regularized regression implemented in **glmnet** (Friedman, Hastie, and Tibshirani 2010). Some modeling algorithms, including tree-based algorithms, do not perform better with sparse input, and then some libraries are not built to take advantage of sparse data structures, even if it would improve performance for those algorithms. We have some computational tools to take advantage of sparsity, but they don't always solve all the problems that come along with big text data sets.

As the size of a corpus increases in terms of words or other tokens, both the sparsity and RAM required to hold the corpus in memory increase. Figure 5.1 shows how this works out; as the corpus grows, there are more words used just a few times included in the corpus. The sparsity increases and approaches 100%, but even more notably, the memory required to store the corpus increases with the square of the number of tokens.

```
get_dfm <- function(frac) {
  complaints %>%
    sample_frac(frac) %>%
    unnest_tokens(word, consumer_complaint_narrative) %>%
    anti_join(get_stopwords(), by = "word") %>%
    mutate(stem = wordStem(word)) %>%
    count(complaint_id, stem) %>%
    cast_dfm(complaint_id, stem, n)
}
```

```
set.seed(123)
tibble(frac = 2 ^ seq(-16, -6, 2)) %>%
```

```
mutate(dfm = map(frac, get_dfm),
       words = map_dbl(dfm, quanteda::nfeat),
       sparsity = map_dbl(dfm, quanteda::sparsity),
       `RAM (in bytes)` = map_dbl(dfm, lobstr::obj_size)) %>%
pivot_longer(sparsity:`RAM (in bytes)`, names_to = "measure") %>%
ggplot(aes(words, value, color = measure)) +
geom_line(size = 1.5, alpha = 0.5) +
geom_point(size = 2) +
facet_wrap(~measure, scales = "free_y") +
scale_x_log10(labels = scales::label_comma()) +
scale_y_continuous(labels = scales::label_comma()) +
theme(legend.position = "none") +
labs(x = "Number of unique words in corpus (log scale)",
     y = NULL)
```

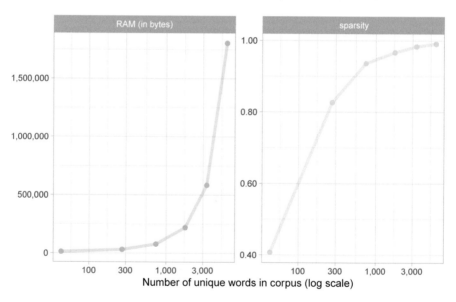

FIGURE 5.1: Memory requirements and sparsity increase with corpus size

Linguists have long worked on vector models for language that can reduce the number of dimensions representing text data based on how people use language; the quote that opened this chapter dates to 1957. These kinds of dense word vectors are often called *word embeddings*.

5.2 Understand word embeddings by finding them yourself

Word embeddings are a way to represent text data as vectors of numbers based on a huge corpus of text, capturing semantic meaning from words' context.

> Modern word embeddings are based on a statistical approach to modeling language, rather than a linguistics or rules-based approach.

We can determine these vectors for a corpus of text using word counts and matrix factorization, as outlined by Moody (2017). This approach is valuable because it allows practitioners to find word vectors for their own collections of text (with no need to rely on pre-trained vectors) using familiar techniques that are not difficult to understand. Let's walk through how to do this using tidy data principles and sparse matrices, on the data set of CFPB complaints. First, let's filter out words that are used only rarely in this data set and create a nested dataframe, with one row per complaint.

```
tidy_complaints <- complaints %>%
  select(complaint_id, consumer_complaint_narrative) %>%
  unnest_tokens(word, consumer_complaint_narrative) %>%
  add_count(word) %>%
  filter(n >= 50) %>%
  select(-n)

nested_words <- tidy_complaints %>%
  nest(words = c(word))

nested_words
```

```
#> # A tibble: 117,170 x 2
#>    complaint_id words
#>           <dbl> <list>
#> 1       3384392 <tibble [18 x 1]>
#> 2       3417821 <tibble [71 x 1]>
#> 3       3433198 <tibble [77 x 1]>
#> 4       3366475 <tibble [69 x 1]>
```

```
#>  5       3385399 <tibble [213 x 1]>
#>  6       3444592 <tibble [19 x 1]>
#>  7       3379924 <tibble [121 x 1]>
#>  8       3446975 <tibble [22 x 1]>
#>  9       3214857 <tibble [64 x 1]>
#> 10       3417374 <tibble [44 x 1]>
#> # ... with 117,160 more rows
```

Next, let's create a `slide_windows()` function, using the `slide()` function from the **slider** package (Vaughan 2021a) that implements fast sliding window computations written in C. Our new function identifies skipgram windows in order to calculate the skipgram probabilities, how often we find each word near each other word. We do this by defining a fixed-size moving window that centers around each word. Do we see `word1` and `word2` together within this window? We can calculate probabilities based on when we do or do not.

One of the arguments to this function is the `window_size`, which determines the size of the sliding window that moves through the text, counting up words that we find within the window. The best choice for this window size depends on your analytical question because it determines what kind of semantic meaning the embeddings capture. A smaller window size, like three or four, focuses on how the word is used and learns what other words are functionally similar. A larger window size, like 10, captures more information about the domain or topic of each word, not constrained by how functionally similar the words are (Levy and Goldberg 2014). A smaller window size is also faster to compute.

```
slide_windows <- function(tbl, window_size) {
  skipgrams <- slider::slide(
    tbl,
    ~.x,
    .after = window_size - 1,
    .step = 1,
    .complete = TRUE
  )

  safe_mutate <- safely(mutate)

  out <- map2(skipgrams,
              1:length(skipgrams),
              ~ safe_mutate(.x, window_id = .y))

  out %>%
    transpose() %>%
    pluck("result") %>%
```

```
    compact() %>%
    bind_rows()
}
```

Now that we can find all the skipgram windows, we can calculate how often words occur on their own, and how often words occur together with other words. We do this using the point-wise mutual information (PMI), a measure of association that measures exactly what we described in the previous sentence; it's the logarithm of the probability of finding two words together, normalized for the probability of finding each of the words alone. We use PMI to measure which words occur together more often than expected based on how often they occurred on their own.

For this example, let's use a window size of *four*.

This next step is the computationally expensive part of finding word embeddings with this method, and can take a while to run. Fortunately, we can use the **furrr** package (Vaughan and Dancho 2021) to take advantage of parallel processing because identifying skipgram windows in one document is independent from all the other documents.

```
library(widyr)
library(furrr)

plan(multisession)  ## for parallel processing

tidy_pmi <- nested_words %>%
  mutate(words = future_map(words, slide_windows, 4L)) %>%
  unnest(words) %>%
  unite(window_id, complaint_id, window_id) %>%
  pairwise_pmi(word, window_id)

tidy_pmi
```

```
#> # A tibble: 4,818,402 x 3
#>    item1    item2          pmi
#>    <chr>    <chr>        <dbl>
#>  1 systems  transworld   7.09
```

```
#>  2 inc     transworld  5.96
#>  3 is      transworld -0.135
#>  4 trying  transworld -0.107
#>  5 to      transworld -0.00206
#>  6 collect transworld  1.07
#>  7 a       transworld -0.516
#>  8 debt    transworld  0.919
#>  9 that    transworld -0.542
#> 10 not     transworld -1.17
#> # ... with 4,818,392 more rows
```

When PMI is high, the two words are associated with each other, i.e., likely
to occur together. When PMI is low, the two words are not associated with
each other, unlikely to occur together.

> The step above used `unite()`, a function from **tidyr** that pastes multiple
> columns into one, to make a new column for `window_id` from the old `win-
> dow_id` plus the `complaint_id`. This new column tells us which combination
> of window and complaint each word belongs to.

We can next determine the word vectors from the PMI values using singular
value decomposition (SVD). SVD is a method for dimensionality reduction
via matrix factorization (Golub and Reinsch 1970) that works by taking our
data and decomposing it onto special orthogonal axes. The first axis is chosen
to capture as much of the variance as possible. Keeping that first axis fixed,
the remaining orthogonal axes are rotated to maximize the variance in the
second. This is repeated for all the remaining axes.

In our application, we will use SVD to factor the PMI matrix into a set of
smaller matrices containing the word embeddings with a size we get to choose.
The embedding size is typically chosen to be in the low hundreds. Thus we get
a matrix of dimension (`n_vocabulary` * `n_dim`) instead of dimension (`n_vocabulary`
* `n_vocabulary`), which can be a vast reduction in size for large vocabularies.
Let's use the `widely_svd()` function in **widyr** (Robinson 2020), creating 100-
dimensional word embeddings. This matrix factorization is much faster than
the previous step of identifying the skipgram windows and calculating PMI.

```
tidy_word_vectors <- tidy_pmi %>%
  widely_svd(
    item1, item2, pmi,
```

```
    nv = 100, maxit = 1000
  )

tidy_word_vectors
```

```
#> # A tibble: 747,500 x 3
#>    item1    dimension    value
#>    <chr>        <int>    <dbl>
#>  1 systems          1   0.0165
#>  2 inc              1   0.0191
#>  3 is               1   0.0202
#>  4 trying           1   0.0423
#>  5 to               1   0.00904
#>  6 collect          1   0.0370
#>  7 a                1   0.0126
#>  8 debt             1   0.0430
#>  9 that             1   0.0136
#> 10 not              1   0.0213
#> # ... with 747,490 more rows
```

tidy_word_vectors is not drastically smaller than tidy_pmi since the vocabulary is not enormous and tidy_pmi is represented in a sparse format.

We have now successfully found word embeddings, with clear and understandable code. This is a real benefit of this approach; this approach is based on counting, dividing, and matrix decomposition and is thus easier to understand and implement than options based on deep learning. Training word vectors or embeddings, even with this straightforward method, still requires a large data set (ideally, hundreds of thousands of documents or more) and a not insignificant investment of time and computational power.

5.3 Exploring CFPB word embeddings

Now that we have determined word embeddings for the data set of CFPB complaints, let's explore them and talk about how they are used in modeling. We have projected the sparse, high-dimensional set of word features into a more dense, 100-dimensional set of features.

Each word can be represented as a numeric vector in this new feature space. A single word is mapped to only one vector, so be aware that all senses of a word are conflated in word embeddings. Because of this, word embeddings are limited for understanding lexical semantics.

Which words are close to each other in this new feature space of word embeddings? Let's create a simple function that will find the nearest words to any given example in using our newly created word embeddings.

```
nearest_neighbors <- function(df, token) {
  df %>%
    widely(
      ~ {
        y <- .[rep(token, nrow(.)), ]
        res <- rowSums(. * y) /
          (sqrt(rowSums(. ^ 2)) * sqrt(sum(.[token, ] ^ 2)))

        matrix(res, ncol = 1, dimnames = list(x = names(res)))
        },
      sort = TRUE
    )(item1, dimension, value) %>%
    select(-item2)
}
```

This function takes the tidy word embeddings as input, along with a word (or token, more strictly) as a string. It uses matrix multiplication and sums to calculate the cosine similarity between the word and all the words in the embedding to find which words are closer or farther to the input word, and returns a dataframe sorted by similarity.

What words are closest to `"error"` in the data set of CFPB complaints, as determined by our word embeddings?

```
tidy_word_vectors %>%
    nearest_neighbors("error")
```

```
#> # A tibble: 7,475 x 2
#>    item1            value
```

```
#>     <chr>              <dbl>
#>  1 error              1
#>  2 mistake            0.683
#>  3 clerical           0.627
#>  4 problem            0.582
#>  5 glitch             0.580
#>  6 errors             0.571
#>  7 miscommunication   0.512
#>  8 misunderstanding   0.486
#>  9 issue              0.478
#> 10 discrepancy        0.474
#> # ... with 7,465 more rows
```

Mistakes, problems, glitches – sounds bad!

What is closest to the word `"month"`?

```
tidy_word_vectors %>%
    nearest_neighbors("month")
```

```
#> # A tibble: 7,475 x 2
#>    item1          value
#>    <chr>          <dbl>
#>  1 month          1
#>  2 year           0.607
#>  3 months         0.593
#>  4 monthly        0.454
#>  5 installments   0.446
#>  6 payment        0.429
#>  7 week           0.406
#>  8 weeks          0.400
#>  9 85.00          0.399
#> 10 bill           0.396
#> # ... with 7,465 more rows
```

We see words about installments and payments, along with other time periods such as years and weeks. Notice that we did not stem this text data (see Chapter 4), but the word embeddings learned that "month," "months," and "monthly" belong together.

What words are closest in this embedding space to `"fee"`?

```
tidy_word_vectors %>%
    nearest_neighbors("fee")
```

```
#> # A tibble: 7,475 x 2
#>     item1      value
#>     <chr>      <dbl>
#>  1 fee        1
#>  2 fees       0.746
#>  3 overdraft  0.678
#>  4 12.00      0.675
#>  5 14.00      0.645
#>  6 37.00      0.632
#>  7 charge     0.630
#>  8 11.00      0.630
#>  9 36.00      0.627
#> 10 28.00      0.624
#> # ... with 7,465 more rows
```

We find a lot of dollar amounts, which makes sense. Let us filter out the numbers to see what non-dollar words are similar to "fee."

```
tidy_word_vectors %>%
  nearest_neighbors("fee") %>%
  filter(str_detect(item1, "[0-9]*.[0-9]{2}", negate = TRUE))
```

```
#> # A tibble: 7,047 x 2
#>     item1      value
#>     <chr>      <dbl>
#>  1 fee        1
#>  2 fees       0.746
#>  3 overdraft  0.678
#>  4 charge     0.630
#>  5 nsf        0.609
#>  6 charged    0.594
#>  7 od         0.552
#>  8 waived     0.547
#>  9 assessed   0.538
#> 10 charges    0.530
#> # ... with 7,037 more rows
```

We now find words about overdrafts and charges. The top two words are "fee" and "fees"; word embeddings can learn that singular and plural forms of words are related and belong together. In fact, word embeddings can accomplish many of the same goals of tasks like stemming (Chapter 4) but more reliably and less arbitrarily.

Since we have found word embeddings via singular value decomposition, we can use these vectors to understand what principal components explain the most variation in the CFPB complaints. The orthogonal axes that SVD used to represent our data were chosen so that the first axis accounts for the most variance, the second axis accounts for the next most variance, and so on. We can now explore which and how much each *original* dimension (tokens in this case) contributed to each of the resulting principal components produced using SVD.

```
tidy_word_vectors %>%
    filter(dimension <= 24) %>%
    group_by(dimension) %>%
    top_n(12, abs(value)) %>%
    ungroup %>%
    mutate(item1 = reorder_within(item1, value, dimension)) %>%
    ggplot(aes(item1, value, fill = dimension)) +
    geom_col(alpha = 0.8, show.legend = FALSE) +
    facet_wrap(~dimension, scales = "free_y", ncol = 4) +
    scale_x_reordered() +
    coord_flip() +
    labs(
      x = NULL,
      y = "Value",
      title = "First 24 principal components for text of CFPB complaints",
      subtitle = paste("Top words contributing to the components that explain",
                       "the most variation")
    )
```

It becomes very clear in Figure 5.2 that stop words have not been removed, but notice that we can learn meaningful relationships in how very common words are used. Component 12 shows us how common prepositions are often used with words like `"regarding"`, `"contacted"`, and `"called"`, while component 9 highlights the use of *different* common words when submitting a complaint about unethical, predatory, and/or deceptive practices. Stop words do carry information, and methods like determining word embeddings can make that information usable.

We created word embeddings and can explore them to understand our text data set, but how do we use this vector representation in modeling? The

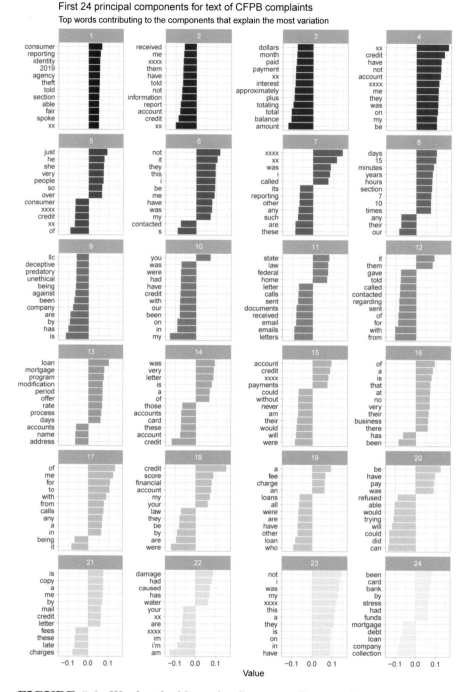

FIGURE 5.2: Word embeddings for Consumer Finance Protection Bureau complaints

classic and simplest approach is to treat each document as a collection of words and summarize the word embeddings into *document embeddings*, either using a mean or sum. This approach loses information about word order but is straightforward to implement. Let's count() to find the sum here in our example.

```
word_matrix <- tidy_complaints %>%
  count(complaint_id, word) %>%
  cast_sparse(complaint_id, word, n)

embedding_matrix <- tidy_word_vectors %>%
  cast_sparse(item1, dimension, value)

doc_matrix <- word_matrix %*% embedding_matrix

dim(doc_matrix)
```

```
#> [1] 117170    100
```

We have a new matrix here that we can use as the input for modeling. Notice that we still have over 100,000 documents (we did lose a few complaints, compared to our example sparse matrices at the beginning of the chapter, when we filtered out rarely used words) but instead of tens of thousands of features, we have exactly 100 features.

> These hundred features are the word embeddings we learned from the text data itself.

If our word embeddings are of high quality, this translation of the high-dimensional space of words to the lower-dimensional space of the word embeddings allows our modeling based on such an input matrix to take advantage of the semantic meaning captured in the embeddings.

This is a straightforward method for finding and using word embeddings, based on counting and linear algebra. It is valuable both for understanding what word embeddings are and how they work, but also in many real-world applications. This is not the method to reach for if you want to publish an academic NLP paper, but is excellent for many applied purposes. Other methods for determining word embeddings include GloVe (Pennington, Socher, and Manning 2014), implemented in R in the **text2vec** package (Selivanov, Bickel, and Wang 2020), word2vec (Mikolov et al. 2013), and FastText (Bojanowski et al. 2017).

5.4   Use pre-trained word embeddings

If your data set is too small, you typically cannot train reliable word embeddings.

> How small is too small? It is hard to make definitive statements because
> being able to determine useful word embeddings depends on the semantic and pragmatic details of *how* words are used in any given data set.
> However, it may be unreasonable to expect good results with data sets
> smaller than about a million words or tokens. (Here, we do not mean
> about a million unique tokens, i.e., the vocabulary size, but instead about
> that many observations in the text data.)

In such situations, we can still use word embeddings for feature creation in
modeling, just not embeddings that we determine ourselves from our own
data set. Instead, we can turn to *pre-trained* word embeddings, such as the
GloVe word vectors trained on six billion tokens from Wikipedia and news
sources. Several pre-trained GloVe vector representations are available in R
via the **textdata** package (Hvitfeldt 2020b). Let's use dimensions = 100, since
we trained 100-dimensional word embeddings in the previous section.

```
library(textdata)

glove6b <- embedding_glove6b(dimensions = 100)
glove6b
```

```
#> # A tibble: 400,000 x 101
#>    token        d1      d2       d3       d4       d5      d6       d7      d8       d9
#>    <chr>     <dbl>   <dbl>    <dbl>    <dbl>    <dbl>   <dbl>    <dbl>   <dbl>    <dbl>
#> 1 "the"   -0.0382 -0.245    0.728   -0.400    0.0832  0.0440 -0.391    0.334  -0.575
#> 2 ","     -0.108   0.111    0.598   -0.544    0.674   0.107   0.0389  0.355   0.0635
#> 3 "."     -0.340   0.209    0.463   -0.648   -0.384   0.0380  0.171   0.160   0.466
#> 4 "of"    -0.153  -0.243    0.898    0.170    0.535   0.488  -0.588  -0.180  -1.36
#> 5 "to"    -0.190   0.0500   0.191   -0.0492  -0.0897  0.210  -0.550   0.0984 -0.201
#> 6 "and"   -0.0720  0.231    0.0237  -0.506    0.339   0.196  -0.329   0.184  -0.181
#> 7 "in"     0.0857 -0.222    0.166    0.134    0.382   0.354   0.0129  0.225  -0.438
#> 8 "a"     -0.271   0.0440  -0.0203  -0.174    0.644   0.712   0.355   0.471  -0.296
```

```
#>  9 "\""   -0.305  -0.236   0.176  -0.729  -0.283  -0.256   0.266   0.0253 -0.0748
#> 10 "'s"    0.589  -0.202   0.735  -0.683  -0.197  -0.180  -0.392   0.342  -0.606
#> # ... with 399,990 more rows, and 91 more variables: d10 <dbl>, d11 <dbl>,
#> #    d12 <dbl>, d13 <dbl>, d14 <dbl>, d15 <dbl>, d16 <dbl>, d17 <dbl>,
#> #    d18 <dbl>, ...
```

We can transform these word embeddings into a more tidy format, using `pivot_longer()` from **tidyr**. Let's also give this tidied version the same column names as `tidy_word_vectors`, for convenience.

```
tidy_glove <- glove6b %>%
  pivot_longer(contains("d"),
                    names_to = "dimension") %>%
  rename(item1 = token)


tidy_glove
```

```
#> # A tibble: 40,000,000 x 3
#>      item1 dimension     value
#>      <chr> <chr>         <dbl>
#>  1 the     d1          -0.0382
#>  2 the     d2          -0.245
#>  3 the     d3           0.728
#>  4 the     d4          -0.400
#>  5 the     d5           0.0832
#>  6 the     d6           0.0440
#>  7 the     d7          -0.391
#>  8 the     d8           0.334
#>  9 the     d9          -0.575
#> 10 the     d10          0.0875
#> # ... with 39,999,990 more rows
```

We've already explored some sets of "synonyms" in the embedding space we determined ourselves from the CPFB complaints. What about this embedding space learned via the GloVe algorithm on a much larger data set? We just need to make one change to our `nearest_neighbors()` function and add `maximum_size = NULL`, because the matrices we are multiplying together are much larger this time.

```
nearest_neighbors <- function(df, token) {
  df %>%
    widely(
      ~ {
        y <- .[rep(token, nrow(.)), ]
        res <- rowSums(. * y) /
          (sqrt(rowSums(. ^ 2)) * sqrt(sum(.[token, ] ^ 2)))
        matrix(res, ncol = 1, dimnames = list(x = names(res)))
        },
      sort = TRUE,
      maximum_size = NULL
    )(item1, dimension, value) %>%
    select(-item2)
}
```

Pre-trained word embeddings are trained on very large, general purpose English language data sets. Commonly used word2vec embeddings[3] are based on the Google News data set, and GloVe embeddings[4] (what we are using here) and FastText embeddings[5] are learned from the text of Wikipedia plus other sources. Keeping that in mind, what words are closest to "error" in the GloVe embeddings?

```
tidy_glove %>%
    nearest_neighbors("error")
```

```
#> # A tibble: 400,000 x 2
#>    item1       value
#>    <chr>       <dbl>
#>  1 error       1
#>  2 errors      0.792
#>  3 mistake     0.664
#>  4 correct     0.621
#>  5 incorrect   0.613
#>  6 fault       0.607
#>  7 difference  0.594
#>  8 mistakes    0.586
#>  9 calculation 0.584
#> 10 probability 0.583
#> # ... with 399,990 more rows
```

---

[3] https://code.google.com/archive/p/word2vec/
[4] https://nlp.stanford.edu/projects/glove/
[5] https://fasttext.cc/docs/en/english-vectors.html

Instead of problems and mistakes like in the CFPB embeddings, we now see words related to sports, especially baseball, where an error is a certain kind of act recorded in statistics. This could present a challenge for using the GloVe embeddings with the CFPB text data. Remember that different senses or uses of the same word are conflated in word embeddings; the high-dimensional space of any set of word embeddings cannot distinguish between different uses of a word, such as the word "error."

What is closest to the word `"month"` in these pre-trained GloVe embeddings?

```
tidy_glove %>%
    nearest_neighbors("month")
```

```
#> # A tibble: 400,000 x 2
#>    item1    value
#>    <chr>    <dbl>
#>  1 month    1
#>  2 week     0.939
#>  3 last     0.924
#>  4 months   0.898
#>  5 year     0.893
#>  6 weeks    0.865
#>  7 earlier  0.859
#>  8 tuesday  0.846
#>  9 ago      0.844
#> 10 thursday 0.841
#> # ... with 399,990 more rows
```

Instead of words about payments, the GloVe results here focus on different time periods only.

What words are closest in the GloVe embedding space to `"fee"`?

```
tidy_glove %>%
    nearest_neighbors("fee")
```

```
#> # A tibble: 400,000 x 2
#>    item1     value
#>    <chr>     <dbl>
#>  1 fee       1
#>  2 fees      0.832
#>  3 payment   0.741
```

```
#>   4 pay            0.711
#>   5 salary         0.700
#>   6 paid           0.668
#>   7 payments       0.653
#>   8 subscription   0.647
#>   9 paying         0.623
#> 10 expenses        0.619
#> # ... with 399,990 more rows
```

The most similar words are, like with the CPFB embeddings, generally financial, but they are largely about salary and pay instead of about charges and
overdrafts.

These examples highlight how pre-trained word embeddings can be useful
because of the incredibly rich semantic relationships they encode, but also
how these vector representations are often less than ideal for specific tasks.

If we do choose to use pre-trained word embeddings, how do we go about
integrating them into a modeling workflow? Again, we can create simple document embeddings by treating each document as a collection of words and
summarizing the word embeddings. The GloVe embeddings do not contain all
the tokens in the CPFB complaints, and vice versa, so let's use inner_join()
to match up our data sets.

```
word_matrix <- tidy_complaints %>%
  inner_join(by = "word",
             tidy_glove %>%
               distinct(item1) %>%
               rename(word = item1)) %>%
  count(complaint_id, word) %>%
  cast_sparse(complaint_id, word, n)

glove_matrix <- tidy_glove %>%
  inner_join(by = "item1",
             tidy_complaints %>%
               distinct(word) %>%
               rename(item1 = word)) %>%
  cast_sparse(item1, dimension, value)

doc_matrix <- word_matrix %*% glove_matrix
```

```
dim(doc_matrix)
```

```
#> [1] 117163     100
```

Since these GloVe embeddings had the same number of dimensions as the word embeddings we found ourselves (100), we end up with the same number of columns as before but with slightly fewer documents in the data set. We have lost documents that contain only words not included in the GloVe embeddings.

> The package **wordsalad** (Hvitfeldt 2020c) provides a unified interface for finding different kinds of word vectors from text using pre-trained embeddings. The options include fastText, GloVe, and word2vec.

5.5 Fairness and word embeddings

Perhaps more than any of the other preprocessing steps this book has covered so far, using word embeddings opens an analysis or model up to the possibility of being influenced by systemic unfairness and bias.

> Embeddings are trained or learned from a large corpus of text data, and whatever human prejudice or bias exists in the corpus becomes imprinted into the vector data of the embeddings.

This is true of all machine learning to some extent (models learn, reproduce, and often amplify whatever biases exist in training data), but this is literally, concretely true of word embeddings. Caliskan, Bryson, and Narayanan (2017) show how the GloVe word embeddings (the same embeddings we used in Section 5.4) replicate human-like semantic biases.

- Typically Black first names are associated with more unpleasant feelings than typically white first names.

- Women's first names are more associated with family and men's first names are more associated with career.

- Terms associated with women are more associated with the arts and terms associated with men are more associated with science.

Results like these have been confirmed over and over again, such as when Bolukbasi et al. (2016) demonstrated gender stereotypes in how word embeddings encode professions or when Google Translate exhibited apparently sexist behavior when translating text from languages with no gendered pronouns[6]. Google has since worked to correct this problem[7], but in 2021 the problem still exists for some languages[8]. Garg et al. (2018) even used the way bias and stereotypes can be found in word embeddings to quantify how social attitudes towards women and minorities have changed over time.

Remember that word embeddings are *learned* or trained from some large data set of text; this training data is the source of the biases we observe when applying word embeddings to NLP tasks. Bender et al. (2021) outline how the very large data sets used in large language models do not mean that such models reflect representative or diverse viewpoints, or even can respond to changing social views. As one concrete example, a common data set used to train large embedding models is the text of Wikipedia, but Wikipedia itself has problems with, for example, gender bias[9]. Some of the gender discrepancies on Wikipedia can be attributed to social and historical factors, but some can be attributed to the site mechanics of Wikipedia itself (Wagner et al. 2016).

It's safe to assume that any large corpus of language will contain latent structure reflecting the biases of the people who generated that language.

When embeddings with these kinds of stereotypes are used as a preprocessing step in training a predictive model, the final model can exhibit racist, sexist, or otherwise biased characteristics. Speer (2017) demonstrated how using pre-trained word embeddings to train a straightforward sentiment analysis model can result in text such as

---

[6] https://twitter.com/seyyedreza/status/935291317252493312

[7] https://www.blog.google/products/translate/reducing-gender-bias-google-translate/

[8] https://twitter.com/doravargha/status/1373211762108076034

[9] https://en.wikipedia.org/wiki/Gender_bias_on_Wikipedia

Let's go get Italian food

being scored much more positively than text such as

Let's go get Mexican food

because of characteristics of the text the word embeddings were trained on.

5.6 Using word embeddings in the real world

Given these profound and fundamental challenges with word embeddings, what options are out there? First, consider not using word embeddings when building a text model. Depending on the particular analytical question you are trying to answer, another numerical representation of text data (such as word frequencies or tf-idf of single words or n-grams) may be more appropriate. Consider this option even more seriously if the model you want to train is already entangled with issues of bias, such as the sentiment analysis example in Section 5.5.

Consider whether finding your own word embeddings, instead of relying on pre-trained embeddings created using an algorithm like GloVe or word2vec, may help you. Building your own vectors is likely to be a good option when the text domain you are working in is *specific* rather than general purpose; some examples of such domains could include customer feedback for a clothing e-commerce site, comments posted on a coding Q&A site, or legal documents.

Learning good quality word embeddings is only realistic when you have a large corpus of text data (say, a million tokens), but if you have that much data, it is possible that embeddings learned from scratch based on your own data may not exhibit the same kind of semantic biases that exist in pre-trained word embeddings. Almost certainly there will be some kind of bias latent in any large text corpus, but when you use your own training data for learning word embeddings, you avoid the problem of *adding* historic, systemic prejudice from general purpose language data sets.

> You can use the same approaches discussed in this chapter to check any new embeddings for dangerous biases such as racism or sexism.

NLP researchers have also proposed methods for debiasing embeddings. Bolukbasi et al. (2016) aim to remove stereotypes by postprocessing pre-trained word vectors, choosing specific sets of words that are reprojected in the vector space so that some specific bias, such as gender bias, is mitigated. This is the most established method for reducing bias in embeddings to date, although other methods have been proposed as well, such as augmenting data with counterfactuals (Lu et al. 2020). Recent work (Ethayarajh, Duvenaud, and Hirst 2019) has explored whether the association tests used to measure bias are even useful, and under what conditions debiasing can be effective.

Other researchers, such as Caliskan, Bryson, and Narayanan (2017), suggest that corrections for fairness should happen at the point of *decision* or action rather than earlier in the process of modeling, such as preprocessing steps like building word embeddings. The concern is that methods for debiasing word embeddings may allow the stereotypes to seep back in, and more recent work shows that this is exactly what can happen. Gonen and Goldberg (2019) highlight how pervasive and consistent gender bias is across different word embedding models, *even after* applying current debiasing methods.

5.7   Summary

Mapping words (or other tokens) to an embedding in a special vector space is a powerful approach in natural language processing. This chapter started from fundamentals to demonstrate how to determine word embeddings from a text data set, but a whole host of highly sophisticated techniques have been built on this foundation. For example, document embeddings can be learned from text directly (Le and Mikolov 2014) rather than summarized from word embeddings. More recently, embeddings have acted as one part of language models with transformers like ULMFiT (Howard and Ruder 2018) and ELMo (Peters et al. 2018). It's important to keep in mind that even more advanced natural language algorithms, such as these language models with transformers, also exhibit such systemic biases (Sheng et al. 2019).

5.7.1 In this chapter, you learned:

- what word embeddings are and why we use them

- how to determine word embeddings from a text data set

- how the vector space of word embeddings encodes word similarity

- about a simple strategy to find document similarity

- how to handle pre-trained word embeddings

- why word embeddings carry historic and systemic bias

- about approaches for debiasing word embeddings

Part II

Machine Learning Methods

Overview

It's time to use what we have discussed and learned in the first five chapters of this book in a supervised machine learning context, to make predictions from text data. In the next two chapters, we will focus on putting into practice such machine learning algorithms as:

- naive Bayes,

- support vector machines (SVM) (Boser, Guyon, and Vapnik 1992), and

- regularized linear models such as implemented in glmnet[10] (Friedman, Hastie, and Tibshirani 2010).

We start in Chapter 6 with exploring regression models and continue in Chapter 7 with classification models. These are different types of prediction problems, but in both, we can use the tools of supervised machine learning to connect our *input*, which may exist entirely or partly as text data, with our *outcome* of interest. Most supervised models for text data are built with one of three purposes in mind:

- The main goal of a **predictive model** is to generate the most accurate predictions possible.

- An **inferential model** is created to test a hypothesis or draw conclusions about a population.

- The main purpose of a **descriptive model** is to describe the properties of the observed data.

Many learning algorithms can be used for more than one of these purposes. Concerns about a model's predictive capacity may be as important for an inferential or descriptive model as for a model designed purely for prediction, and model interpretability and explainability may be important for a solely predictive or descriptive model as well as for an inferential model. We will use

---

[10]https://glmnet.stanford.edu/

the tidymodels[11] framework to address all of these issues, with its consistent approach to resampling, preprocessing, fitting, and evaluation.

> The **tidymodels** framework (Kuhn and Wickham 2021a) is a collection of R packages for modeling and machine learning using tidyverse principles (Wickham et al. 2019). These packages facilitate resampling, preprocessing, modeling, and evaluation. There are core packages that you can load all together via `library(tidymodels)` and then extra packages for more specific tasks.

As you read through these next chapters, notice the modeling *process* moving through these stages; we'll discuss the structure of this process in more detail in the overview for the deep learning chapters.

Before we starting fitting these models to real data sets, let's consider how to think about algorithmic bias for predictive modeling. Rachel Thomas proposed a checklist at ODSC West 2019[12] for algorithmic bias in machine learning.

Should we even be doing this?

This is always the first step. Machine learning algorithms involve math and data, but that does not mean they are neutral. They can be used for purposes that are helpful, harmful, or even unethical.

What bias is already in the data?

Chapter 6 uses a data set of United States Supreme Court opinions, with an uneven distribution of years. There are many more opinions from more recent decades than from earlier ones. Bias like this is extremely common in data sets and must be considered in modeling. In this case, we show how using regularized linear models results in better predictions across years than other approaches (Section 6.3).

---

[11] https://www.tidymodels.org/

[12] https://opendatascience.com/odsc-west-2019-keynote-rachel-thomas-on-algorithmic-bias/

Can the code and data be audited?

In the case of this book, the code and data are all publicly available. You as a reader can audit our methods and what kinds of bias exist in the data sets. When you take what you have learned in this book and apply it your real-world work, consider how accessible your code and data are to internal and external stakeholders.

What are the error rates for sub-groups?

In Section 7.6 we demonstrate how to measure model performance for a multiclass classifier, but you can also compute model metrics for sub-groups that are not explicitly in your model as class labels or predictors. Using tidy data principles and the **yardstick** package makes this task well within the reach of data practitioners.

> In **tidymodels**, the **yardstick** package (Kuhn and Vaughan 2021a) has functions for model evaluation.

What is the accuracy of a simple rule-based alternative?

Chapter 7 shows how to train models to predict the category of a user complaint using sophisticated preprocessing steps and machine learning algorithms, but such a complaint could be categorized using simple regular expressions (Appendix A), perhaps combined with other rules. Straightforward heuristics are easy to implement, maintain, and audit, compared to machine learning models; consider comparing the accuracy of models to simpler options.

What processes are in place to handle appeals or mistakes?

If models such as those built in Chapter 7 were put into production by an organization, what would happen if a complaint was classified incorrectly? We as data practitioners typically (hopefully) have a reasonable estimate of the true positive rate and true negative rate for models we train, so processes to handle misclassifications can be built with a good understanding of how often they will be used.

How diverse is the team that built it?

The two-person team that wrote this book includes perspectives from a man and woman, and from someone who has always lived inside the United States and someone who is from a European country. However, we are both white with similar educational backgrounds. We must be aware of how the limited life experiences of individuals training and assessing machine learning models can cause unintentional harm.

6

Regression

In this chapter, we will use machine learning to predict *continuous values* that are associated with text data. Like in all predictive modeling tasks, this chapter demonstrates how to use learning algorithms to find and model relationships between an outcome or target variable and other input features. What is unique about the focus of this book is that our features are created from text data following the techniques laid out in Chapters 1 through 5, and what is unique about the focus of this particular chapter is that our outcome is numeric and continuous. For example, let's consider a sample of opinions from the United States Supreme Court, available in the **scotus** (Hvitfeldt 2019b) package.

```
library(tidyverse)
library(scotus)

scotus_filtered %>%
  as_tibble()
```

```
#> # A tibble: 10,000 x 5
#>    year  case_name               docket_number       id text
#>    <chr> <chr>                   <chr>            <dbl> <chr>
#>  1 1903  Clara Perry, Plff. In Err~ 16             80304 "No. 16.\n State Repor~
#>  2 1987  West v. Conrail         85-1804          96216 "No. 85-1804.\n\n     ~
#>  3 1957  Roth v. United States   582              89930 "Nos. 582, 61.\nNo. 61~
#>  4 1913  McDermott v. Wisconsin  Nos. 112 and ~   82218 "Nos. 112 and 113.\nMr~
#>  5 1826  Wetzell v. Bussard      <NA>             52899 "Feb. 7th.\nThis cause~
#>  6 1900  Forsyth v. Vehmeyer     180              79609 "No. 180.\nMr. Edward ~
#>  7 1871  Reed v. United States   <NA>             57846 "APPEAL and cross appe~
#>  8 1833  United States v. Mills  <NA>             53394 "CERTIFICATE of Divisi~
#>  9 1940  Puerto Rico v. Rubert Her~ 582           87714 "No. 582.\nMr. Wm. Cat~
#> 10 1910  Williams v. First Nat. Ba~ 130           81588 "No. 130.\nThe defenda~
#> # ... with 9,990 more rows
```

This data set contains the entire text of each opinion in the text column, along with the case_name and docket_number. Notice that we also have the year that each case was decided by the Supreme Court; this is basically a continuous variable (rather than a group membership of discrete label).

 If we want to build a model to predict which court opinions were written in which years, we would build a regression model.

- A **classification model** predicts a class label or group membership.

- A **regression model** predicts a numeric or continuous value.

In text modeling, we use text data (such as the text of the court opinions), sometimes combined with other structured, non-text data, to predict the continuous value of interest (such as year of the court opinion). The goal of predictive modeling with text input features and a continuous outcome is to learn and model the relationship between the input features and the numeric target (outcome).

6.1   A first regression model

Let's build our first regression model using this sample of Supreme Court opinions. Before we start, let's check out how many opinions we have for each decade in Figure 6.1.

```
scotus_filtered %>%
  mutate(year = as.numeric(year),
         year = 10 * (year %/% 10)) %>%
  count(year) %>%
  ggplot(aes(year, n)) +
  geom_col() +
  labs(x = "Year", y = "Number of opinions per decade")
```

This sample of opinions reflects the distribution over time of available opinions for analysis; there are many more opinions per year in this data set after about 1850 than before. This is an example of bias already in our data, as we discussed in the overview to these chapters, and we will need to account for that in choosing a model and understanding our results.

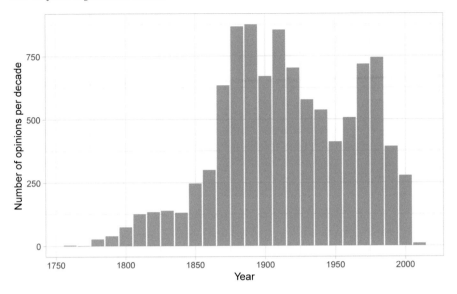

FIGURE 6.1: Supreme Court opinions per decade in sample

6.1.1 Building our first regression model

Our first step in building a model is to split our data into training and testing sets. We use functions from **tidymodels** for this; we use initial_split() to set up *how* to split the data, and then we use the functions training() and testing() to create the data sets we need. Let's also convert the year to a numeric value since it was originally stored as a character, and remove the ' character because of its effect on one of the models[1] we want to try out.

```
library(tidymodels)
set.seed(1234)
scotus_split <- scotus_filtered %>%
  mutate(year = as.numeric(year),
         text = str_remove_all(text, "'")) %>%
  initial_split()

scotus_train <- training(scotus_split)
scotus_test <- testing(scotus_split)
```

---

[1]The random forest implementation in the **ranger** package, demonstrated in Section 6.3, does not handle special characters in columns names well.

Next, let's preprocess our data to get it ready for modeling using a recipe. We'll use both general preprocessing functions from **tidymodels** and specialized functions just for text from **textrecipes** in this preprocessing.

> The **recipes** package (Kuhn and Wickham 2021b) is part of **tidymodels** and provides functions for data preprocessing and feature engineering. The **textrecipes** package (Hvitfeldt 2020a) extends **recipes** by providing steps that create features for modeling from text, as we explored in the first five chapters of this book.

What are the steps in creating this recipe?

- First, we must specify in our initial `recipe()` statement the form of our model (with the formula `year ~ text`, meaning we will predict the year of each opinion from the text of that opinion) and what our training data is.

- Then, we tokenize (Chapter 2) the text of the court opinions.

- Next, we filter to only keep the top 1000 tokens by term frequency. We filter out those less frequent words because we expect them to be too rare to be reliable, at least for our first attempt. (We are *not* removing stop words yet; we'll explore removing them in Section 6.4.)

- The recipe step `step_tfidf()`, used with defaults here, weights each token frequency by the inverse document frequency.

- As a last step, we normalize (center and scale) these tf-idf values. This centering and scaling is needed because we're going to use a support vector machine model.

```
library(textrecipes)

scotus_rec <- recipe(year ~ text, data = scotus_train) %>%
  step_tokenize(text) %>%
  step_tokenfilter(text, max_tokens = 1e3) %>%
  step_tfidf(text) %>%
  step_normalize(all_predictors())

scotus_rec
```

```
#> Data Recipe
#>
#> Inputs:
#>
#>          role #variables
#>       outcome           1
#>     predictor           1
#>
#> Operations:
#>
#> Tokenization for text
#> Text filtering for text
#> Term frequency-inverse document frequency with text
#> Centering and scaling for all_predictors()
```

Now that we have a full specification of the preprocessing recipe, we can prep() this recipe to estimate all the necessary parameters for each step using the training data and bake() it to apply the steps to data, like the training data (with new_data = NULL), testing data, or new data at prediction time.

```
scotus_prep <- prep(scotus_rec)
scotus_bake <- bake(scotus_prep, new_data = NULL)

dim(scotus_bake)
```

```
#> [1] 7500 1001
```

For most modeling tasks, you will not need to prep() or bake() your recipe directly; instead you can build up a tidymodels workflow() to bundle together your modeling components.

> In **tidymodels**, the **workflows** package (Vaughan 2021b) offers infrastructure for bundling model components. A *model workflow* is a convenient way to combine different modeling components (a preprocessor plus a model specification); when these are bundled explicitly, it can be easier to keep track of your modeling plan, as well as fit your model and predict on new data.

Let's create a workflow() to bundle together our recipe with any model specifications we may want to create later. First, let's create an empty workflow() and then only add the data preprocessor scotus_rec to it.

```
scotus_wf <- workflow() %>%
  add_recipe(scotus_rec)

scotus_wf
```

```
#> == Workflow ===============================================================
#> Preprocessor: Recipe
#> Model: None
#>
#> -- Preprocessor -----------------------------------------------------------
#> 4 Recipe Steps
#>
#> * step_tokenize()
#> * step_tokenfilter()
#> * step_tfidf()
#> * step_normalize()
```

Notice that there is no model yet: Model: None. It's time to specify the model we will use! Let's build a support vector machine (SVM) model. While they don't see widespread use in cutting-edge machine learning research today, they are frequently used in practice and have properties that make them well-suited for text classification (Joachims 1998) and can give good performance (Van-Tu and Anh-Cuong 2016).

An SVM model can be used for either regression or classification, and linear SVMs often work well with text data. Even better, linear SVMs typically do not need to be tuned (see Section 7.4 for tuning model hyperparameters).

Before fitting, we set up a model specification. There are three components to specifying a model using tidymodels: the model algorithm (a linear SVM here), the mode (typically either classification or regression), and the computational engine we are choosing to use. For our linear SVM, let's use the **LiblineaR** engine (Helleputte 2021).

```
svm_spec <- svm_linear() %>%
  set_mode("regression") %>%
  set_engine("LiblineaR")
```

Everything is now ready for us to fit our model. Let's add our model to the workflow with `add_model()` and fit to our training data `scotus_train`.

```
svm_fit <- scotus_wf %>%
  add_model(svm_spec) %>%
  fit(data = scotus_train)
```

We have successfully fit an SVM model to this data set of Supreme Court opinions. What does the result look like? We can access the fit using `pull_workflow_fit()`, and even `tidy()` the model coefficient results into a convenient dataframe format.

```
svm_fit %>%
  pull_workflow_fit() %>%
  tidy() %>%
  arrange(-estimate)
```

```
#> # A tibble: 1,001 x 2
#>    term                 estimate
#>    <chr>                   <dbl>
#>  1 Bias                   1920.
#>  2 tfidf_text_later        1.50
#>  3 tfidf_text_appeals      1.48
#>  4 tfidf_text_see          1.39
#>  5 tfidf_text_noted        1.38
#>  6 tfidf_text_example      1.27
#>  7 tfidf_text_petitioner   1.26
#>  8 tfidf_text_even         1.23
#>  9 tfidf_text_rather       1.21
#> 10 tfidf_text_including    1.13
#> # ... with 991 more rows
```

The term Bias here means the same thing as an intercept. We see here what terms contribute to a Supreme Court opinion being written more recently, like "appeals" and "petitioner."

What terms contribute to a Supreme Court opinion being written further in the past, for this first attempt at a model?

```
svm_fit %>%
  pull_workflow_fit() %>%
  tidy() %>%
  arrange(estimate)
```

```
#> # A tibble: 1,001 x 2
#>    term                    estimate
#>    <chr>                      <dbl>
#>  1 tfidf_text_ought           -2.77
#>  2 tfidf_text_1st             -1.94
#>  3 tfidf_text_but             -1.63
#>  4 tfidf_text_same            -1.62
#>  5 tfidf_text_the             -1.57
#>  6 tfidf_text_therefore       -1.54
#>  7 tfidf_text_it              -1.46
#>  8 tfidf_text_which           -1.40
#>  9 tfidf_text_this            -1.39
#> 10 tfidf_text_be              -1.33
#> # ... with 991 more rows
```

Here we see words like "ought" and "therefore."

6.1.2   Evaluation

One option for evaluating our model is to predict one time on the testing set to measure performance.

> The testing set is extremely valuable data, however, and in real-world situations, we advise that you only use this precious resource one time (or at most, twice).

The purpose of the testing data is to estimate how your final model will perform on new data; we set aside a proportion of the data available and pretend that it is not available to us for training the model so we can use it to estimate model performance on strictly out-of-sample data. Often during the process of modeling, we want to compare models or different model parameters. If we use the test set for these kinds of tasks, we risk fooling ourselves that we are doing better than we really are.

Another option for evaluating models is to predict one time on the training set to measure performance. This is the *same data* that was used to train the model, however, and evaluating on the training data often results in performance estimates that are too optimistic. This is especially true for powerful machine learning algorithms that can learn subtle patterns from data; we risk overfitting to the training set.

Yet another option for evaluating or comparing models is to use a separate validation set. In this situation, we split our data *not* into two sets (training and testing) but into three sets (testing, training, and validation). The validation set is used for computing performance metrics to compare models or model parameters. This can be a great option if you have enough data for it, but often we as machine learning practitioners are not so lucky.

What are we to do, then, if we want to train multiple models and find the best one? Or compute a reliable estimate for how our model has performed without wasting the valuable testing set? We can use **resampling**. When we resample, we create new simulated data sets from the training set for the purpose of, for example, measuring model performance.

Let's estimate the performance of the linear SVM regression model we just fit. We can do this using resampled data sets built from the training set.

In **tidymodels**, the package for data splitting and resampling is **rsample** (Silge et al. 2021).

Let's create 10-fold cross-validation sets, and use these resampled sets for performance estimates.

```
set.seed(123)
scotus_folds <- vfold_cv(scotus_train)

scotus_folds
```

```
#> #  10-fold cross-validation
#> # A tibble: 10 x 2
#>    splits            id
#>    <list>            <chr>
#>  1 <split [6750/750]> Fold01
#>  2 <split [6750/750]> Fold02
#>  3 <split [6750/750]> Fold03
```

```
#>  4 <split [6750/750]> Fold04
#>  5 <split [6750/750]> Fold05
#>  6 <split [6750/750]> Fold06
#>  7 <split [6750/750]> Fold07
#>  8 <split [6750/750]> Fold08
#>  9 <split [6750/750]> Fold09
#> 10 <split [6750/750]> Fold10
```

Each of these "splits" contains information about how to create cross-validation folds from the original training data. In this example, 90% of the training data is included in each fold for analysis and the other 10% is held out for assessment. Since we used cross-validation, each Supreme Court opinion appears in only one of these held-out assessment sets.

In Section 6.1.1, we fit one time to the training data as a whole. Now, to estimate how well that model performs, let's fit many times, once to each of these resampled folds, and then evaluate on the heldout part of each resampled fold.

```
set.seed(123)
svm_rs <- fit_resamples(
  scotus_wf %>% add_model(svm_spec),
  scotus_folds,
  control = control_resamples(save_pred = TRUE)
)

svm_rs
```

```
#> # Resampling results
#> # 10-fold cross-validation
#> # A tibble: 10 x 5
#>    splits              id     .metrics       .notes         .predictions
#>    <list>              <chr>  <list>         <list>         <list>
#>  1 <split [6750/750]> Fold01 <tibble [2 x 4]> <tibble [0 x 1]> <tibble [750 x 4~
#>  2 <split [6750/750]> Fold02 <tibble [2 x 4]> <tibble [0 x 1]> <tibble [750 x 4~
#>  3 <split [6750/750]> Fold03 <tibble [2 x 4]> <tibble [0 x 1]> <tibble [750 x 4~
#>  4 <split [6750/750]> Fold04 <tibble [2 x 4]> <tibble [0 x 1]> <tibble [750 x 4~
#>  5 <split [6750/750]> Fold05 <tibble [2 x 4]> <tibble [0 x 1]> <tibble [750 x 4~
#>  6 <split [6750/750]> Fold06 <tibble [2 x 4]> <tibble [0 x 1]> <tibble [750 x 4~
#>  7 <split [6750/750]> Fold07 <tibble [2 x 4]> <tibble [0 x 1]> <tibble [750 x 4~
#>  8 <split [6750/750]> Fold08 <tibble [2 x 4]> <tibble [0 x 1]> <tibble [750 x 4~
#>  9 <split [6750/750]> Fold09 <tibble [2 x 4]> <tibble [0 x 1]> <tibble [750 x 4~
#> 10 <split [6750/750]> Fold10 <tibble [2 x 4]> <tibble [0 x 1]> <tibble [750 x 4~
```

These results look a lot like the resamples, but they have some additional columns, like the .metrics that we can use to measure how well this model performed and the .predictions we can use to explore that performance more deeply. What results do we see, in terms of performance metrics?

```
collect_metrics(svm_rs)
```

```
#> # A tibble: 2 x 6
#>   .metric .estimator   mean     n std_err .config
#>   <chr>   <chr>       <dbl> <int>   <dbl> <chr>
#> 1 rmse    standard   15.6      10 0.216   Preprocessor1_Model1
#> 2 rsq     standard    0.895    10 0.00244 Preprocessor1_Model1
```

The default performance metrics to be computed for regression models are RMSE (root mean squared error) and R^2 (coefficient of determination). RMSE is a metric that is in the same units as the original data, so in units of *years*, in our case; the RMSE of this first regression model is 15.6 years.

RSME and R^2 are performance metrics used for regression models.

RSME is a measure of the difference between the predicted and observed values; if the model fits the data well, RMSE is lower. To compute RMSE, you take the mean values of the squared difference between the predicted and observed values, then take the square root.

R^2 is the squared correlation between the predicted and observed values. When the model fits the data well, the predicted and observed values are closer together with a higher correlation between them. The correlation between two variables is bounded between -1 and 1, so the closer R^2 is to one, the better.

These values are quantitative estimates for how well our model performed, and can be compared across different kinds of models. Figure 6.2 shows the predicted years for these Supreme Court opinions plotted against the true years when they were published, for all the resampled data sets.

```
svm_rs %>%
  collect_predictions() %>%
  ggplot(aes(year, .pred, color = id)) +
```

```
geom_abline(lty = 2, color = "gray80", size = 1.5) +
geom_point(alpha = 0.3) +
labs(
  x = "Truth",
  y = "Predicted year",
  color = NULL,
  title = "Predicted and true years for Supreme Court opinions",
  subtitle = "Each cross-validation fold is shown in a different color"
)
```

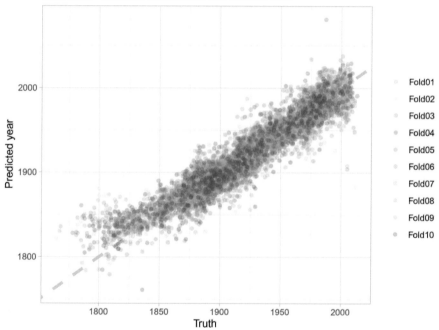

FIGURE 6.2: Most Supreme Court opinions are near the dashed line, indicating good agreement between our SVM regression predictions and the real years

The average spread of points in this plot above and below the dashed line corresponds to RMSE, which is 15.6 years for this model. When RMSE is better (lower), the points will be closer to the dashed line. This first model we have tried did not do a great job for Supreme Court opinions from before 1850, but for opinions after 1850, this looks pretty good!

Hopefully you are convinced that using resampled data sets for measuring performance is the right choice, but it can be computationally expensive. Instead of fitting once, we must fit the model one time for *each* resample. The resamples are independent of each other, so this is a great fit for parallel processing. The tidymodels framework is designed to work fluently with parallel processing in R, using multiple cores or multiple machines. The implementation details of parallel processing are operating system specific, so look at tidymodels' documentation for how to get started[2].

6.2 Compare to the null model

One way to assess a model like this one is to compare its performance to a "null model."

A null model is a simple, non-informative model that always predicts the largest class (for classification) or the mean (such as the mean year of Supreme Court opinions, in our specific regression case)[3].

We can use the same function `fit_resamples()` and the same preprocessing recipe as before, switching out our SVM model specification for the `null_model()` specification.

```
null_regression <- null_model() %>%
  set_engine("parsnip") %>%
  set_mode("regression")

null_rs <- fit_resamples(
  scotus_wf %>% add_model(null_regression),
  scotus_folds,
```

---

[2]https://tune.tidymodels.org/articles/extras/optimizations.html
[3]This is sometimes called a "baseline model."

```
  metrics = metric_set(rmse)
)

null_rs
```

```
#> # Resampling results
#> # 10-fold cross-validation
#> # A tibble: 10 x 4
#>    splits            id     .metrics         .notes
#>    <list>            <chr>  <list>           <list>
#>  1 <split [6750/750]> Fold01 <tibble [1 x 4]> <tibble [0 x 1]>
#>  2 <split [6750/750]> Fold02 <tibble [1 x 4]> <tibble [0 x 1]>
#>  3 <split [6750/750]> Fold03 <tibble [1 x 4]> <tibble [0 x 1]>
#>  4 <split [6750/750]> Fold04 <tibble [1 x 4]> <tibble [0 x 1]>
#>  5 <split [6750/750]> Fold05 <tibble [1 x 4]> <tibble [0 x 1]>
#>  6 <split [6750/750]> Fold06 <tibble [1 x 4]> <tibble [0 x 1]>
#>  7 <split [6750/750]> Fold07 <tibble [1 x 4]> <tibble [0 x 1]>
#>  8 <split [6750/750]> Fold08 <tibble [1 x 4]> <tibble [0 x 1]>
#>  9 <split [6750/750]> Fold09 <tibble [1 x 4]> <tibble [0 x 1]>
#> 10 <split [6750/750]> Fold10 <tibble [1 x 4]> <tibble [0 x 1]>
```

What results do we obtain from the null model, in terms of performance
metrics?

```
collect_metrics(null_rs)
```

```
#> # A tibble: 1 x 6
#>    .metric .estimator  mean      n std_err .config
#>    <chr>   <chr>      <dbl>  <int>   <dbl> <chr>
#> 1 rmse    standard    47.9     10   0.294 Preprocessor1_Model1
```

The RMSE indicates that this null model is dramatically worse than our first
model. Even our first very attempt at a regression model (using only unigrams
and very little specialized preprocessing) did much better than the null model;
the text of the Supreme Court opinions has enough information in it related
to the year the opinions were published that we can build successful models.

6.3 Compare to a random forest model

Random forest models are broadly used in predictive modeling contexts because they are low-maintenance and perform well. For example, see Caruana, Karampatziakis, and Yessenalina (2008) and Olson et al. (2018) for comparisons of the performance of common models such as random forest, decision tree, support vector machines, etc. trained on benchmark data sets; random forest models were one of the best overall. Let's see how a random forest model performs with our data set of Supreme Court opinions.

First, let's build a random forest model specification, using the ranger implementation. Random forest models are known for performing well without hyperparameter tuning, so we will just make sure we have enough trees.

```
rf_spec <- rand_forest(trees = 1000) %>%
  set_engine("ranger") %>%
  set_mode("regression")

rf_spec
```

```
#> Random Forest Model Specification (regression)
#>
#> Main Arguments:
#>   trees = 1000
#>
#> Computational engine: ranger
```

Now we can fit this random forest model. Let's use fit_resamples() again, so we can evaluate the model performance. We will use three arguments to this function:

- Our modeling workflow(), with the same preprocessing recipe we have been using so far in this chapter plus our new random forest model specification

- Our cross-validation resamples of the Supreme Court opinions

- A control argument to specify that we want to keep the predictions, to explore after fitting

```
rf_rs <- fit_resamples(
  scotus_wf %>% add_model(rf_spec),
  scotus_folds,
  control = control_resamples(save_pred = TRUE)
)
```

We can use `collect_metrics()` to obtain and format the performance metrics for this random forest model.

```
collect_metrics(rf_rs)
```

```
#> # A tibble: 2 x 6
#>    .metric .estimator   mean     n std_err .config
#>    <chr>   <chr>       <dbl> <int>   <dbl> <chr>
#> 1 rmse    standard    15.0     10 0.264   Preprocessor1_Model1
#> 2 rsq     standard     0.919   10 0.00283 Preprocessor1_Model1
```

This looks pretty promising, so let's explore the predictions for this random forest model.

```
collect_predictions(rf_rs) %>%
  ggplot(aes(year, .pred, color = id)) +
  geom_abline(lty = 2, color = "gray80", size = 1.5) +
  geom_point(alpha = 0.3) +
  labs(
    x = "Truth",
    y = "Predicted year",
    color = NULL,
    title = paste("Predicted and true years for Supreme Court opinions using",
                  "a random forest model", sep = "\n"),
    subtitle = "Each cross-validation fold is shown in a different color"
  )
```

Figure 6.3 shows some of the strange behavior from our fitted model. The overall performance metrics look pretty good, but predictions are too high and too low around certain threshold years.

It is very common to run into problems when using tree-based models like random forests with text data. One of the defining characteristics of text data is that it is *sparse*, with many features but most features not occurring in most observations. Tree-based models such as random forests are often

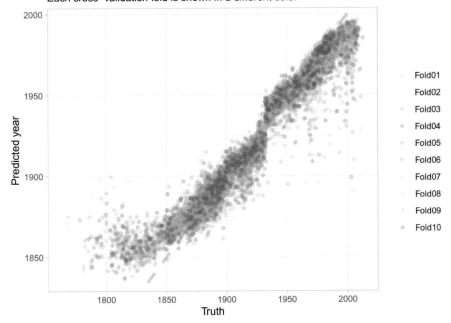

FIGURE 6.3: The random forest model did not perform very sensibly across years, compared to our first attempt using a linear SVM model

not well-suited to sparse data because of how decision trees model outcomes (Tang, Garreau, and Luxburg 2018).

Models that work best with text tend to be models designed for or otherwise appropriate for sparse data.

Algorithms that work well with sparse data are less important when text has been transformed to a non-sparse representation, such as with word embeddings (Chapter 5).

6.4   Case study: removing stop words

We did not remove stop words (Chapter 3) in any of our models so far in this chapter. What impact will removing stop words have, and how do we know which stop word list is the best to use? The best way to answer these questions is with experimentation.

Removing stop words is part of data preprocessing, so we define this step as part of our preprocessing recipe. Let's use the best model we've found so far (the linear SVM model from Section 6.1.2) and switch in a different recipe in our modeling workflow.

Let's build a small recipe wrapper helper function so we can pass a value `stopword_name` to `step_stopwords()`.

```r
stopword_rec <- function(stopword_name) {
  recipe(year ~ text, data = scotus_train) %>%
    step_tokenize(text) %>%
    step_stopwords(text, stopword_source = stopword_name) %>%
    step_tokenfilter(text, max_tokens = 1e3) %>%
    step_tfidf(text) %>%
    step_normalize(all_predictors())
}
```

For example, now we can create a recipe that removes the Snowball stop words list by calling this function.

```r
stopword_rec("snowball")
```

```
#> Data Recipe
#>
#> Inputs:
#>
#>        role #variables
#>     outcome          1
#>   predictor          1
#>
#> Operations:
#>
#> Tokenization for text
```

```
#> Stop word removal for text
#> Text filtering for text
#> Term frequency-inverse document frequency with text
#> Centering and scaling for all_predictors()
```

Next, let's set up a new workflow that has a model only, using `add_model()`. We start with the empty `workflow()` and then add our linear SVM regression model.

```
svm_wf <- workflow() %>%
  add_model(svm_spec)

svm_wf
```

```
#> == Workflow ========================================================
#> Preprocessor: None
#> Model: svm_linear()
#>
#> -- Model -------------------   ---------------------------------------------
#> Linear Support Vector Machine Specification (regression)
#>
#> Computational engine: LiblineaR
```

Notice that for this workflow, there is no preprocessor yet: `Preprocessor: None`. This workflow uses the same linear SVM specification that we used in Section 6.1, but we are going to combine several different preprocessing recipes with it, one for each stop word lexicon we want to try.

Now we can put this all together and fit these models that include stop word removal. We could create a little helper function for fitting like we did for the recipe, but we have printed out all three calls to `fit_resamples()` for extra clarity. Notice for each one that there are two arguments:

- A workflow, which consists of the linear SVM model specification and a data preprocessing recipe with stop word removal

- The same cross-validation folds we created earlier

```
set.seed(123)
snowball_rs <- fit_resamples(
  svm_wf %>% add_recipe(stopword_rec("snowball")),
```

```
  scotus_folds
)

set.seed(234)
smart_rs <- fit_resamples(
  svm_wf %>% add_recipe(stopword_rec("smart")),
  scotus_folds
)

set.seed(345)
stopwords_iso_rs <- fit_resamples(
  svm_wf %>% add_recipe(stopword_rec("stopwords-iso")),
  scotus_folds
)
```

After fitting models to each of the cross-validation folds, these sets of results contain metrics computed for removing that set of stop words.

```
collect_metrics(smart_rs)
```

```
#> # A tibble: 2 x 6
#>    .metric .estimator    mean     n std_err .config
#>    <chr>   <chr>        <dbl> <int>   <dbl> <chr>
#> 1 rmse    standard    17.2      10 0.199   Preprocessor1_Model1
#> 2 rsq     standard     0.876    10 0.00261 Preprocessor1_Model1
```

We can explore whether one of these sets of stop words performed better than the others by comparing the performance, for example in terms of RMSE as shown Figure 6.4. This plot shows the five best models for each set of stop words, using show_best() applied to each via purrr::map_dfr().

```
word_counts <- tibble(name = c("snowball", "smart", "stopwords-iso")) %>%
  mutate(words = map_int(name, ~length(stopwords::stopwords(source = .))))

list(snowball = snowball_rs,
     smart = smart_rs,
     `stopwords-iso` = stopwords_iso_rs) %>%
  map_dfr(show_best, "rmse", .id = "name") %>%
  left_join(word_counts, by = "name") %>%
  mutate(name = paste0(name, " (", words, " words)"),
```

```
            name = fct_reorder(name, words)) %>%
  ggplot(aes(name, mean, color = name)) +
  geom_crossbar(aes(ymin = mean - std_err, ymax = mean + std_err), alpha = 0.6) +
  geom_point(size = 3, alpha = 0.8) +
  theme(legend.position = "none") +
  labs(x = NULL, y = "RMSE",
       title = "Model performance for three stop word lexicons",
       subtitle = "For this data set, the Snowball lexicon performed best")
```

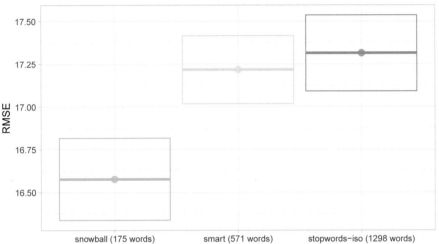

FIGURE 6.4: Comparing model performance for predicting the year of Supreme Court opinions with three different stop word lexicons

The Snowball lexicon contains the smallest number of words (see Figure 3.1) and, in this case, results in the best performance. Removing fewer stop words results in the best performance.

This result is not generalizable to all data sets and contexts, but the approach outlined in this section **is** generalizable.

This approach can be used to compare different lexicons and find the best one for a specific data set and model. Notice how the results for all stop word lexicons are worse than removing no stop words at all (remember that the

RMSE was 15.6 years in Section 6.1.2). This indicates that, for this particular data set, removing even a small stop word list is not a great choice.

When removing stop words does appear to help a model, it's good to know that removing stop words isn't computationally slow or difficult so the cost for this improvement is low.

6.5   Case study: varying n-grams

Each model trained so far in this chapter has involved single words or *unigrams*, but using n-grams (Section 2.2.3) can integrate different kinds of information into a model. Bigrams and trigrams (or even higher-order n-grams) capture concepts that span single words, as well as effects from word order, that can be predictive.

This is another part of data preprocessing, so we again define this step as part of our preprocessing recipe. Let's build another small recipe wrapper helper function so we can pass a list of options ngram_options to step_tokenize(). We'll use it with the same model as the previous section.

```
ngram_rec <- function(ngram_options) {
  recipe(year ~ text, data = scotus_train) %>%
    step_tokenize(text, token = "ngrams", options = ngram_options) %>%
    step_tokenfilter(text, max_tokens = 1e3) %>%
    step_tfidf(text) %>%
    step_normalize(all_predictors())
}
```

There are two options we can specify, n and n_min, when we are using engine = "tokenizers". We can set up a recipe with only n = 1 to tokenize and only extract the unigrams.

```
ngram_rec(list(n = 1))
```

We can use n = 3, n_min = 1 to identify the set of all trigrams, bigrams, *and* unigrams.

```
ngram_rec(list(n = 3, n_min = 1))
```

Including n-grams of different orders in a model (such as trigrams, bi-grams, plus unigrams) allows the model to learn at different levels of linguistic organization and context.

We can reuse the same workflow svm_wf from our earlier case study; these types of modular components are a benefit to adopting this approach to supervised machine learning. This workflow provides the linear SVM specification. Let's put it all together and create a helper function to use fit_resamples() with this model plus our helper recipe function.

```
fit_ngram <- function(ngram_options) {
  fit_resamples(
    svm_wf %>% add_recipe(ngram_rec(ngram_options)),
    scotus_folds
  )
}
```

We could have created this type of small function for trying out differ-ent stop word lexicons in Section 6.4, but there we showed each call to fit_resamples() for extra clarity.

With this helper function, let's try out predicting the year of Supreme Court opinions using:

- only unigrams

- bigrams and unigrams

- trigrams, bigrams, and unigrams

```
set.seed(123)
unigram_rs <- fit_ngram(list(n = 1))

set.seed(234)
bigram_rs <- fit_ngram(list(n = 2, n_min = 1))

set.seed(345)
trigram_rs <- fit_ngram(list(n = 3, n_min = 1))
```

These sets of results contain metrics computed for the model with that tokenization strategy.

```
collect_metrics(bigram_rs)
```

```
#> # A tibble: 2 x 6
#>   .metric .estimator   mean     n std_err .config
#>   <chr>   <chr>       <dbl> <int>   <dbl> <chr>
#> 1 rmse    standard   15.9     10 0.225   Preprocessor1_Model1
#> 2 rsq     standard    0.892   10 0.00240 Preprocessor1_Model1
```

We can compare the performance of these models in terms of RMSE as shown Figure 6.5.

```
list(`1` = unigram_rs,
     `1 and 2` = bigram_rs,
     `1, 2, and 3` = trigram_rs) %>%
  map_dfr(collect_metrics, .id = "name") %>%
  filter(.metric == "rmse") %>%
  ggplot(aes(name, mean, color = name)) +
  geom_crossbar(aes(ymin = mean - std_err, ymax = mean + std_err), alpha = 0.6) +
  geom_point(size = 3, alpha = 0.8) +
  theme(legend.position = "none") +
  labs(
    x = "Degree of n-grams",
    y = "RMSE",
    title = "Model performance for different degrees of n-gram tokenization",
    subtitle = "For the same number of tokens, unigrams performed best"
  )
```

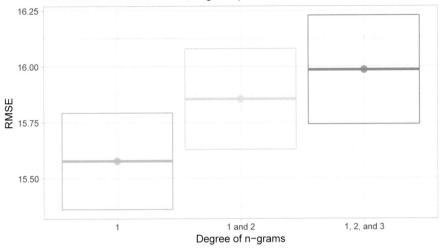

FIGURE 6.5: Comparing model performance for predicting the year of Supreme Court opinions with three different degrees of n-grams

Each of these models was trained with `max_tokens = 1e3`, i.e., including only the top 1000 tokens for each tokenization strategy. Holding the number of tokens constant, using unigrams alone performs best for this corpus of Supreme Court opinions. To be able to incorporate the more complex information in bigrams or trigrams, we would need to increase the number of tokens in the model considerably.

Keep in mind that adding n-grams is computationally expensive to start with, especially compared to the typical improvement in model performance gained. We can benchmark the whole model workflow, including preprocessing and modeling. Using bigrams plus unigrams takes more than twice as long to train than only unigrams (number of tokens held constant), and adding in trigrams as well takes almost five times as long as training on unigrams alone.

6.6 Case study: lemmatization

As we discussed in Section 4.6, we can normalize words to their roots or **lemmas** based on each word's context and the structure of a language. Table 6.1 shows both the original words and the lemmas for one sentence from a

Supreme Court opinion, using lemmatization implemented via the spaCy[4] library as made available through the **spacyr** R package (Benoit and Matsuo 2020).

Notice several things about lemmatization that are different from the kind of default tokenization (Chapter 2) you may be more familiar with.

- Words are converted to lowercase except for proper nouns.

- The lemma for pronouns is -PRON-.

- Words are converted from their existing form in the text to their canonical roots, like "disagree" and "conclude."

- Irregular verbs are converted to their canonical form ("did" to "do").

Using lemmatization instead of a more straightforward tokenization strategy is slower because of the increased complexity involved, but it can be worth it. Let's explore how to train a model using *lemmas* instead of *words*.

Lemmatization is, like choices around n-grams and stop words, part of data preprocessing so we define how to set up lemmatization as part of our preprocessing recipe. We use `engine = "spacyr"` for tokenization (instead of the default) and add `step_lemma()` to our preprocessing. This step extracts the lemmas from the parsing done by the tokenization engine.

```
spacyr::spacy_initialize(entity = FALSE)
```

```
#> NULL
```

```
lemma_rec <- recipe(year ~ text, data = scotus_train) %>%
  step_tokenize(text, engine = "spacyr") %>%
  step_lemma(text) %>%
  step_tokenfilter(text, max_tokens = 1e3) %>%
  step_tfidf(text) %>%
  step_normalize(all_predictors())
```

```
lemma_rec
```

---

[4] https://spacy.io/

Lemmatization of one sentence from a Supreme Court opinion

original word	lemma
However	however
,	,
the	the
Court	Court
of	of
Appeals	Appeals
disagreed	disagree
with	with
the	the
District	District
Court	Court
's	's
construction	construction
of	of
the	the
state	state
statute	statute
,	,
concluding	conclude
that	that
it	it
did	do
authorize	authorize
issuance	issuance
of	of
the	the
orders	order
to	to
withhold	withhold
to	to
the	the
Postal	Postal
Service	Service
.	.

```
#> Data Recipe
#>
#> Inputs:
#>
#>         role #variables
#>    outcome          1
#>  predictor          1
#>
#> Operations:
#>
#> Tokenization for text
#> Lemmatization for text
#> Text filtering for text
#> Term frequency-inverse document frequency with text
#> Centering and scaling for all_predictors()
```

Let's combine this lemmatized text with our linear SVM workflow. We can then fit our workflow to our resampled data sets and estimate performance using lemmatization.

```
lemma_rs <- fit_resamples(
  svm_wf %>% add_recipe(lemma_rec),
  scotus_folds
)
```

How did this model perform?

```
collect_metrics(lemma_rs)
```

```
#> # A tibble: 2 x 6
#>    .metric .estimator    mean      n std_err .config
#>    <chr>   <chr>        <dbl>  <int>   <dbl> <chr>
#> 1 rmse    standard     14.2      10   0.276  Preprocessor1_Model1
#> 2 rsq     standard      0.913    10   0.00304 Preprocessor1_Model1
```

The best value for RMSE at 14.2 shows us that using lemmatization can have a significant benefit for model performance, compared to 15.6 from fitting a non-lemmatized linear SVM model in Section 6.1.2. The best model using lemmatization is better than the best model without. However, this comes at a cost of much slower training because of the procedure involved in identifying lemmas; adding step_lemma() to our preprocessing increases the overall time to train the workflow by over 10-fold.

We can use engine = "spacyr" to assign part-of-speech tags to the tokens during tokenization, and this information can be used in various useful ways in text modeling. One approach is to filter tokens to only retain a certain part of speech, like nouns. An example of how to do this is illustrated in this **textrecipes** blogpost[5] and can be performed with step_pos_filter().

6.7   Case study: feature hashing

The models we have created so far have used tokenization (Chapter 2) to split apart text data into tokens that are meaningful to us as human beings (words, bigrams) and then weighted these tokens by simple counts with word frequencies or weighted counts with tf-idf. A problem with these methods is that the output space can be vast and dynamic. We have limited ourselves to 1000 tokens so far in this chapter, but we could easily have more than 10,000 features in our training set. We may run into computational problems with memory or long processing times; deciding how many tokens to include can become a trade-off between computational time and information. This style of approach also doesn't let us take advantage of new tokens we didn't see in our training data.

One method that has gained popularity in the machine learning field is the **hashing trick**. This method addresses many of the challenges outlined above and is very fast with a low memory footprint.

Let's start with the basics of feature hashing. First proposed by Weinberger et al. (2009), feature hashing was introduced as a dimensionality reduction method with a simple premise. We begin with a hashing function that we then apply to our tokens.

A hashing function takes input of variable size and maps it to output of a fixed size. Hashing functions are commonly used in cryptography.

---

[5] https://www.hvitfeldt.me/blog/tidytuesday-pos-textrecipes-the-office/

We will use the `hash()` function from the **rlang** package to illustrate the behavior of hashing functions. The `rlang::hash()` function uses the XXH128 hash algorithm of the xxHash library, which generates a 128-bit hash. This is a more complex hashing function than what is normally used for the hashing trick. The 32-bit version of MurmurHash3 (Appleby 2008) is often used for its speed and good properties.

Hashing functions are typically very fast and have certain properties. For example, the output of a hash function is expected to be uniform, with the whole output space filled evenly. The "avalanche effect" describes how similar strings are hashed in such a way that their hashes are not similar in the output space.

Suppose we have many country names in a character vector. We can apply the hashing function to each of the country names to project them into an integer space defined by the hashing function.

Since `hash()` creates hashes that are very long, let's create `small_hash()` for demonstration purposes here that generates slightly smaller hashes. (The specific details of what hashes are generated are not important here.)

```
library(rlang)
countries <- c("Palau", "Luxembourg", "Vietnam", "Guam", "Argentina",
               "Mayotte", "Bouvet Island", "South Korea", "San Marino",
               "American Samoa")

small_hash <- function(x) {
  strtoi(substr(hash(x), 26, 32), 16)
}

map_int(countries, small_hash)
```

```
#>  [1]   4292706   2881716 242176357 240902473 204438359  88787026 230339508
#>  [8]  15112074  96146649 192775182
```

Our `small_hash()` function uses 7 * 4 = 28 bits, so the number of possible values is 2^28 = 268435456. This is admittedly not much of an improvement over 10 country names. Let's take the modulo of these big integer values to project them down to a more manageable space.

```
map_int(countries, small_hash) %% 24
```

```
#>   [1] 18 12 13  1 23 10 12 18  9  6
```

Now we can use these values as indices when creating a matrix.

```
#> 10 x 24 sparse Matrix of class "ngCMatrix"
#>
#> Palau           . . . . . . . . . . . . . . . . . | . . . . . .
#> Luxembourg      . . . . . . . . . . . . | . . . . . . . . . . . .
#> Vietnam         . . . . . . . . . . . . | . . . . . . . . . . . .
#> Guam            | . . . . . . . . . . . . . . . . . . . . . . .
#> Argentina       . . . . . . . . . . . . . . . . . . . . . . | .
#> Mayotte         . . . . . . . . . | . . . . . . . . . . . . . .
#> Bouvet Island   . . . . . . . . . . . . | . . . . . . . . . . .
#> South Korea     . . . . . . . . . . . . . . . . . | . . . . . .
#> San Marino      . . . . . . . . | . . . . . . . . . . . . . . .
#> American Samoa  . . . . . | . . . . . . . . . . . . . . . . . .
```

This method is very fast; both the hashing and modulo can be performed independently for each input since neither need information about the full corpus. Since we are reducing the space, there is a chance that multiple words are hashed to the same value. This is called a collision and, at first glance, it seems like it would be a big problem for a model. However, research finds that using feature hashing has roughly the same accuracy as a simple bag-of-words model, and the effect of collisions is quite minor (Forman and Kirshenbaum 2008).

Another step that is taken to avoid the negative effects of hash collisions is to use a *second* hashing function that returns 1 and −1. This determines if we are adding or subtracting the index we get from the first hashin function. Suppose both the words "outdoor" and "pleasant" hash to the integer value 583. Without the second hashing they would collide to 2. Using signed hashing, we have a 50% chance that they will cancel each other out, which tries to stop one feature from growing too much.

There are downsides to using feature hashing. Feature hashing:

- still has one tuning parameter, and

- cannot be reversed.

The number of buckets you have correlates with computation speed and collision rate, which in turn affects performance. It is your job to find the output that best suits your needs. Increasing the number of buckets will decrease the collision rate but will, in turn, return a larger output data set, which increases model fitting time. The number of buckets is tunable in tidymodels using the **tune** package.

Perhaps the more important downside to using feature hashing is that the operation can't be reversed. We are not able to detect if a collision occurs and it is difficult to understand the effect of any word in the model. Remember that we are left with n columns of *hashes* (not tokens), so if we find that the 274th column is a highly predictive feature, we cannot know in general which tokens contribute to that column. We cannot directly connect model values to words or tokens at all. We could go back to our training set and create a paired list of the tokens and what hashes they map to. Sometimes we might find only one token in that list, but it may have two (or three or four or more!) different tokens contributing. This feature hashing method is used because of its speed and scalability, not because it is interpretable.

Feature hashing on tokens is available in tidymodels using the `step_texthash()` step from **textrecipes**. Let's `prep()` and `bake()` this recipe for demonstration purposes.

```
scotus_hash <- recipe(year ~ text, data = scotus_train) %>%
  step_tokenize(text) %>%
  step_texthash(text, signed = TRUE, num_terms = 512) %>%
  prep() %>%
  bake(new_data = NULL)

dim(scotus_hash)
```

```
#> [1] 7500  513
```

There are many columns in the results. Let's take a `glimpse()` at the first 10 columns.

```
scotus_hash %>%
  select(num_range("text_hash00", 1:9)) %>%
  glimpse()
```

```
#> Rows: 7,500
#> Columns: 9
#> $ text_hash001 <dbl> -16, -5, -12, -10, -10, -2, -7, -13, -16, -18, -1, -2, -1~
#> $ text_hash002 <dbl> -1, 1, 3, -2, 0, 0, 5, -1, 1, 6, 0, 2, 0, 0, 0, -3, 1, 2,~
#> $ text_hash003 <dbl> -2, 0, 4, -1, -1, 1, -5, -2, -2, 0, 0, -1, 1, 6, 0, 0, -3~
#> $ text_hash004 <dbl> -2, 0, -1, 0, 0, 0, -14, -14, -4, -2, 0, -10, -1, -2, 0, ~
#> $ text_hash005 <dbl> 0, 0, 0, 0, 0, 0, -2, -1, 2, 1, 0, -1, 0, -1, 0, 0, -1, 0~
#> $ text_hash006 <dbl> 24, 2, 4, 6, 7, 2, 14, 13, 13, 22, 1, 41, 2, 49, 9, 1, 17~
#> $ text_hash007 <dbl> 13, 1, 1, -3, 0, -6, -2, -4, -8, -1, 0, 0, -4, -11, 0, 0,~
#> $ text_hash008 <dbl> -8, 3, 1, 1, 1, 0, -19, 0, 1, 0, 1, -1, 1, 1, -2, 1, -8, ~
#> $ text_hash009 <dbl> -2, 0, -1, 1, 0, 0, 0, -1, -1, -1, 0, -1, -1, -1, 0, 0, -~
```

By using `step_texthash()` we can quickly generate machine-ready data with a consistent number of variables. This typically results in a slight loss of performance compared to using a traditional bag-of-words representation. An example of this loss is illustrated in this **textrecipes** blogpost[6].

6.7.1 Text normalization

When working with text, you will inevitably run into problems with encodings and related irregularities. These kinds of problems have a significant influence on feature hashing, as well as other preprocessing steps. Consider the German word "schön." The o with an umlaut (two dots over it) is a fairly simple character, but it can be represented in a couple of different ways. We can either use a single character \U00f6[7] to represent the letter with an umlaut. Alternatively, we can use two characters, one for the o and one character to denote the presence of two dots over the previous character \U0308[8].

```
s1 <- "sch\U00f6n"
s2 <- "scho\U0308n"
```

These two strings will print the same for us as human readers.

---

[6] https://www.hvitfeldt.me/blog/textrecipes-series-featurehashing/
[7] https://www.fileformat.info/info/unicode/char/00f6/index.htm
[8] https://www.fileformat.info/info/unicode/char/0308/index.htm

```
s1
```

```
#> [1] "schön"
```

```
s2
```

```
#> [1] "schön"
```

However, they are not equal.

```
s1 == s2
```

```
#> [1] FALSE
```

This poses a problem for the avalanche effect, which is needed for feature hashing to perform correctly. The avalanche effect will result in these two words (which should be identical) hashing to completely different values.

```
small_hash(s1)
```

```
#> [1] 180735918
```

```
small_hash(s2)
```

```
#> [1] 3013209
```

We can deal with this problem by performing **text normalization** on our text before feeding it into our preprocessing engine. One library to perform text normalization is the **stringi** package, which includes many different text normalization methods. How these methods work is beyond the scope of this book, but know that the text normalization functions make text like our two versions of "schön" equivalent. We will use `stri_trans_nfc()` for this example, which performs canonical decomposition, followed by canonical composition, but we could also use `textrecipes::step_text_normalize()` within a tidymodels recipe for the same task.

```
library(stringi)
```

```
stri_trans_nfc(s1) == stri_trans_nfc(s2)
```

```
#> [1] TRUE
```

```
small_hash(stri_trans_nfc(s1))
```

```
#> [1] 180735918
```

```
small_hash(stri_trans_nfc(s2))
```

```
#> [1] 180735918
```

Now we see that the strings are equal after normalization.

This issue of text normalization can be important even if you don't use feature hashing in your machine learning.

Since these words are encoded in different ways, they will be counted separately when we are counting token frequencies. Representing what should be a single token in multiple ways will split the counts. This will introduce noise in the best case, and in worse cases, some tokens will fall below the cutoff when we select tokens, leading to a loss of potentially informative words.

Luckily this is easily addressed by using `stri_trans_nfc()` on our text columns *before* starting preprocessing, or perhaps more conveniently, by using `tex-trecipes::step_text_normalize()` *within* a preprocessing recipe.

6.8 What evaluation metrics are appropriate?

We have focused on using RMSE and R^2 as metrics for our models in this chapter, the defaults in the tidymodels framework. Other metrics can also be appropriate for regression models. Another common set of regression metric options are the various flavors of mean absolute error.

If you know before you fit your model that you want to compute one or more of these metrics, you can specify them in a call to metric_set(). Let's set up a tuning grid for mean absolute error (mae) and mean absolute percent error (mape).

```
lemma_rs <- fit_resamples(
  svm_wf %>% add_recipe(lemma_rec),
  scotus_folds,
  metrics = metric_set(mae, mape)
)
```

If you have already fit your model, you can still compute and explore non-default metrics as long as you saved the predictions for your resampled data sets using control_resamples(save_pred = TRUE).

Let's go back to the first linear SVM model we tuned in Section 6.1.2, with results in svm_rs. We can compute the overall mean absolute percent error.

```
svm_rs %>%
  collect_predictions() %>%
  mape(year, .pred)
```

```
#> # A tibble: 1 x 3
#>    .metric .estimator .estimate
#>    <chr>   <chr>          <dbl>
#> 1 mape    standard       0.616
```

We can also compute the mean absolute percent error for each resample.

```
svm_rs %>%
  collect_predictions() %>%
  group_by(id) %>%
  mape(year, .pred)
```

```
#> # A tibble: 10 x 4
#>    id      .metric .estimator .estimate
#>    <chr>   <chr>   <chr>          <dbl>
#> 1 Fold01 mape    standard       0.603
```

```
#>  2 Fold02 mape   standard    0.660
#>  3 Fold03 mape   standard    0.596
#>  4 Fold04 mape   standard    0.639
#>  5 Fold05 mape   standard    0.618
#>  6 Fold06 mape   standard    0.611
#>  7 Fold07 mape   standard    0.618
#>  8 Fold08 mape   standard    0.602
#>  9 Fold09 mape   standard    0.604
#> 10 Fold10 mape   standard    0.605
```

Similarly, we can do the same for the mean absolute error, which gives a result in units of the original data (years, in this case) instead of relative units.

```
svm_rs %>%
  collect_predictions() %>%
  group_by(id) %>%
  mae(year, .pred)
```

```
#> # A tibble: 10 x 4
#>    id      .metric .estimator .estimate
#>    <chr>   <chr>   <chr>          <dbl>
#>  1 Fold01 mae     standard        11.5
#>  2 Fold02 mae     standard        12.6
#>  3 Fold03 mae     standard        11.4
#>  4 Fold04 mae     standard        12.2
#>  5 Fold05 mae     standard        11.8
#>  6 Fold06 mae     standard        11.7
#>  7 Fold07 mae     standard        11.9
#>  8 Fold08 mae     standard        11.5
#>  9 Fold09 mae     standard        11.6
#> 10 Fold10 mae     standard        11.6
```

For the full set of regression metric options, see the yardstick documentation[9].

---

[9] https://yardstick.tidymodels.org/reference/

6.9   The full game: regression

In this chapter, we started from the beginning and then explored both different types of models and different data preprocessing steps. Let's take a step back and build one final model, using everything we've learned. For our final model, let's again use a linear SVM regression model, since it performed better than the other options we looked at. We will:

- train on the same set of cross-validation resamples used throughout this chapter,

- *tune* the number of tokens used in the model to find a value that fits our needs,

- include both unigrams and bigrams,

- choose not to use lemmatization, to demonstrate what is possible for situations when training time makes lemmatization an impractical choice, and

- finally evaluate on the testing set, which we have not touched at all yet.

We will include a much larger number of tokens than before, which should give us the latitude to include both unigrams and bigrams, despite the result we saw in Section 6.5.

6.9.1   Preprocess the data

First, let's create the data preprocessing recipe. By setting the tokenization options to `list(n = 2, n_min = 1)`, we will include both unigrams and bigrams in our model.

When we set `max_tokens = tune()`, we can train multiple models with different numbers of maximum tokens and then compare these models' performance to choose the best value. Previously, we set `max_tokens = 1e3` to choose a specific value for the number of tokens included in our model, but here we are going to try multiple different values.

```
final_rec <- recipe(year ~ text, data = scotus_train) %>%
  step_tokenize(text, token = "ngrams", options = list(n = 2, n_min = 1)) %>%
  step_tokenfilter(text, max_tokens = tune()) %>%
  step_tfidf(text) %>%
  step_normalize(all_predictors())

final_rec
```

```
#> Data Recipe
#>
#> Inputs:
#>
#>        role #variables
#>     outcome          1
#>   predictor          1
#>
#> Operations:
#>
#> Tokenization for text
#> Text filtering for text
#> Term frequency-inverse document frequency with text
#> Centering and scaling for all_predictors()
```

6.9.2 Specify the model

Let's use the same linear SVM regression model specification we have used multiple times in this chapter, and set it up here again to remind ourselves.

```
svm_spec <- svm_linear() %>%
  set_mode("regression") %>%
  set_engine("LiblineaR")

svm_spec
```

```
#> Linear Support Vector Machine Specification (regression)
#>
#> Computational engine: LiblineaR
```

We can combine the preprocessing recipe and the model specification in a tunable workflow. We can't fit this workflow right away to training data, because the value for max_tokens hasn't been chosen yet.

```
tune_wf <- workflow() %>%
  add_recipe(final_rec) %>%
  add_model(svm_spec)

tune_wf
```

```
#> == Workflow ========================================================
#> Preprocessor: Recipe
#> Model: svm_linear()
#>
#> -- Preprocessor ----------------------------------------------------
#> 4 Recipe Steps
#>
#> * step_tokenize()
#> * step_tokenfilter()
#> * step_tfidf()
#> * step_normalize()
#>
#> -- Model -----------------------------------------------------------
#> Linear Support Vector Machine Specification (regression)
#>
#> Computational engine: LiblineaR
```

6.9.3   Tune the model

Before we tune the model, we need to set up a set of possible parameter values
to try.

There is *one* tunable parameter in this model, the maximum number of
tokens included in the model.

Let's include different possible values for this parameter starting from the
value we've already tried, for a combination of six models.

```
final_grid <- grid_regular(
  max_tokens(range = c(1e3, 6e3)),
  levels = 6
)
final_grid
```

```
#> # A tibble: 6 x 1
#>    max_tokens
#>         <int>
#> 1       1000
#> 2       2000
#> 3       3000
#> 4       4000
#> 5       5000
#> 6       6000
```

Now it's time for tuning. Instead of using `fit_resamples()` as we have through-out this chapter, we are going to use `tune_grid()`, a function that has a very similar set of arguments. We pass this function our workflow (which holds our preprocessing recipe and SVM model), our resampling folds, and also the grid of possible parameter values to try. Let's save the predictions so we can explore them in more detail, and let's also set custom metrics instead of using the defaults. Let's compute RMSE, mean absolute error, and mean absolute percent error during tuning.

```
final_rs <- tune_grid(
  tune_wf,
  scotus_folds,
  grid = final_grid,
  metrics = metric_set(rmse, mae, mape),
  control = control_resamples(save_pred = TRUE)
)

final_rs
```

```
#> # Tuning results
#> # 10-fold cross-validation
#> # A tibble: 10 x 5
#>    splits            id     .metrics        .notes          .predictions
#>    <list>            <chr>  <list>          <list>          <list>
#>  1 <split [6750/750]> Fold01 <tibble [18 x 5]> <tibble [0 x 1]> <tibble [4,500 ~
#>  2 <split [6750/750]> Fold02 <tibble [18 x 5]> <tibble [0 x 1]> <tibble [4,500 ~
#>  3 <split [6750/750]> Fold03 <tibble [18 x 5]> <tibble [0 x 1]> <tibble [4,500 ~
#>  4 <split [6750/750]> Fold04 <tibble [18 x 5]> <tibble [0 x 1]> <tibble [4,500 ~
#>  5 <split [6750/750]> Fold05 <tibble [18 x 5]> <tibble [0 x 1]> <tibble [4,500 ~
#>  6 <split [6750/750]> Fold06 <tibble [18 x 5]> <tibble [0 x 1]> <tibble [4,500 ~
#>  7 <split [6750/750]> Fold07 <tibble [18 x 5]> <tibble [0 x 1]> <tibble [4,500 ~
#>  8 <split [6750/750]> Fold08 <tibble [18 x 5]> <tibble [0 x 1]> <tibble [4,500 ~
#>  9 <split [6750/750]> Fold09 <tibble [18 x 5]> <tibble [0 x 1]> <tibble [4,500 ~
#> 10 <split [6750/750]> Fold10 <tibble [18 x 5]> <tibble [0 x 1]> <tibble [4,500 ~
```

We trained all these models!

6.9.4   Evaluate the modeling

Now that all of the models with possible parameter values have been trained, we can compare their performance. Figure 6.6 shows us the relationship between performance (as measured by the metrics we chose) and the number of tokens.

```
final_rs %>%
  collect_metrics() %>%
  ggplot(aes(max_tokens, mean, color = .metric)) +
  geom_line(size = 1.5, alpha = 0.5) +
  geom_point(size = 2, alpha = 0.9) +
  facet_wrap(~.metric, scales = "free_y", ncol = 1) +
  theme(legend.position = "none") +
  labs(
    x = "Number of tokens",
    title = "Linear SVM performance across number of tokens",
    subtitle = "Performance improves as we include more tokens"
  )
```

Since this is our final version of this model, we want to choose final parameters and update our model object so we can use it with new data. We have several options for choosing our final parameters, such as selecting the numerically best model (which would be one of the ones with the most tokens in our situation here) or the simplest model within some limit around the numerically best result. In this situation, we likely want to choose a simpler model with fewer tokens that gives close-to-best performance.

Let's choose by percent loss compared to the best model, with the default 2% loss.

```
chosen_mae <- final_rs %>%
  select_by_pct_loss(metric = "mae", max_tokens)

chosen_mae
```

```
#> # A tibble: 1 x 9
#>   max_tokens .metric .estimator mean     n std_err .config        .best .loss
#>        <int> <chr>   <chr>      <dbl> <int>   <dbl> <chr>          <dbl> <dbl>
#> 1       5000 mae     standard   10.1    10  0.0680 Preprocessor5_M~ 9.98 0.795
```

Linear SVM performance across number of tokens

Performance improves as we include more tokens

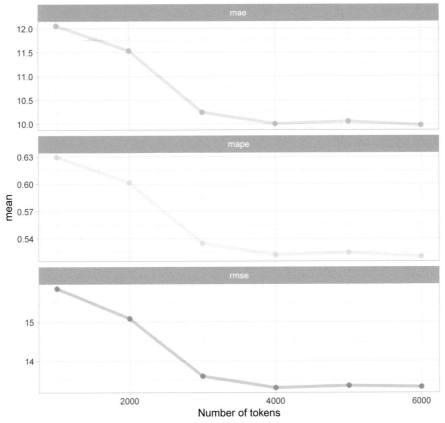

FIGURE 6.6: Performance improves significantly at about 4000 tokens

After we have those parameters, `penalty` and `max_tokens`, we can finalize our earlier tunable workflow, by updating it with this value.

```
final_wf <- finalize_workflow(tune_wf, chosen_mae)

final_wf
```

```
#> == Workflow ==================================================================
#> Preprocessor: Recipe
#> Model: svm_linear()
#>
#> -- Preprocessor ---------------------------------------------------------------
#> 4 Recipe Steps
#>
#> * step_tokenize()
#> * step_tokenfilter()
#> * step_tfidf()
#> * step_normalize()
#>
#> -- Model ----------------------------------------------------------------------
#> Linear Support Vector Machine Specification (regression)
#>
#> Computational engine: LiblineaR
```

The `final_wf` workflow now has a finalized value for `max_tokens`.

We can now fit this finalized workflow on training data and *finally* return to our testing data.

> Notice that this is the first time we have used our testing data during this entire chapter; we compared and now tuned models using resampled data sets instead of touching the testing set.

We can use the function `last_fit()` to **fit** our model one last time on our training data and **evaluate** it on our testing data. We only have to pass this function our finalized model/workflow and our data split.

```
final_fitted <- last_fit(final_wf, scotus_split)

collect_metrics(final_fitted)
```

```
#> # A tibble: 2 x 4
#>   .metric .estimator .estimate .config
#>   <chr>   <chr>          <dbl> <chr>
#> 1 rmse    standard      13.8   Preprocessor1_Model1
#> 2 rsq     standard       0.921 Preprocessor1_Model1
```

The metrics for the test set look about the same as the resampled training data and indicate we did not overfit during tuning. The RMSE of our final model has improved compared to our earlier models, both because we are combining multiple preprocessing steps and because we have tuned the number of tokens.

The output of last_fit() also contains a fitted model (a workflow, to be more specific), that has been trained on the *training* data. We can tidy() this final result to understand what the most important variables are in the predictions, shown in Figure 6.7.

```r
scotus_fit <- pull_workflow_fit(final_fitted$.workflow[[1]])

scotus_fit %>%
  tidy() %>%
  filter(term != "Bias") %>%
  mutate(
    sign = case_when(estimate > 0 ~ "Later (after mean year)",
                     TRUE ~ "Earlier (before mean year)"),
    estimate = abs(estimate),
    term = str_remove_all(term, "tfidf_text_")
  ) %>%
  group_by(sign) %>%
  top_n(20, estimate) %>%
  ungroup() %>%
  ggplot(aes(x = estimate,
             y = fct_reorder(term, estimate),
             fill = sign)) +
  geom_col(show.legend = FALSE) +
  scale_x_continuous(expand = c(0, 0)) +
  facet_wrap(~sign, scales = "free") +
  labs(
    y = NULL,
    title = paste("Variable importance for predicting year of",
                  "Supreme Court opinions"),
    subtitle = paste("These features are the most importance",
                     "in predicting the year of an opinion")
  )
```

The tokens (unigrams or bigrams) that contribute in the positive direction, like "court said" and "constitutionally," are associated with higher, later years; those that contribute in the negative direction, like "ought" and "the judges," are associated with lower, earlier years for these Supreme Court opinions.

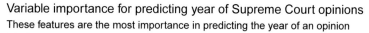

Variable importance for predicting year of Supreme Court opinions

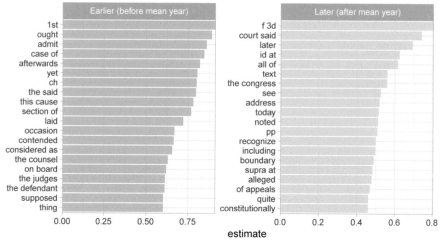

FIGURE 6.7: Some words or bigrams increase a Supreme Court opinion's probability of being written later (more recently) while some increase its probability of being written earlier

Some of these features are unigrams and some are bigrams, and stop words are included because we did not remove them from the model.

We can also examine how the true and predicted years compare for the testing set. Figure 6.8 shows us that, like for our earlier models on the resampled training data, we can predict the year of Supreme Court opinions for the testing data starting from about 1850. Predictions are less reliable before that year. This is an example of finding different error rates across sub-groups of observations, like we discussed in the overview to these chapters; these differences can lead to unfairness and algorithmic bias when models are applied in the real world.

```
final_fitted %>%
  collect_predictions() %>%
  ggplot(aes(year, .pred)) +
  geom_abline(lty = 2, color = "gray80", size = 1.5) +
  geom_point(alpha = 0.3) +
  labs(
```

```
  x = "Truth",
  y = "Predicted year",
  title = paste("Predicted and true years for the testing set of",
                "Supreme Court opinions"),
  subtitle = "For the testing set, predictions are more reliable after 1850"
)
```

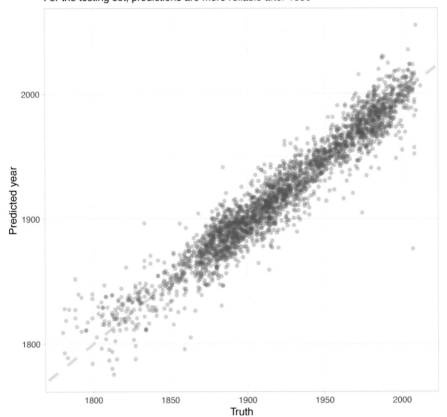

Predicted and true years for the testing set of Supreme Court opinions
For the testing set, predictions are more reliable after 1850

FIGURE 6.8: Predicted and true years from a linear SVM regression model with bigrams and unigrams

Finally, we can gain more insight into our model and how it is behaving by looking at observations from the test set that have been *mispredicted*. Let's bind together the predictions on the test set with the original Supreme Court opinion test data and filter to observations with a prediction that is more than 25 years wrong.

```
scotus_bind <- collect_predictions(final_fitted) %>%
  bind_cols(scotus_test %>% select(-year, -id)) %>%
  filter(abs(year - .pred) > 25)
```

There isn't too much training data to start with for the earliest years, so we are unlikely to quickly gain insight from looking at the oldest opinions. However, what do the more recent opinions that were predicted inaccurately look like?

```
scotus_bind %>%
  arrange(-year) %>%
  select(year, .pred, case_name, text)
```

```
#> # A tibble: 168 x 4
#>    year .pred case_name                                      text
#>   <dbl> <dbl> <chr>                                          <chr>
#>  1  2009 2055. Nijhawan v. Holder                  "Supreme Court of Unite~
#>  2  2008 1957. Green v. Johnson                    "           Cite ~
#>  3  2008 1952. Dalehite v. United States           "Supreme Court of Unite~
#>  4  2008 1982. Preston v. Ferrer                   "Supreme Court of Unite~
#>  5  2007 1876. Quebec Bank of Toronto v. Hellman   "Supreme Court of Unite~
#>  6  2004 2035. Illinois v. Lidster                 "No. 02-1060.\nPolice s~
#>  7  2002 1969. Borgner v. Florida Board of Dentistry "No. 02-165.\nCERTIORAR~
#>  8  2000 1974. Ohler v. United States              "OHLERv.UNITED STATES\n~
#>  9  2000 1955. Bush v. Palm Beach County Canvassing Bd. "No. 00-836\nON WRIT OF~
#> 10  1999 1964. Dickinson v. Zurko                  "No. 98 377\nQ. TODD DI~
#> # ... with 158 more rows
```

There are some interesting examples here where we can understand why the model would mispredict:

- *Dalehite v. United States* was a case about a fertilizer explosion that is mislabeled in our dataset; it was decided in 1953, not 2008 as we see in our data, and we predict a year of 1952, very close to the true decision date.

- *Bush v. Palm Beach County Canvassing Board* in 2000 was part of the fallout of the 2000 presidential election and dealt with historical issues like the due process clause of the U.S. Constitution; these "old" textual elements push its prediction much earlier than its true date.

Looking at examples that your model does not perform well for is well worth your time, for similar reasons that exploratory data analysis is valuable before you begin training your model.

6.10 Summary

You can use regression modeling to predict a continuous variable from a data set, including a text data set. Linear support vector machine models, along with regularized linear models (which we will cover in the next chapter), often work well for text data sets, while tree-based models such as random forest often behave poorly in practice. There are many possible preprocessing steps for text data, from removing stop words to n-gram tokenization strategies to lemmatization, that may improve your model. Resampling data sets and careful use of metrics allow you to make good choices among these possible options, given your own concerns and priorities.

6.10.1 In this chapter, you learned:

- what kind of quantities can be modeled using regression

- to evaluate a model using resampled data

- how to compare different model types

- about measuring the impact of n-gram tokenization on models

- how to implement lemmatization and stop word removal with text models

- how feature hashing can be used as a fast alternative to bag-of-words

- about performance metrics for regression models

7

Classification

In Chapter 6, we focused on modeling to predict *continuous values* for documents, such as what year a Supreme Court opinion was published. This is an example of a regression model. We can also use machine learning to predict *labels* on documents using a classification model. For both types of prediction questions, we develop a learner or model to describe the relationship between a target or outcome variable and our input features; what is different about a classification model is the nature of that outcome.

- A **regression model** predicts a numeric or continuous value.

- A **classification model** predicts a class label or group membership.

For our classification example in this chapter, let's consider the data set of consumer complaints submitted to the US Consumer Finance Protection Bureau. Let's read in the complaint data (Section B.3) with `read_csv()`.

```
library(tidyverse)
complaints <- read_csv("data/complaints.csv.gz")
```

We can start by taking a quick `glimpse()` at the data to see what we have to work with. This data set contains a text field with the complaint, along with information regarding what it was for, how and when it was filed, and the response from the bureau.

```
glimpse(complaints)
```

```
#> Rows: 117,214
#> Columns: 18
#> $ date_received    <date> 2019-09-24, 2019-10-25, 2019-11-08, 2019~
#> $ product          <chr> "Debt collection", "Credit reporting, cre~
#> $ sub_product      <chr> "I do not know", "Credit reporting", "I d~
#> $ issue            <chr> "Attempts to collect debt not owed", "Inc~
```

```
#> $ sub_issue                  <chr> "Debt is not yours", "Information belongs~
#> $ consumer_complaint_narrative <chr> "transworld systems inc. \nis trying to c~
#> $ company_public_response     <chr> NA, "Company has responded to the consume~
#> $ company                     <chr> "TRANSWORLD SYSTEMS INC", "TRANSUNION INT~
#> $ state                       <chr> "FL", "CA", "NC", "RI", "FL", "TX", "SC",~
#> $ zip_code                    <chr> "335XX", "937XX", "275XX", "029XX", "333X~
#> $ tags                        <chr> NA, NA, NA, NA, NA, NA, NA, NA, NA, NA, N~
#> $ consumer_consent_provided   <chr> "Consent provided", "Consent provided", "~
#> $ submitted_via               <chr> "Web", "Web", "Web", "Web", "Web", "Web",~
#> $ date_sent_to_company        <date> 2019-09-24, 2019-10-25, 2019-11-08, 2019~
#> $ company_response_to_consumer <chr> "Closed with explanation", "Closed with e~
#> $ timely_response             <chr> "Yes", "Yes", "Yes", "Yes", "Yes", "Yes",~
#> $ consumer_disputed           <chr> "N/A", "N/A", "N/A", "N/A", "N/A", "N/A",~
#> $ complaint_id                <dbl> 3384392, 3417821, 3433198, 3366475, 33853~
```

In this chapter, we will build classification models to predict what type of financial `product` the complaints are referring to, i.e., a label or categorical variable. The goal of predictive modeling with text input features and a categorical outcome is to learn and model the relationship between those input features, typically created through steps as outlined in Chapters 1 through 5, and the class label or categorical outcome. Most classification models do predict the probability of a class (a numeric output), but the particular characteristics of this output make classification models different enough from regression models that we handle them differently.

7.1   A first classification model

For our first model, let's build a binary classification model to predict whether a submitted complaint is about "Credit reporting, credit repair services, or other personal consumer reports" or not.

 This kind of "yes or no" binary classification model is both common and useful in real-world text machine learning problems.

The outcome variable `product` contains more categories than this, so we need to transform this variable to only contain the values "Credit reporting, credit repair services, or other personal consumer reports" and "Other."

It is always a good idea to look at your data! Here are the first six complaints:

```
head(complaints$consumer_complaint_narrative)
```

```
#> [1] "transworld systems inc. \nis trying to collect a debt that is not mine,
not owed and is inaccurate."
#> [2] "I would like to request the suppression of the following items from my
credit report, which are the result of my falling victim to identity theft.
This information does not relate to [ transactions that I have made/accounts
that I have opened ], as the attached supporting documentation can attest. As
such, it should be blocked from appearing on my credit report pursuant to
section 605B of the Fair Credit Reporting Act."
#> [3] "Over the past 2 weeks, I have been receiving excessive amounts of
telephone calls from the company listed in this complaint. The calls occur
between XXXX XXXX and XXXX XXXX to my cell and at my job. The company does not
have the right to harass me at work and I want this to stop. It is extremely
distracting to be told 5 times a day that I have a call from this collection
agency while at work."
#> [4] "I was sold access to an event digitally, of which I have all the
screenshots to detail the transactions, transferred the money and was provided
with only a fake of a ticket. I have reported this to paypal and it was for the
amount of {$21.00} including a {$1.00} fee from paypal. \n\nThis occured on
XX/XX/2019, by paypal user who gave two accounts : 1 ) XXXX 2 ) XXXX XXXX"
#> [5] "While checking my credit report I noticed three collections by a
company called ARS that i was unfamiliar with. I disputed these collections
with XXXX, and XXXX and they both replied that they contacted the creditor and
the creditor verified the debt so I asked for proof which both bureaus replied
that they are not required to prove anything. I then mailed a certified letter
to ARS requesting proof of the debts n the form of an original aggrement, or a
proof of a right to the debt, or even so much as the process as to how the bill
was calculated, to which I was simply replied a letter for each collection
claim that listed my name an account number and an amount with no other
information to verify the debts after I sent a clear notice to provide me
evidence. Afterwards I recontacted both XXXX, and XXXX, to redispute on the
premise that it is not my debt if evidence can not be drawn up, I feel as if I
am being personally victimized by ARS on my credit report for debts that are
not owed to them or any party for that matter, and I feel discouraged that the
credit bureaus who control many aspects of my personal finances are so
negligent about my information."
#> [6] "I would like the credit bureau to correct my XXXX XXXX XXXX XXXX
balance. My correct balance is XXXX"
```

The complaint narratives contain many series of capital "x"'s. These strings (like "XX/XX" or "XXXX XXXX XXXX XXXX") are used to to protect personally identifiable information (PII) in this publicly available data set. This is not a universal censoring mechanism; censoring and PII protection will vary from source to source. Hopefully you will be able to find information on PII censoring in a data dictionary, but you should always look at the data yourself to verify.

We also see that monetary amounts are surrounded by curly brackets (like "{$21.00}"); this is another text preprocessing step that has been taken care of for us. We could craft a regular expression to extract all the dollar amounts.

```
complaints$consumer_complaint_narrative %>%
  str_extract_all("\\{\\$[0-9\\.]*\\}") %>%
  compact() %>%
  head()
```

```
#> [[1]]
#> [1] "{$21.00}" "{$1.00}"
#>
#> [[2]]
#> [1] "{$2300.00}"
#>
#> [[3]]
#> [1] "{$200.00}"  "{$5000.00}" "{$5000.00}" "{$770.00}"  "{$800.00}"
#> [6] "{$5000.00}"
#>
#> [[4]]
#> [1] "{$15000.00}" "{$11000.00}" "{$420.00}"   "{$15000.00}"
#>
#> [[5]]
#> [1] "{$0.00}" "{$0.00}" "{$0.00}" "{$0.00}"
#>
#> [[6]]
#> [1] "{$650.00}"
```

In Section 7.9, we will use an approach like this for custom feature engineering from the text.

7.1.1 Building our first classification model

This data set includes more possible predictors than the text alone, but for this first model we will only use the text variable consumer_complaint_narrative.

Let's create a factor outcome variable product with two levels, "Credit" and "Other." Then, we split the data into training and testing data sets. We can use the initial_split() function from **rsample** to create this binary split of the data. The strata argument ensures that the distribution of product is similar in the training set and testing set. Since the split uses random sampling, we set a seed so we can reproduce our results.

```
library(tidymodels)

set.seed(1234)
complaints2class <- complaints %>%
  mutate(product = factor(if_else(
    product == paste("Credit reporting, credit repair services,",
                     "or other personal consumer reports"),
    "Credit", "Other"
  )))

complaints_split <- initial_split(complaints2class, strata = product)

complaints_train <- training(complaints_split)
complaints_test <- testing(complaints_split)
```

The dimensions of the two splits show that this first step worked as we planned.

```
dim(complaints_train)
```

```
#> [1] 87910     18
```

```
dim(complaints_test)
```

```
#> [1] 29304     18
```

Next we need to preprocess this data to prepare it for modeling; we have text data, and we need to build numeric features for machine learning from that text.

The **recipes** package, part of tidymodels, allows us to create a specification of preprocessing steps we want to perform. These transformations are estimated (or "trained") on the training set so that they can be applied in the same way on the testing set or new data at prediction time, without data leakage. We initialize our set of preprocessing transformations with the `recipe()` function, using a formula expression to specify the variables, our outcome plus our predictor, along with the data set.

```
complaints_rec <-
  recipe(product ~ consumer_complaint_narrative, data = complaints_train)
```

Now we add steps to process the text of the complaints; we use **textrecipes** to handle the `consumer_complaint_narrative` variable. First we tokenize the text to words with `step_tokenize()`. By default this uses `tokenizers::tokenize_words()`. Before we calculate tf-idf we use `step_tokenfilter()` to only keep the 1000 most frequent tokens, to avoid creating too many variables in our first model. To finish, we use `step_tfidf()` to compute tf-idf.

```
library(textrecipes)

complaints_rec <- complaints_rec %>%
  step_tokenize(consumer_complaint_narrative) %>%
  step_tokenfilter(consumer_complaint_narrative, max_tokens = 1e3) %>%
  step_tfidf(consumer_complaint_narrative)
```

Now that we have a full specification of the preprocessing recipe, we can build up a tidymodels `workflow()` to bundle together our modeling components.

```
complaint_wf <- workflow() %>%
  add_recipe(complaints_rec)
```

Let's start with a naive Bayes model (S. Kim et al. 2006; Kibriya et al. 2005; Frank and Bouckaert 2006), which is available in the tidymodels package **discrim**. One of the main advantages of a naive Bayes model is its ability to handle a large number of features, such as those we deal with when using word count methods. Here we have only kept the 1000 most frequent tokens, but we could have kept more tokens and a naive Bayes model would still be able to handle such predictors well. For now, we will limit the model to a moderate number of tokens.

In **tidymodels**, the package for creating model specifications is **parsnip** (Kuhn and Vaughan 2021b). The **parsnip** package provides the functions for creating all the models we have used so far, but other extra packages provide more. The **discrim** package is an extension package for **parsnip** that contains model definitions for various discriminant analysis models, including naive Bayes.

```
library(discrim)
nb_spec <- naive_Bayes() %>%
  set_mode("classification") %>%
  set_engine("naivebayes")

nb_spec
```

```
#> Naive Bayes Model Specification (classification)
#>
#> Computational engine: naivebayes
```

Now we have everything we need to fit our first classification model. We can add the naive Bayes model to our workflow, and then we can fit this workflow to our training data.

```
nb_fit <- complaint_wf %>%
  add_model(nb_spec) %>%
  fit(data = complaints_train)
```

We have trained our first classification model!

7.1.2 Evaluation

Like we discussed in Section 6.1.2, we should not use the test set to compare models or different model parameters. The test set is a precious resource that should only be used at the end of the model training process to estimate performance on new data. Instead, we will use *resampling* methods to evaluate our model.

Let's use resampling to estimate the performance of the naive Bayes classification model we just fit. We can do this using resampled data sets built from the training set. Let's create 10-fold cross-validation sets, and use these resampled sets for performance estimates.

```
set.seed(234)
complaints_folds <- vfold_cv(complaints_train)

complaints_folds
```

```
#> #  10-fold cross-validation
#> # A tibble: 10 x 2
#>     splits               id
#>     <list>               <chr>
#>  1 <split [79119/8791]> Fold01
#>  2 <split [79119/8791]> Fold02
#>  3 <split [79119/8791]> Fold03
#>  4 <split [79119/8791]> Fold04
#>  5 <split [79119/8791]> Fold05
#>  6 <split [79119/8791]> Fold06
#>  7 <split [79119/8791]> Fold07
#>  8 <split [79119/8791]> Fold08
#>  9 <split [79119/8791]> Fold09
#> 10 <split [79119/8791]> Fold10
```

Each of these splits contains information about how to create cross-validation folds from the original training data. In this example, 90% of the training data is included in each fold, and the other 10% is held out for evaluation.

For convenience, let's again use a `workflow()` for our resampling estimates of performance.

> Using a `workflow()` isn't required (you can fit or tune a model plus a preprocessor), but it can make your code easier to read and organize.

```
nb_wf <- workflow() %>%
  add_recipe(complaints_rec) %>%
  add_model(nb_spec)

nb_wf
```

```
#> == Workflow =========================================================
#> Preprocessor: Recipe
#> Model: naive_Bayes()
#>
#> -- Preprocessor ----------------------------------------------------
#> 3 Recipe Steps
#>
#> * step_tokenize()
#> * step_tokenfilter()
#> * step_tfidf()
#>
#> -- Model -----------------------------------------------------------
#> Naive Bayes Model Specification (classification)
#>
#> Computational engine: naivebayes
```

In the last section, we fit one time to the training data as a whole. Now, to estimate how well that model performs, let's fit the model many times, once to each of these resampled folds, and then evaluate on the heldout part of each resampled fold.

```
nb_rs <- fit_resamples(
  nb_wf,
  complaints_folds,
  control = control_resamples(save_pred = TRUE)
)
```

We can extract the relevant information using `collect_metrics()` and `collect_predictions()`.

```
nb_rs_metrics <- collect_metrics(nb_rs)
nb_rs_predictions <- collect_predictions(nb_rs)
```

What results do we see, in terms of performance metrics?

```
nb_rs_metrics
```

```
#> # A tibble: 2 x 6
#>   .metric  .estimator  mean     n std_err .config
#>   <chr>    <chr>      <dbl> <int>   <dbl> <chr>
#> 1 accuracy binary     0.802    10 0.00434 Preprocessor1_Model1
#> 2 roc_auc  binary     0.881    10 0.00150 Preprocessor1_Model1
```

The default performance parameters for binary classification are accuracy and ROC AUC (area under the receiver operator characteristic curve). For these resamples, the average accuracy is 80.2%.

Accuracy and ROC AUC are performance metrics used for classification models. For both, values closer to 1 are better.

Accuracy is the proportion of the data that is predicted correctly. Be aware that accuracy can be misleading in some situations, such as for imbalanced data sets.

ROC AUC measures how well a classifier performs at different thresholds. The ROC curve plots the true positive rate against the false positive rate; AUC closer to 1 indicates a better-performing model, while AUC closer to 0.5 indicates a model that does no better than random guessing.

Figure 7.1 shows the ROC curve, a visualization of how well a classification model can distinguish between classes, for our first classification model on each of the resampled data sets.

```
nb_rs_predictions %>%
  group_by(id) %>%
  roc_curve(truth = product, .pred_Credit) %>%
  autoplot() +
  labs(
    color = NULL,
    title = "ROC curve for US Consumer Finance Complaints",
    subtitle = "Each resample fold is shown in a different color"
  )
```

The area under each of these curves is the roc_auc metric we have computed. If the curve was close to the diagonal line, then the model's predictions would be no better than random guessing.

Another way to evaluate our model is to evaluate the confusion matrix. A confusion matrix tabulates a model's false positives and false negatives for each class. The function conf_mat_resampled() computes a separate confusion matrix for each resample and takes the average of the cell counts. This allows us to visualize an overall confusion matrix rather than needing to examine each resample individually.

ROC curve for US Consumer Finance Complaints
Each resample fold is shown in a different color

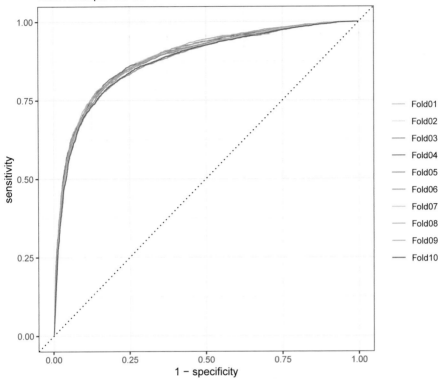

FIGURE 7.1: ROC curve for naive Bayes classifier with resamples of US Consumer Finance Bureau complaints

```
conf_mat_resampled(nb_rs, tidy = FALSE) %>%
  autoplot(type = "heatmap")
```

In Figure 7.2, the squares for "Credit"/"Credit" and "Other"/"Other" have a darker shade than the off-diagonal squares. This is a good sign, meaning that our model is right more often than not! However, this first model is struggling somewhat since many observations from the "Credit" class are being mispredicted as "Other."

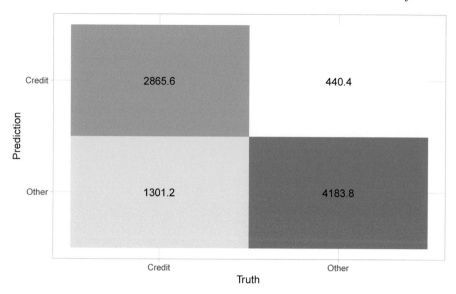

FIGURE 7.2: Confusion matrix for naive Bayes classifier, showing some bias toward predicting the credit category

One metric alone cannot give you a complete picture of how well your classification model is performing. The confusion matrix is a good starting point to get an overview of your model performance, as it includes rich information.

This is real data from a government agency, and these kinds of performance metrics must be interpreted in the context of how such a model would be used. What happens if the model we trained gets a classification wrong for a consumer complaint? What impact will it have if more "Other" complaints are correctly identified than "Credit" complaints, either for consumers or for policymakers?

7.2   Compare to the null model

Like we did in Section 6.2, we can assess a model like this one by comparing its performance to a "null model" or baseline model, a simple, non-informative model that always predicts the largest class for classification. Such a model is perhaps the simplest heuristic or rule-based alternative that we can consider as we assess our modeling efforts.

We can build a classification null_model() specification and add it to a workflow() with the same preprocessing recipe we used in the previous section, to estimate performance.

```
null_classification <- null_model() %>%
  set_engine("parsnip") %>%
  set_mode("classification")

null_rs <- workflow() %>%
  add_recipe(complaints_rec) %>%
  add_model(null_classification) %>%
  fit_resamples(
    complaints_folds
  )
```

What results do we obtain from the null model, in terms of performance metrics?

```
null_rs %>%
  collect_metrics()
```

```
#> # A tibble: 2 x 6
#>    .metric  .estimator  mean     n std_err .config
#>    <chr>    <chr>      <dbl> <int>   <dbl> <chr>
#> 1 accuracy binary     0.526    10 0.00143 Preprocessor1_Model1
#> 2 roc_auc  binary     0.5      10 0       Preprocessor1_Model1
```

The accuracy and ROC AUC indicate that this null model is, like in the regression case, dramatically worse than even our first model. The text of the CFPB complaints is predictive relative to the category we are building models for.

7.3 Compare to a lasso classification model

Regularized linear models are a class of statistical model that can be used in regression and classification tasks. Linear models are not considered cutting edge in NLP research, but are a workhorse in real-world practice. Here we will use a lasso regularized model (Tibshirani 1996), where the regularization method also performs variable selection. In text analysis, we typically have many tokens, which are the features in our machine learning problem.

> Using regularization helps us choose a simpler model that we expect to generalize better to new observations, and variable selection helps us identify which features to include in our model.

Lasso regression or classification learns how much of a *penalty* to put on some features (sometimes penalizing all the way down to zero) so that we can select only some features out of the high-dimensional space of original possible variables (tokens) for the final model.

Let's create a specification of a lasso regularized model. Remember that in tidymodels, specifying a model has three components: the algorithm, the mode, and the computational engine.

```
lasso_spec <- logistic_reg(penalty = 0.01, mixture = 1) %>%
  set_mode("classification") %>%
  set_engine("glmnet")

lasso_spec
```

```
#> Logistic Regression Model Specification (classification)
#>
#> Main Arguments:
#>   penalty = 0.01
#>   mixture = 1
#>
#> Computational engine: glmnet
```

Then we can create another workflow() object with the lasso specification. Notice that we can reuse our text preprocessing recipe.

```
lasso_wf <- workflow() %>%
  add_recipe(complaints_rec) %>%
  add_model(lasso_spec)

lasso_wf
```

```
#> == Workflow ====================================================================
#> Preprocessor: Recipe
#> Model: logistic_reg()
#>
#> -- Preprocessor --------------------------------------------------------------
#> 3 Recipe Steps
#>
#> * step_tokenize()
#> * step_tokenfilter()
#> * step_tfidf()
#>
#> -- Model ---------------------------------------------------------------------
#> Logistic Regression Model Specification (classification)
#>
#> Main Arguments:
#>   penalty = 0.01
#>   mixture = 1
#>
#> Computational engine: glmnet
```

Now we estimate the performance of this first lasso classification model with `fit_resamples()`.

```
set.seed(2020)
lasso_rs <- fit_resamples(
  lasso_wf,
  complaints_folds,
  control = control_resamples(save_pred = TRUE)
)
```

Let's again extract the relevant information using `collect_metrics()` and `collect_predictions()`

```
lasso_rs_metrics <- collect_metrics(lasso_rs)
lasso_rs_predictions <- collect_predictions(lasso_rs)
```

Now we can see that `lasso_rs_metrics` contains the same default performance metrics we have been using so far in this chapter.

```
lasso_rs_metrics
```

```
#> # A tibble: 2 x 6
#>   .metric  .estimator  mean      n  std_err  .config
#>   <chr>    <chr>       <dbl> <int>    <dbl>  <chr>
#> 1 accuracy binary      0.870    10 0.00124   Preprocessor1_Model1
#> 2 roc_auc  binary      0.939    10 0.000646  Preprocessor1_Model1
```

This looks pretty promising, considering we haven't yet done any tuning of the lasso hyperparameters. Figure 7.3 shows the ROC curves for this regularized model on each of the resampled data sets.

```
lasso_rs_predictions %>%
  group_by(id) %>%
  roc_curve(truth = product, .pred_Credit) %>%
  autoplot() +
  labs(
    color = NULL,
    title = "ROC curve for US Consumer Finance Complaints",
    subtitle = "Each resample fold is shown in a different color"
  )
```

Let's finish this section by generating a confusion matrix, shown in Figure 7.4. Our lasso model is better at separating the classes than the naive Bayes model in Section 7.1.1, and our results are more symmetrical than those for the naive Bayes model in Figure 7.2.

```
conf_mat_resampled(lasso_rs, tidy = FALSE) %>%
  autoplot(type = "heatmap")
```

7.4   Tuning lasso hyperparameters

The value `penalty = 0.01` for regularization in Section 7.3 was picked somewhat arbitrarily. How do we know the *right* or *best* regularization parameter penalty? This is a model hyperparameter, and we cannot learn its best value during model training, but we can estimate the best value by training many models on resampled data sets and exploring how well all these models perform. Let's build a new model specification for **model tuning**.

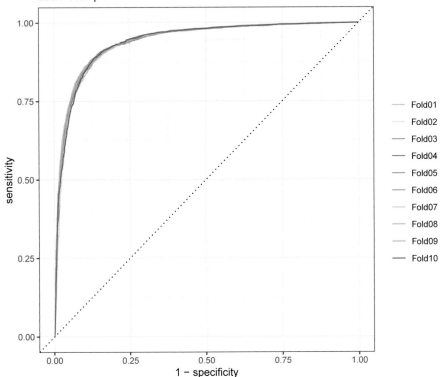

FIGURE 7.3: ROC curve for lasso regularized classifier with resamples of US Consumer Finance Bureau complaints

```
tune_spec <- logistic_reg(penalty = tune(), mixture = 1) %>%
  set_mode("classification") %>%
  set_engine("glmnet")

tune_spec

#> Logistic Regression Model Specification (classification)
#>
#> Main Arguments:
#>   penalty = tune()
#>   mixture = 1
#>
#> Computational engine: glmnet
```

FIGURE 7.4: Confusion matrix for a lasso regularized classifier, with more symmetric results

After the tuning process, we can select a single best numeric value.

  Think of `tune()` here as a placeholder for the regularization penalty.

We can create a regular grid of values to try, using a convenience function for `penalty()`.

```
lambda_grid <- grid_regular(penalty(), levels = 30)
lambda_grid
```

```
#> # A tibble: 30 x 1
#>     penalty
#>       <dbl>
#>  1 1   e-10
#>  2 2.21e-10
#>  3 4.89e-10
#>  4 1.08e- 9
#>  5 2.40e- 9
```

```
#>  6 5.30e- 9
#>  7 1.17e- 8
#>  8 2.59e- 8
#>  9 5.74e- 8
#> 10 1.27e- 7
#> # ... with 20 more rows
```

The function `grid_regular()` is from the **dials** package. It chooses sensible values to try for a parameter like the regularization penalty; here, we asked for 30 different possible values.

Now it is time to tune! Let's use `tune_grid()` to fit a model at each of the values for the regularization penalty in our regular grid.

In **tidymodels**, the package for tuning is called **tune**. Tuning a model uses a similar syntax compared to fitting a model to a set of resampled data sets for the purposes of evaluation (`fit_resamples()`) because the two tasks are so similar. The difference is that when you tune, each model that you fit has *different* parameters and you want to find the best one.

We add our tunable model specification `tune_spec` to a workflow with the same preprocessing recipe we've been using so far, and then fit it to every possible parameter in `lambda_grid` and every resample in `complaints_folds` with `tune_grid()`.

```
tune_wf <- workflow() %>%
  add_recipe(complaints_rec) %>%
  add_model(tune_spec)

set.seed(2020)
tune_rs <- tune_grid(
  tune_wf,
  complaints_folds,
  grid = lambda_grid,
  control = control_resamples(save_pred = TRUE)
)

tune_rs
```

```
#> # Tuning results
#> # 10-fold cross-validation
#> # A tibble: 10 x 5
#>    splits              id     .metrics         .notes         .predictions
#>    <list>              <chr>  <list>           <list>         <list>
#>  1 <split [79119/8791]> Fold01 <tibble [60 x 5]> <tibble [0 x 1]> <tibble [263,~
#>  2 <split [79119/8791]> Fold02 <tibble [60 x 5]> <tibble [0 x 1]> <tibble [263,~
#>  3 <split [79119/8791]> Fold03 <tibble [60 x 5]> <tibble [0 x 1]> <tibble [263,~
#>  4 <split [79119/8791]> Fold04 <tibble [60 x 5]> <tibble [0 x 1]> <tibble [263,~
#>  5 <split [79119/8791]> Fold05 <tibble [60 x 5]> <tibble [0 x 1]> <tibble [263,~
#>  6 <split [79119/8791]> Fold06 <tibble [60 x 5]> <tibble [0 x 1]> <tibble [263,~
#>  7 <split [79119/8791]> Fold07 <tibble [60 x 5]> <tibble [0 x 1]> <tibble [263,~
#>  8 <split [79119/8791]> Fold08 <tibble [60 x 5]> <tibble [0 x 1]> <tibble [263,~
#>  9 <split [79119/8791]> Fold09 <tibble [60 x 5]> <tibble [0 x 1]> <tibble [263,~
#> 10 <split [79119/8791]> Fold10 <tibble [60 x 5]> <tibble [0 x 1]> <tibble [263,~
```

 Like when we used `fit_resamples()`, tuning in tidymodels can use multiple cores or multiple machines via parallel processing, because the resampled data sets and possible parameters are independent of each other. A discussion of parallel processing for all possible operating systems is beyond the scope of this book, but it is well worth your time to learn how to parallelize your machine learning tasks on *your* system.

Now, instead of one set of metrics, we have a set of metrics for each value of the regularization penalty.

```
collect_metrics(tune_rs)
```

```
#> # A tibble: 60 x 7
#>    penalty .metric  .estimator  mean     n std_err .config
#>      <dbl> <chr>    <chr>      <dbl> <int>   <dbl> <chr>
#>  1 1       e-10 accuracy binary   0.890    10 0.000820 Preprocessor1_Model01
#>  2 1       e-10 roc_auc  binary   0.953    10 0.000522 Preprocessor1_Model01
#>  3 2.21e-10 accuracy binary   0.890    10 0.000820 Preprocessor1_Model02
#>  4 2.21e-10 roc_auc  binary   0.953    10 0.000522 Preprocessor1_Model02
#>  5 4.89e-10 accuracy binary   0.890    10 0.000820 Preprocessor1_Model03
#>  6 4.89e-10 roc_auc  binary   0.953    10 0.000522 Preprocessor1_Model03
#>  7 1.08e- 9 accuracy binary   0.890    10 0.000820 Preprocessor1_Model04
#>  8 1.08e- 9 roc_auc  binary   0.953    10 0.000522 Preprocessor1_Model04
#>  9 2.40e- 9 accuracy binary   0.890    10 0.000820 Preprocessor1_Model05
```

```
#> 10 2.40e- 9 roc_auc  binary      0.953    10 0.000522 Preprocessor1_Model05
#> # ... with 50 more rows
```

Let's visualize these metrics, accuracy and ROC AUC, in Figure 7.5 to see what the best model is.

```
autoplot(tune_rs) +
  labs(
    title = "Lasso model performance across regularization penalties",
    subtitle = "Performance metrics can be used to identity the best penalty"
  )
```

We can view the best results with show_best() and a choice for the metric, such as ROC AUC.

```
tune_rs %>%
  show_best("roc_auc")
```

```
#> # A tibble: 5 x 7
#>       penalty .metric .estimator   mean     n  std_err .config
#>         <dbl> <chr>   <chr>       <dbl> <int>    <dbl> <chr>
#> 1 0.000788      roc_auc binary    0.953    10 0.000505 Preprocessor1_Model21
#> 2 0.000356      roc_auc binary    0.953    10 0.000510 Preprocessor1_Model20
#> 3 0.000161      roc_auc binary    0.953    10 0.000517 Preprocessor1_Model19
#> 4 0.0000728     roc_auc binary    0.953    10 0.000520 Preprocessor1_Model18
#> 5 0.0000000001 roc_auc binary    0.953    10 0.000522 Preprocessor1_Model01
```

The best value for ROC AUC from this tuning run is 0.953. We can extract the best regularization parameter for this value of ROC AUC from our tuning results with select_best(), or a simpler model with higher regularization with select_by_pct_loss() or select_by_one_std_err() Let's choose the model with the best ROC AUC within one standard error of the numerically best model (Breiman et al. 1984).

```
chosen_auc <- tune_rs %>%
  select_by_one_std_err(metric = "roc_auc", -penalty)

chosen_auc
```

Lasso model performance across regularization penalties
Performance metrics can be used to identity the best penalty

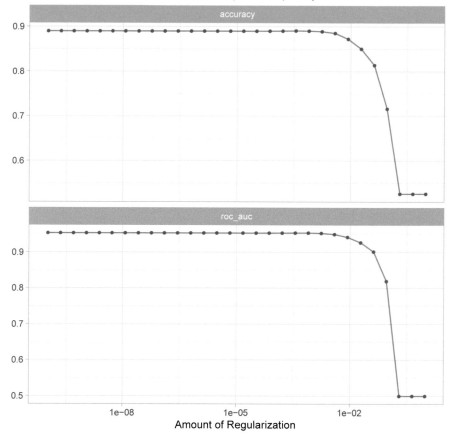

FIGURE 7.5: We can identify the best regularization penalty from model performance metrics, for example, at the highest ROC AUC. Note the logarithmic scale for the regularization penalty.

```
#> # A tibble: 1 x 9
#>    penalty .metric .estimator  mean     n std_err .config          .best .bound
#>      <dbl> <chr>   <chr>       <dbl> <int>   <dbl> <chr>            <dbl>  <dbl>
#> 1 0.000788 roc_auc binary      0.953    10 0.000505 Preprocessor1_M~ 0.953  0.953
```

Next, let's finalize our tunable workflow with this particular regularization penalty. This is the regularization penalty that our tuning results indicate give us the best model.

```
final_lasso <- finalize_workflow(tune_wf, chosen_auc)

final_lasso
```

```
#> == Workflow ======================================================
#> Preprocessor: Recipe
#> Model: logistic_reg()
#>
#> -- Preprocessor --------------------------------------------------
#> 3 Recipe Steps
#>
#> * step_tokenize()
#> * step_tokenfilter()
#> * step_tfidf()
#>
#> -- Model ---------------------------------------------------------
#> Logistic Regression Model Specification (classification)
#>
#> Main Arguments:
#>   penalty = 0.000788046281566992
#>   mixture = 1
#>
#> Computational engine: glmnet
```

Instead of `penalty = tune()` like before, now our workflow has finalized values for all arguments. The preprocessing recipe has been evaluated on the training data, and we tuned the regularization penalty so that we have a penalty value of 0.00079. This workflow is ready to go! It can now be fit to our training data.

```
fitted_lasso <- fit(final_lasso, complaints_train)
```

What does the result look like? We can access the fit using `pull_workflow_fit()`, and even `tidy()` the model coefficient results into a convenient dataframe format.

```
fitted_lasso %>%
  pull_workflow_fit() %>%
  tidy() %>%
  arrange(-estimate)
```

```
#> # A tibble: 1,001 x 3
#>    term                                            estimate  penalty
#>    <chr>                                              <dbl>    <dbl>
#>  1 tfidf_consumer_complaint_narrative_funds            27.6 0.000788
#>  2 tfidf_consumer_complaint_narrative_appraisal        22.9 0.000788
#>  3 tfidf_consumer_complaint_narrative_escrow           21.0 0.000788
#>  4 tfidf_consumer_complaint_narrative_bonus            20.7 0.000788
#>  5 tfidf_consumer_complaint_narrative_debt             18.5 0.000788
#>  6 tfidf_consumer_complaint_narrative_emailed          16.4 0.000788
#>  7 tfidf_consumer_complaint_narrative_money            16.1 0.000788
#>  8 tfidf_consumer_complaint_narrative_interest         15.7 0.000788
#>  9 tfidf_consumer_complaint_narrative_afford           15.5 0.000788
#> 10 tfidf_consumer_complaint_narrative_merchant         14.9 0.000788
#> # ... with 991 more rows
```

We see here, for the penalty we chose, what terms contribute the most to a complaint *not* being about credit. The words are largely about mortgages and other financial products.

What terms contribute to a complaint being about credit reporting, for this tuned model? Here we see the names of the credit reporting agencies and words about credit inquiries.

```
fitted_lasso %>%
  pull_workflow_fit() %>%
  tidy() %>%
  arrange(estimate)
```

```
#> # A tibble: 1,001 x 3
#>    term                                            estimate  penalty
#>    <chr>                                              <dbl>    <dbl>
#>  1 tfidf_consumer_complaint_narrative_reseller        -90.9 0.000788
#>  2 tfidf_consumer_complaint_narrative_experian        -56.9 0.000788
#>  3 tfidf_consumer_complaint_narrative_transunion      -50.1 0.000788
#>  4 tfidf_consumer_complaint_narrative_equifax         -48.1 0.000788
#>  5 tfidf_consumer_complaint_narrative_compliant       -23.7 0.000788
#>  6 tfidf_consumer_complaint_narrative_reporting       -21.1 0.000788
#>  7 tfidf_consumer_complaint_narrative_freeze          -20.9 0.000788
#>  8 tfidf_consumer_complaint_narrative_inquiries       -19.0 0.000788
#>  9 tfidf_consumer_complaint_narrative_report          -18.6 0.000788
#> 10 tfidf_consumer_complaint_narrative_method          -16.3 0.000788
#> # ... with 991 more rows
```

Since we are using a linear model, the model coefficients are directly interpretable and transparently give us variable importance. Many models useful for machine learning with text do *not* have such transparent variable importance; in those situations, you can use other model-independent or model-agnostic approaches like permutation variable importance[1].

7.5 Case study: sparse encoding

We can change how our text data is represented to take advantage of its sparsity, especially for models like lasso regularized models. The regularized regression model we have been training in previous sections used `set_engine("glmnet")`; this computational engine can be more efficient when text data is transformed to a sparse matrix (Section 5.1), rather than a dense dataframe or tibble representation.

To keep our text data sparse throughout modeling and use the sparse capabilities of `set_engine("glmnet")`, we need to explicitly set a non-default preprocessing blueprint, using the package **hardhat** (Vaughan and Kuhn 2020).

The **hardhat** package is used by other tidymodels packages like recipes and parsnip under the hood. As a tidymodels user, you typically don't use hardhat functions directly. The exception is when you need to customize something about your model or preprocessing, like in this sparse data example.

```
library(hardhat)
sparse_bp <- default_recipe_blueprint(composition = "dgCMatrix")
```

This "blueprint" lets us specify during modeling how we want our data passed around from the preprocessing into the model. The composition `"dgCMatrix"` is

---

[1] https://juliasilge.com/blog/last-airbender/

the most common sparse matrix type, from the Matrix package (Bates and Maechler 2021), used in R for modeling. We can use this `blueprint` argument when we add our recipe to our modeling workflow, to define how the data should be passed into the model.

```
sparse_wf <- workflow() %>%
  add_recipe(complaints_rec, blueprint = sparse_bp) %>%
  add_model(tune_spec)

sparse_wf
```

```
#> == Workflow ====================================================================
#> Preprocessor: Recipe
#> Model: logistic_reg()
#>
#> -- Preprocessor ----------------------------------------------------------------
#> 3 Recipe Steps
#>
#> * step_tokenize()
#> * step_tokenfilter()
#> * step_tfidf()
#>
#> -- Model -----------------------------------------------------------------------
#> Logistic Regression Model Specification (classification)
#>
#> Main Arguments:
#>   penalty = tune()
#>   mixture = 1
#>
#> Computational engine: glmnet
```

The last time we tuned a lasso model, we used the defaults for the penalty parameter and 30 levels. Let's restrict the values this time using the `range` argument, so we don't test out as small values for regularization, and only try 20 levels.

```
smaller_lambda <- grid_regular(penalty(range = c(-5, 0)), levels = 20)
smaller_lambda
```

```
#> # A tibble: 20 x 1
#>      penalty
#>        <dbl>
#>  1 0.00001
#>  2 0.0000183
#>  3 0.0000336
#>  4 0.0000616
#>  5 0.000113
#>  6 0.000207
#>  7 0.000379
#>  8 0.000695
#>  9 0.00127
#> 10 0.00234
#> 11 0.00428
#> 12 0.00785
#> 13 0.0144
#> 14 0.0264
#> 15 0.0483
#> 16 0.0886
#> 17 0.162
#> 18 0.298
#> 19 0.546
#> 20 1
```

We can tune this lasso regression model, in the same way that we did in Section 7.4. We will fit and assess each possible regularization parameter on each resampling fold, to find the best amount of regularization.

```
set.seed(2020)
sparse_rs <- tune_grid(
  sparse_wf,
  complaints_folds,
  grid = smaller_lambda
)

sparse_rs
```

```
#> # Tuning results
#> # 10-fold cross-validation
#> # A tibble: 10 x 4
#>    splits                id     .metrics        .notes
#>    <list>                <chr>  <list>          <list>
#>  1 <split [79119/8791]>  Fold01 <tibble [40 x 5]> <tibble [0 x 1]>
```

```
#>  2 <split [79119/8791]> Fold02 <tibble [40 x 5]> <tibble [0 x 1]>
#>  3 <split [79119/8791]> Fold03 <tibble [40 x 5]> <tibble [0 x 1]>
#>  4 <split [79119/8791]> Fold04 <tibble [40 x 5]> <tibble [0 x 1]>
#>  5 <split [79119/8791]> Fold05 <tibble [40 x 5]> <tibble [0 x 1]>
#>  6 <split [79119/8791]> Fold06 <tibble [40 x 5]> <tibble [0 x 1]>
#>  7 <split [79119/8791]> Fold07 <tibble [40 x 5]> <tibble [0 x 1]>
#>  8 <split [79119/8791]> Fold08 <tibble [40 x 5]> <tibble [0 x 1]>
#>  9 <split [79119/8791]> Fold09 <tibble [40 x 5]> <tibble [0 x 1]>
#> 10 <split [79119/8791]> Fold10 <tibble [40 x 5]> <tibble [0 x 1]>
```

How did this model turn out, especially compared to the tuned model that did not use the sparse capabilities of `set_engine("glmnet")`?

```
sparse_rs %>%
  show_best("roc_auc")
```

```
#> # A tibble: 5 x 7
#>    penalty .metric .estimator  mean     n std_err .config
#>      <dbl> <chr>   <chr>      <dbl> <int>   <dbl> <chr>
#> 1 0.000695 roc_auc binary     0.953    10 0.000506 Preprocessor1_Model08
#> 2 0.000379 roc_auc binary     0.953    10 0.000510 Preprocessor1_Model07
#> 3 0.000207 roc_auc binary     0.953    10 0.000515 Preprocessor1_Model06
#> 4 0.00127  roc_auc binary     0.953    10 0.000504 Preprocessor1_Model09
#> 5 0.000113 roc_auc binary     0.953    10 0.000519 Preprocessor1_Model05
```

The best ROC AUC is nearly identical; the best ROC AUC for the non-sparse tuned lasso model in Section 7.4 was 0.953. The best regularization parameter (`penalty`) is a little different (the best value in Section 7.4 was 0.00079), but we used a different grid so didn't try out exactly the same values. We ended up with nearly the same performance and best tuned model.

Importantly, this tuning also took a bit less time to complete.

- The *preprocessing* was not much faster, because tokenization and computing tf-idf take a long time.

- The *model fitting* was much faster, because for highly sparse data, this implementation of regularized regression is much faster for sparse matrix input than any dense input.

Overall, the whole tuning workflow is about 10% faster using the sparse preprocessing blueprint. Depending on how computationally expensive your preprocessing is relative to your model and how sparse your data is, you may expect to see larger (or smaller) gains from moving to a sparse data representation.

Since our model performance is about the same and we see gains in training time, let's use this sparse representation for the rest of this chapter.

7.6 Two-class or multiclass?

Most of this chapter focuses on binary classification, where we have two classes in our outcome variable (such as "Credit" and "Other") and each observation can either be one or the other. This is a simple scenario with straightforward evaluation strategies because the results only have a two-by-two contingency matrix. However, it is not always possible to limit a modeling question to two classes. Let's explore how to deal with situations where we have more than two classes. The CFPB complaints data set in this chapter has nine different product classes. In decreasing frequency, they are:

- Credit reporting, credit repair services, or other personal consumer reports

- Debt collection

- Credit card or prepaid card

- Mortgage

- Checking or savings account

- Student loan

- Vehicle loan or lease

- Money transfer, virtual currency, or money service

- Payday loan, title loan, or personal loan

We assume that there is a reason why these product classes have been created in this fashion by this government agency. Perhaps complaints from different classes are handled by different people or organizations. Whatever the reason, in this section we would like to build a multiclass classifier to identify these nine specific product classes.

We need to create a new split of the data using `initial_split()` on the unmodified `complaints` data set.

```
set.seed(1234)

multicomplaints_split <- initial_split(complaints, strata = product)

multicomplaints_train <- training(multicomplaints_split)
multicomplaints_test <- testing(multicomplaints_split)
```

Before we continue, let us take a look at the number of cases in each of the classes.

```
multicomplaints_train %>%
  count(product, sort = TRUE) %>%
  select(n, product)
```

```
#> # A tibble: 9 x 2
#>        n product
#>    <int> <chr>
#> 1 41714 Credit reporting, credit repair services, or other personal consumer re~
#> 2 16784 Debt collection
#> 3  8637 Credit card or prepaid card
#> 4  7067 Mortgage
#> 5  5164 Checking or savings account
#> 6  2932 Student loan
#> 7  2014 Vehicle loan or lease
#> 8  1942 Money transfer, virtual currency, or money service
#> 9  1656 Payday loan, title loan, or personal loan
```

There is significant imbalance between the classes that we must address, with over 20 times more cases of the majority class than there is of the smallest class. This kind of imbalance is a common problem with multiclass classification, with few multiclass data sets in the real world exhibiting balance between classes.

Compared to binary classification, there are several additional issues to keep in mind when working with multiclass classification:

- Many machine learning algorithms do not handle imbalanced data well and are likely to have a hard time predicting minority classes.

- Not all machine learning algorithms are built for multiclass classification at all.

- Many evaluation metrics need to be reformulated to describe multiclass predictions.

When you have multiple classes in your data, it is possible to formulate the multiclass problem in two ways. With one approach, any given observation can belong to multiple classes. With the other approach, an observation can belong to one and only one class. We will be sticking to the second, "one class per observation" model formulation in this section.

There are many different ways to deal with imbalanced data. We will demonstrate one of the simplest methods, downsampling, where observations from the majority classes are removed during training to achieve a balanced class distribution. We will be using the **themis** (Hvitfeldt 2020d) add-on package for recipes which provides the `step_downsample()` function to perform downsampling.

The **themis** package provides many more algorithms to deal with imbalanced data during data preprocessing.

We have to create a new recipe specification from scratch, since we are dealing with new training data this time. The specification `multicomplaints_rec` is similar to what we created in Section 7.1. The only changes are that different data is passed to the `data` argument in the `recipe()` function (it is now `multicomplaints_train`) and we have added `step_downsample(product)` to the end of the recipe specification to downsample after all the text preprocessing. We want to downsample last so that we still generate features on the full training data set. The downsampling will then *only* affect the modeling step, not the preprocessing steps, with hopefully better results.

```
library(themis)

multicomplaints_rec <-
  recipe(product ~ consumer_complaint_narrative,
         data = multicomplaints_train) %>%
```

```
step_tokenize(consumer_complaint_narrative) %>%
step_tokenfilter(consumer_complaint_narrative, max_tokens = 1e3) %>%
step_tfidf(consumer_complaint_narrative) %>%
step_downsample(product)
```

We also need a new cross-validation object since we are using a different data set.

```
multicomplaints_folds <- vfold_cv(multicomplaints_train)
```

We cannot reuse the tuneable lasso classification specification from Section 7.4 because it only works for binary classification. Some model algorithms and computational engines (examples are most random forests and SVMs) automatically detect when we perform multiclass classification from the number of classes in the outcome variable and do not require any changes to our model specification. For lasso regularization, we need to create a new special model specification just for the multiclass class using `multinom_reg()`.

```
multi_spec <- multinom_reg(penalty = tune(), mixture = 1) %>%
  set_mode("classification") %>%
  set_engine("glmnet")

multi_spec
```

```
#> Multinomial Regression Model Specification (classification)
#>
#> Main Arguments:
#>   penalty = tune()
#>   mixture = 1
#>
#> Computational engine: glmnet
```

We used the same arguments for `penalty` and `mixture` as in Section 7.4, as well as the same mode and engine, but this model specification is set up to handle more than just two classes. We can combine this model specification with our preprocessing recipe for multiclass data in a `workflow()`.

```
multi_lasso_wf <- workflow() %>%
    add_recipe(multicomplaints_rec, blueprint = sparse_bp) %>%
    add_model(multi_spec)

multi_lasso_wf
```

```
#> == Workflow ======================================================
#> Preprocessor: Recipe
#> Model: multinom_reg()
#>
#> -- Preprocessor ---------------------------------------------------
#> 4 Recipe Steps
#>
#> * step_tokenize()
#> * step_tokenfilter()
#> * step_tfidf()
#> * step_downsample()
#>
#> -- Model ----------------------------------------------------------
#> Multinomial Regression Model Specification (classification)
#>
#> Main Arguments:
#>    penalty = tune()
#>    mixture = 1
#>
#> Computational engine: glmnet
```

Now we have everything we need to tune the regularization penalty and find an appropriate value. Note that we specify save_pred = TRUE, so we can create ROC curves and a confusion matrix later. This is especially beneficial for multiclass classification.

```
multi_lasso_rs <- tune_grid(
    multi_lasso_wf,
    multicomplaints_folds,
    grid = smaller_lambda,
    control = control_resamples(save_pred = TRUE)
)

multi_lasso_rs
```

```
#> # Tuning results
#> # 10-fold cross-validation
#> # A tibble: 10 x 5
#>     splits               id       .metrics          .notes          .predictions
#>     <list>               <chr>    <list>            <list>          <list>
#>  1 <split [79119/8791]> Fold01 <tibble [40 x 5]> <tibble [0 x 1]> <tibble [175,~
#>  2 <split [79119/8791]> Fold02 <tibble [40 x 5]> <tibble [0 x 1]> <tibble [175,~
#>  3 <split [79119/8791]> Fold03 <tibble [40 x 5]> <tibble [0 x 1]> <tibble [175,~
#>  4 <split [79119/8791]> Fold04 <tibble [40 x 5]> <tibble [0 x 1]> <tibble [175,~
#>  5 <split [79119/8791]> Fold05 <tibble [40 x 5]> <tibble [0 x 1]> <tibble [175,~
#>  6 <split [79119/8791]> Fold06 <tibble [40 x 5]> <tibble [0 x 1]> <tibble [175,~
#>  7 <split [79119/8791]> Fold07 <tibble [40 x 5]> <tibble [0 x 1]> <tibble [175,~
#>  8 <split [79119/8791]> Fold08 <tibble [40 x 5]> <tibble [0 x 1]> <tibble [175,~
#>  9 <split [79119/8791]> Fold09 <tibble [40 x 5]> <tibble [1 x 1]> <tibble [175,~
#> 10 <split [79119/8791]> Fold10 <tibble [40 x 5]> <tibble [0 x 1]> <tibble [175,~
```

What do we see, in terms of performance metrics?

```
best_acc <- multi_lasso_rs %>%
  show_best("accuracy")

best_acc
```

```
#> # A tibble: 5 x 7
#>    penalty .metric  .estimator  mean     n std_err .config
#>      <dbl> <chr>    <chr>      <dbl> <int>   <dbl> <chr>
#> 1 0.00234  accuracy multiclass 0.754    10 0.00155 Preprocessor1_Model10
#> 2 0.00428  accuracy multiclass 0.751    10 0.00147 Preprocessor1_Model11
#> 3 0.00127  accuracy multiclass 0.749    10 0.00150 Preprocessor1_Model09
#> 4 0.00785  accuracy multiclass 0.741    10 0.00135 Preprocessor1_Model12
#> 5 0.000695 accuracy multiclass 0.736    10 0.00139 Preprocessor1_Model08
```

The accuracy metric naturally extends to multiclass tasks, but even the very best value is quite low at 75.4%, significantly lower than for the binary case in Section 7.4. This is expected since multiclass classification is a harder task than binary classification.

In binary classification, there is one right answer and one wrong answer; in this multiclass case, there is one right answer and *eight* wrong answers.

To get a more detailed view of how our classifier is performing, let us look at one of the confusion matrices in Figure 7.6.

```
multi_lasso_rs %>%
  collect_predictions() %>%
  filter(penalty == best_acc$penalty) %>%
  filter(id == "Fold01") %>%
  conf_mat(product, .pred_class) %>%
  autoplot(type = "heatmap") +
  scale_y_discrete(labels = function(x) str_wrap(x, 20)) +
  scale_x_discrete(labels = function(x) str_wrap(x, 20))
```

Prediction	Checking or savings account	Credit card or prepaid card	Credit reporting, credit repair services, or other personal consumer reports	Debt collection	Money transfer, virtual currency, or money service	Mortgage	Payday loan, title loan, or personal loan	Student loan	Vehicle loan or lease
Checking or savings account	408	62	33	25	26	11	8	5	3
Credit card or prepaid card	38	651	216	84	8	3	5	5	4
Credit reporting, credit repair services, or other personal consumer reports	1	33	3002	149	2	12	4	6	9
Debt collection	3	17	402	1224	2	7	9	10	9
Money transfer, virtual currency, or money service	47	29	27	20	181	7	5	4	3
Mortgage	6	14	85	44	5	613	1	6	3
Payday loan, title loan, or personal loan	8	27	82	87	7	35	100	24	19
Student loan	1	3	92	26	1	6	4	259	1
Vehicle loan or lease	4	20	171	43	1	11	16	5	142

Truth

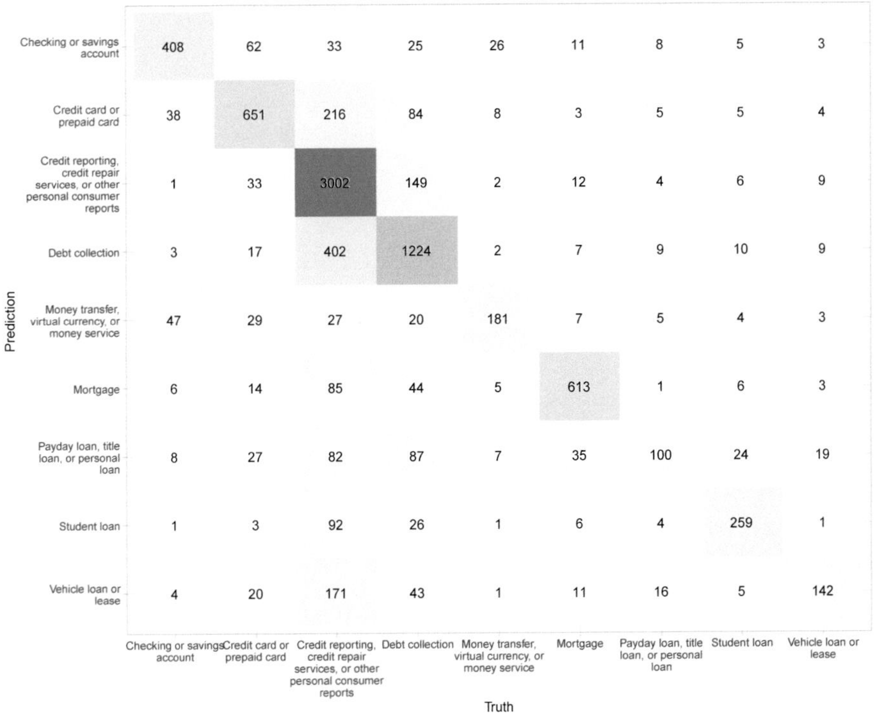

FIGURE 7.6: Confusion matrix for multiclass lasso regularized classifier, with most of the classifications along the diagonal

The diagonal is fairly well populated, which is a good sign. This means that the model generally predicted the right class. The off-diagonal numbers are all the failures and where we should direct our focus. It is a little hard to see these cases well since the majority class affects the scale. A trick to deal with this problem is to remove all the correctly predicted observations.

```
multi_lasso_rs %>%
  collect_predictions() %>%
  filter(penalty == best_acc$penalty) %>%
  filter(id == "Fold01") %>%
  filter(.pred_class != product) %>%
  conf_mat(product, .pred_class) %>%
  autoplot(type = "heatmap") +
  scale_y_discrete(labels = function(x) str_wrap(x, 20)) +
  scale_x_discrete(labels = function(x) str_wrap(x, 20))
```

Prediction \ Truth	Checking or savings account	Credit card or prepaid card	Credit reporting, credit repair services, or other personal consumer reports	Debt collection	Money transfer, virtual currency, or money service	Mortgage	Payday loan, title loan, or personal loan	Student loan	Vehicle loan or lease
Checking or savings account	0	62	33	25	26	11	8	5	3
Credit card or prepaid card	38	0	216	84	8	3	5	5	4
Credit reporting, credit repair services, or other personal consumer reports	1	33	0	149	2	12	4	6	9
Debt collection	3	17	402	0	2	7	9	10	9
Money transfer, virtual currency, or money service	47	29	27	20	0	7	5	4	3
Mortgage	6	14	85	44	5	0	1	6	3
Payday loan, title loan, or personal loan	8	27	82	87	7	35	0	24	19
Student loan	1	3	92	26	1	6	4	0	1
Vehicle loan or lease	4	20	171	43	1	11	16	5	0

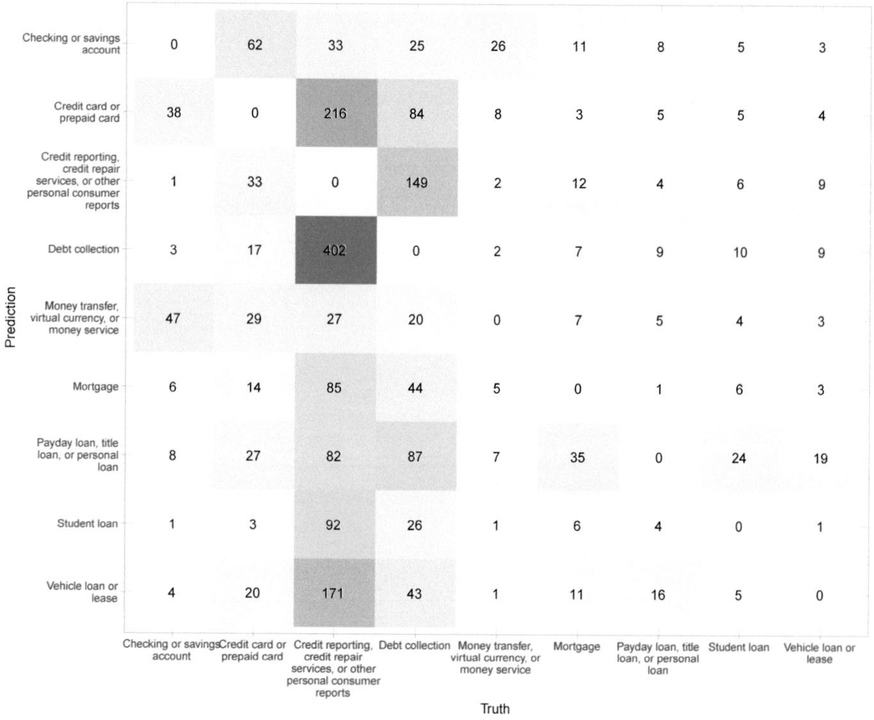

FIGURE 7.7: Confusion matrix for multiclass lasso regularized classifier without diagonal

Now we can more clearly see where our model breaks down in Figure 7.7. Some of the most common errors are "Credit reporting, credit repair services, or other personal consumer reports" complaints being wrongly being predicted as "Debt collection" or "Credit card of prepaid card" complaints. Those mistakes by the model are not hard to understand since all deal with credit and debt and do have overlap in vocabulary. Knowing what the problem is helps us figure out how to improve our model. The next step for improving our model is to revisit the data preprocessing steps and model selection. We can look at different models or model engines that might be able to more easily separate the classes.

Now that we have an idea of where the model isn't working, we can look more closely at the data and attempt to create features that could distinguish between these classes. In Section 7.9 we will demonstrate how you can create your own custom features.

7.7 Case study: including non-text data

We are building a model from a data set that includes more than text data alone. Annotations and labels have been added by the CFPB that we can use during modeling, but we need to ensure that only information that would be available at the time of prediction is included in the model. Otherwise we will be very disappointed once our model is used to predict on new data! The variables we identify as available for use as predictors are:

- `date_received`

- `issue`

- `sub_issue`

- `consumer_complaint_narrative`

- `company`

- `state`

- `zip_code`

- `tags`

- `submitted_via`

Let's try including `date_received` in our modeling, along with the text variable we have already used, `consumer_complaint_narrative`, and a new variable `tags`. The `submitted_via` variable could have been a viable candidate, but all the entries are "web." The other variables like ZIP code could be of use too, but

they are categorical variables with many values so we will exclude them for
now.

```
more_vars_rec <-
  recipe(product ~ date_received + tags + consumer_complaint_narrative,
       data = complaints_train)
```

How should we preprocess the `date_received` variable? We can use the
`step_date()` function to extract the month and day of the week (`"dow"`). Then
we remove the original date variable and convert the new month and day-of-
the-week columns to indicator variables with `step_dummy()`.

> Categorical variables like the month can be stored as strings or factors,
> but for some kinds of models, they must be converted to indicator or
> dummy variables. These are numeric binary variables for the levels of the
> original categorical variable. For example, a variable called `December` would
> be created that is all zeroes and ones specifying which complaints were
> submitted in December, plus a variable called `November`, a variable called
> `October`, and so on.

```
more_vars_rec <- more_vars_rec %>%
  step_date(date_received, features = c("month", "dow"), role = "dates") %>%
  step_rm(date_received) %>%
  step_dummy(has_role("dates"))
```

The `tags` variable has some missing data. We can deal with this by using
`step_unknown()`, which adds a new level to this factor variable for cases of missing
data. Then we "dummify" (create dummy/indicator variables) the variable
with `step_dummy()`.

```
more_vars_rec <- more_vars_rec %>%
  step_unknown(tags) %>%
  step_dummy(tags)
```

Now we add steps to process the text of the complaints, as before.

```
more_vars_rec <- more_vars_rec %>%
  step_tokenize(consumer_complaint_narrative) %>%
  step_tokenfilter(consumer_complaint_narrative, max_tokens = 1e3) %>%
  step_tfidf(consumer_complaint_narrative)
```

Let's combine this more extensive preprocessing recipe that handles more variables together with the tuneable lasso regularized classification model specification.

```
more_vars_wf <- workflow() %>%
  add_recipe(more_vars_rec, blueprint = sparse_bp) %>%
  add_model(tune_spec)

more_vars_wf
```

```
#> == Workflow ===========================================================
#> Preprocessor: Recipe
#> Model: logistic_reg()
#>
#> -- Preprocessor ------------------------------------------------------
#> 8 Recipe Steps
#>
#> * step_date()
#> * step_rm()
#> * step_dummy()
#> * step_unknown()
#> * step_dummy()
#> * step_tokenize()
#> * step_tokenfilter()
#> * step_tfidf()
#>
#> -- Model -------------------------------------------------------------
#> Logistic Regression Model Specification (classification)
#>
#> Main Arguments:
#>   penalty = tune()
#>   mixture = 1
#>
#> Computational engine: glmnet
```

Let's tune this `workflow()` with our resampled data sets, find a good value for the regularization penalty, and estimate the model's performance.

```
set.seed(123)
more_vars_rs <- tune_grid(
  more_vars_wf,
  complaints_folds,
  grid = smaller_lambda,
)
```

We can extract the metrics for the best-performing regularization penalties from these results with show_best() with an option like "roc_auc" or "accuracy" if we prefer. How did our chosen performance metric turn out for our model that included more than just the text data?

```
more_vars_rs %>%
  show_best("roc_auc")
```

```
#> # A tibble: 5 x 7
#>     penalty .metric .estimator  mean     n std_err .config
#>       <dbl> <chr>   <chr>      <dbl> <int>   <dbl> <chr>
#> 1 0.000695 roc_auc binary     0.953    10 0.000514 Preprocessor1_Model08
#> 2 0.000379 roc_auc binary     0.953    10 0.000515 Preprocessor1_Model07
#> 3 0.000207 roc_auc binary     0.953    10 0.000520 Preprocessor1_Model06
#> 4 0.00127  roc_auc binary     0.953    10 0.000511 Preprocessor1_Model09
#> 5 0.000113 roc_auc binary     0.953    10 0.000525 Preprocessor1_Model05
```

We see here that including more predictors did not measurably improve our model performance or even change the regularization. With only text features in Section 7.5 and the same grid and sparse encoding, we achieved an accuracy of 0.953, the same as what we see now by including the features dealing with dates and tags as well. The best regularization penalty in Section 7.5 was 0.0007 and is about the same here. We can use tidy() and some **dplyr** manipulation to find at what rank (term_rank) any of the date or tag variables were included in the regularized results, by absolute value of the model coefficient.

```
finalize_workflow(more_vars_wf,
                  select_best(more_vars_rs, "roc_auc")) %>%
  fit(complaints_train) %>%
  pull_workflow_fit() %>%
  tidy() %>%
  arrange(-abs(estimate)) %>%
  mutate(term_rank = row_number()) %>%
  filter(!str_detect(term, "tfidf"))
```

```
#> # A tibble: 21 x 4
#>    term                     estimate  penalty term_rank
#>    <chr>                        <dbl>    <dbl>     <int>
#>  1 (Intercept)                  0.326 0.000695       701
#>  2 date_received_month_Dec     -0.271 0.000695       716
#>  3 date_received_month_Aug     -0.105 0.000695       746
#>  4 date_received_dow_Mon        0.102 0.000695       748
#>  5 date_received_month_Apr     0.0763 0.000695       756
#>  6 date_received_month_Feb    -0.0547 0.000695       761
#>  7 tags_Servicemember         -0.0426 0.000695       765
#>  8 date_received_dow_Tue       0.0329 0.000695       766
#>  9 date_received_dow_Fri       0.0147 0.000695       770
#> 10 date_received_month_May    0.00337 0.000695       774
#> # ... with 11 more rows
```

In our example here, some of the non-text predictors are included in the model
with non-zero coefficients but ranked down in the 700s of all model terms, with
smaller coefficients than many text terms. They are not that important.

This whole book focuses on supervised machine learning for text data, but
models can combine *both* text predictors and other kinds of predictors.

7.8 Case study: data censoring

The complaints data set already has sensitive information (PII) censored or
protected using strings such as "XXXX" and "XX." This data censoring can
be viewed as data *annotation*; specific account numbers and birthdays are
protected, but we know they were there. These values would be mostly unique
anyway, and likely filtered out in their original form.

Figure 7.8 shows the most frequent trigrams (Section 2.2.3) in our training
data set.

```
library(tidytext)

complaints_train %>%
  slice(1:1000) %>%
```

```
unnest_tokens(trigrams,
              consumer_complaint_narrative, token = "ngrams",
              collapse = NULL) %>%
count(trigrams, sort = TRUE) %>%
mutate(censored = str_detect(trigrams, "xx")) %>%
slice(1:20) %>%
ggplot(aes(n, reorder(trigrams, n), fill = censored)) +
geom_col() +
scale_fill_manual(values = c("grey40", "firebrick")) +
labs(y = "Trigrams", x = "Count")
```

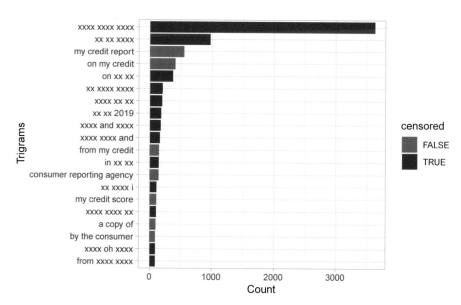

FIGURE 7.8: Many of the most frequent trigrams feature censored information

The vast majority of trigrams in Figure 7.8 include one or more censored words. Not only do the most used trigrams include some kind of censoring, but the censoring itself is informative as it is not used uniformly across the product classes. In Figure 7.9, we take the top-25 most frequent trigrams that include censoring, and plot the proportions for "Credit" and "Other."

```
top_censored_trigrams <- complaints_train %>%
  slice(1:1000) %>%
  unnest_tokens(trigrams,
                consumer_complaint_narrative, token = "ngrams",
```

```
                    collapse = NULL) %>%
    count(trigrams, sort = TRUE) %>%
    filter(str_detect(trigrams, "xx")) %>%
    slice(1:25)

plot_data <- complaints_train %>%
    unnest_tokens(trigrams,
                    consumer_complaint_narrative, token = "ngrams",
                    collapse = NULL) %>%
    right_join(top_censored_trigrams, by = "trigrams") %>%
    count(trigrams, product, .drop = FALSE)

plot_data %>%
    ggplot(aes(n, trigrams, fill = product)) +
    geom_col(position = "fill")
```

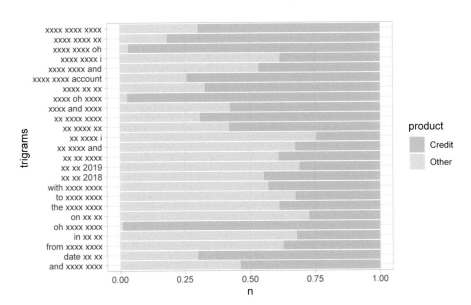

FIGURE 7.9: Many of the most frequent trigrams feature censored words, but there is a difference in how often they are used within each class

There is a difference in these proportions across classes. Tokens like "on xx xx" are used when referencing a date, e.g., "we had a problem on 06/25/2018." Remember that the current tokenization engine strips punctuation before tokenizing. This means that the above example will be turned into "we had a problem on 06 25 2018" before creating n-grams[2].

---

[2]The censored trigrams that include "oh" seem mysterious but upon closer examination,

To crudely simulate what the data might look like before it was censored, we can replace all cases of "XX" and "XXXX" with random integers. This isn't quite right since dates will be given values between 00 and 99, and we don't know for sure that only numerals have been censored, but it gives us a place to start. Below is a simple function uncensor_vec() that locates all instances of "xx" and replaces them with a number between 11 and 99. We don't need to handle the special case of xxxx as it automatically being handled.

```r
uncensor <- function(n) {
  as.character(sample(seq(10 ^ (n - 1), 10 ^ n - 1), 1))
}


uncensor_vec <- function(x) {
  locs <- str_locate_all(x, "XX")
  map2_chr(x, locs, ~ {
    for (i in seq_len(nrow(.y))) {
      str_sub(.x, .y[i, 1], .y[i, 2]) <- uncensor(2)
    }
    .x
  })
}
```

We can run a quick test to see how it works.

```r
uncensor_vec("In XX/XX/XXXX I leased a XXXX vehicle")
```

```r
#> [1] "In 33/64/4458 I leased a 7595 vehicle"
```

Now we can produce the same visualization as Figure 7.8 but can also apply our uncensoring function to the text before tokenizing.

```r
complaints_train %>%
  slice(1:1000) %>%
  mutate(text = uncensor_vec(consumer_complaint_narrative)) %>%
  unnest_tokens(trigrams, text, token = "ngrams",
                collapse = NULL) %>%
  count(trigrams, sort = TRUE) %>%
```

---

they come from censored addresses, with "oh" representing the US state of Ohio. Most two-letter state abbreviations are censored, but this one is not since it is ambiguous. This highlights the real challenge of anonymizing text.

```
mutate(censored = str_detect(trigrams, "xx")) %>%
slice(1:20) %>%
ggplot(aes(n, reorder(trigrams, n), fill = censored)) +
geom_col() +
scale_fill_manual(values = c("grey40", "firebrick")) +
labs(y = "Trigrams", x = "Count")
```

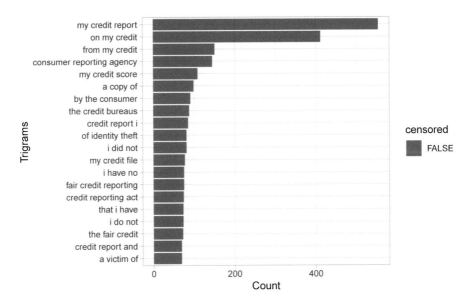

FIGURE 7.10: Trigrams without numbers float to the top as the uncensored tokens are too spread out

Here in Figure 7.10, we see the same trigrams that appeared in Figure 7.8. However, none of the uncensored words appear, because of our uncensoring function. This is expected, because while `"xx xx 2019"` appears in the first plot indicating a date in the year 2019, after we uncensor it, it is split into 365 buckets (actually more, since we used numerical values between `00` and `99`). Censoring the dates in these complaints gives more power to a date as a general construct.

What happens when we use these censored dates as a feature in supervised machine learning? We have a higher chance of understanding if dates in the complaint text are important to predicting the class, but we are blinded to the possibility that certain dates and months are more important.

Data censoring can be a form of preprocessing in your data pipeline. For example, it is highly unlikely to be useful (or ethical/legal) to have any specific person's social security number, credit card number, or any other kind of PII embedded into your model. Such values appear rarely and are most likely highly correlated with other known variables in your data set. More importantly, that information can become embedded in your model and begin to leak as demonstrated by Carlini et al. (2019), Matthew Fredrikson et al. (2014), and Matt Fredrikson, Jha, and Ristenpart (2015). Both of these issues are important, and one of them could land you in a lot of legal trouble. Exposing such PII to modeling is an example of where we should all stop to ask, "Should we even be doing this?" as we discussed in the overview to these chapters.

If you have social security numbers in text data, you should definitely not pass them on to your machine learning model, but you may consider the option of annotating the *presence* of a social security number. Since a social security number has a very specific form, we can easily construct a regular expression (Appendix A) to locate them.

A social security number comes in the form AAA-BB-CCCC where AAA is a number between 001 and 899 excluding 666, BB is a number between 01 and 99 and CCCC is a number between 0001 and 9999. This gives us the following regex:

```
(?!000|666)[0-8][0-9]{2}-(?!00)[0-9]{2}-(?!0000)[0-9]{4}
```

We can use a function to replace each social security number with an indicator that can be detected later by preprocessing steps. It's a good idea to use a "word" that won't be accidentally broken up by a tokenizer.

```
ssn_text <- c("My social security number is 498-08-6333",
              "No way, mine is 362-60-9159",
              "My parents numbers are 575-32-6985 and 576-36-5202")

ssn_pattern <-  "(?!000|666)[0-8][0-9]{2}-(?!00)[0-9]{2}-(?!0000)[0-9]{4}"

str_replace_all(string = ssn_text,
                pattern = ssn_pattern,
                replacement = "ssnindicator")
```

```
#> [1] "My social security number is ssnindicator"
```

```
#> [2] "No way, mine is ssnindicator"
#> [3] "My parents numbers are ssnindicator and ssnindicator"
```

This technique isn't useful only for personally identifiable information but can be used anytime you want to gather similar words in the same bucket; hashtags, email addresses, and usernames can sometimes benefit from being annotated in this way.

> The practice of data re-identification or de-anonymization, where seemingly or partially "anonymized" data sets are mined to identify individuals, is out of scope for this section and our book. However, this is a significant and important issue for any data practitioner dealing with PII, and we encourage readers to familiarize themselves with results such as Sweeney (2000) and current best practices to protect against such mining.

7.9 Case study: custom features

Most of what we have looked at so far has boiled down to counting tokens and weighting them in one way or another. This approach is quite broad and domain agnostic, but you as a data practitioner often have specific knowledge about your data set that you should use in feature engineering. Your domain knowledge allows you to build more predictive features than the naive search of simple tokens. As long as you can reasonably formulate what you are trying to count, chances are you can write a function that can detect it. This is where having a little bit of knowledge about regular expressions pays off.

> The **textfeatures** (Kearney 2019) package includes functions to extract useful features from text, from the number of digits to the number of second-person pronouns and more. These features can be used in textrecipes data preprocessing with the `step_textfeature()` function.

Your specific domain knowledge may provide specific guidance about feature engineering for text. Such custom features can be simple such as the number of URLs or the number of punctuation marks. They can also be more engineered, such as the percentage of capitalization, whether the text ends with a hashtag, or whether two people's names are both mentioned in a document.

For our CFPB complaints data, certain patterns may not have adequately been picked up by our model so far, such as the data censoring and the curly bracket annotation for monetary amounts that we saw in Section 7.1. Let's walk through how to create data preprocessing functions to build the features to:

- detect credit cards,

- calculate percentage censoring, and

- detect monetary amounts.

7.9.1   Detect credit cards

A credit card number is represented as four groups of four capital Xs in this data set. Since the data is fairly well processed we are fairly sure that spacing will not be an issue and all credit cards will be represented as "XXXX XXXX XXXX XXXX." A first naive attempt may be to use str_detect() with "XXXX XXXX XXXX XXXX" to find all the credit cards.

It is a good idea to create a small example regular expression where you know the answer, and then prototype your function before moving to the main data set.

We start by creating a vector with two positives, one negative, and one potential false positive. The last string is more tricky since it has the same shape as a credit card but has one too many groups.

```
credit_cards <- c("my XXXX XXXX XXXX XXXX balance, and XXXX XXXX XXXX XXXX.",
                  "card with number XXXX XXXX XXXX XXXX.",
                  "at XX/XX 2019 my first",
                  "live at XXXX XXXX XXXX XXXX XXXX SC")
```

```
str_detect(credit_cards, "XXXX XXXX XXXX XXXX")
```

```
#> [1]  TRUE  TRUE FALSE  TRUE
```

As we feared, the last vector was falsely detected to be a credit card. Sometimes you will have to accept a certain number of false positives and/or false negatives, depending on the data and what you are trying to detect. In this case, we can make the regex a little more complicated to avoid that specific false positive. We need to make sure that the word coming before the X's doesn't end in a capital X and the word following the last X doesn't start with a capital X. We place spaces around the credit card and use some negated character classes (Appendix A.3) to detect anything BUT a capital X.

```
str_detect(credit_cards, "[^X] XXXX XXXX XXXX XXXX [^X]")
```

```
#> [1]  TRUE FALSE FALSE FALSE
```

Hurray! This fixed the false positive. But it gave us a false negative in return. Turns out that this regex doesn't allow the credit card to be followed by a period since it requires a space. We can fix this with an alteration to match for a period or a space and a non-X.

```
str_detect(credit_cards, "[^X] +XXXX XXXX XXXX XXXX(\\.| [^X])")
```

```
#> [1]  TRUE  TRUE FALSE FALSE
```

Now that we have a regular expression we are happy with we can wrap it up in a function we can use. We can extract the presence of a credit card with `str_detect()` and the number of credit cards with `str_count()`.

```
creditcard_indicator <- function(x) {
  str_detect(x, "[^X] +XXXX XXXX XXXX XXXX(\\.| [^X])")
}

creditcard_count <- function(x) {
  str_count(x, "[^X] +XXXX XXXX XXXX XXXX(\\.| [^X])")
}

creditcard_indicator(credit_cards)
```

```
#> [1]  TRUE  TRUE FALSE FALSE
```

```
creditcard_count(credit_cards)
```

```
#> [1] 2 1 0 0
```

7.9.2   Calculate percentage censoring

Some of the complaints contain a high proportion of censoring, and we can build a feature to measure the percentage of the text that is censored.

There are often many ways to get to the same solution when working with regular expressions.

Let's attack this problem by counting the number of X's in each string, then count the number of alphanumeric characters and divide the two to get a percentage.

```
str_count(credit_cards, "X")
```

```
#> [1] 32 16  4 20
```

```
str_count(credit_cards, "[:alnum:]")
```

```
#> [1] 44 30 17 28
```

```
str_count(credit_cards, "X") / str_count(credit_cards, "[:alnum:]")
```

```
#> [1] 0.7272727 0.5333333 0.2352941 0.7142857
```

We can finish up by creating a function.

```
percent_censoring <- function(x) {
  str_count(x, "X") / str_count(x, "[:alnum:]")
}
```

```
percent_censoring(credit_cards)
```

```
#> [1] 0.7272727 0.5333333 0.2352941 0.7142857
```

7.9.3 Detect monetary amounts

We have already constructed a regular expression that detects the monetary amount from the text in Section 7.1, so now we can look at how to use this information. Let's start by creating a little example and see what we can extract.

```
dollar_texts <- c("That will be {$20.00}",
                  "{$3.00}, {$2.00} and {$7.00}",
                  "I have no money")
```

```
str_extract_all(dollar_texts, "\\{\\$[0-9\\.]*\\}")
```

```
#> [[1]]
#> [1] "{$20.00}"
#>
#> [[2]]
#> [1] "{$3.00}" "{$2.00}" "{$7.00}"
#>
#> [[3]]
#> character(0)
```

We can create a function that simply detects the dollar amount, and we can count the number of times each amount appears. Each occurrence also has a value, so it would be nice to include that information as well, such as the mean, minimum, or maximum.

First, let's extract the number from the strings. We could write a regular expression for this, but the `parse_number()` function from the readr package does a really good job of pulling out numbers.

```
str_extract_all(dollar_texts, "\\{\\$[0-9\\.]*\\}") %>%
  map(readr::parse_number)
```

```
#> [[1]]
#> [1] 20
#>
#> [[2]]
#> [1] 3 2 7
#>
#> [[3]]
#> numeric(0)
```

Now that we have the numbers we can iterate over them with the function of our choice. Since we are going to have texts with no monetary amounts, we need to handle the case with zero numbers. Defaults for some functions with vectors of length zero can be undesirable; we don't want -Inf to be a value. Let's extract the maximum value and give cases with no monetary amounts a maximum of zero.

```
max_money <- function(x) {
  str_extract_all(x, "\\{\\$[0-9\\.]*\\}") %>%
    map(readr::parse_number) %>%
    map_dbl(~ ifelse(length(.x) == 0, 0, max(.x)))
}

max_money(dollar_texts)
```

```
#> [1] 20  7  0
```

Now that we have created some feature engineering functions, we can use them to (hopefully) make our classification model better.

7.10   What evaluation metrics are appropriate?

We have focused on using accuracy and ROC AUC as metrics for our classification models so far. These are not the only classification metrics available, and your choice will often depend on how much you care about false positives compared to false negatives.

If you know before you fit your model that you want to compute one or more metrics, you can specify them in a call to metric_set(). Let's set up a tuning grid for two new classification metrics, recall and precision, that focuses not on the overall proportion of observations that are predicted correctly but instead on false positives and false negatives.

```
nb_rs <- fit_resamples(
  nb_wf,
  complaints_folds,
  metrics = metric_set(recall, precision)
)
```

If you have already fit your model, you can still compute and explore non-default metrics as long as you saved the predictions for your resampled data sets using control_resamples(save_pred = TRUE).

Let's go back to the naive Bayes model we tuned in Section 7.1.1, with predictions stored in nb_rs_predictions. We can compute the overall recall.

```
nb_rs_predictions %>%
  recall(product, .pred_class)
```

```
#> # A tibble: 1 x 3
#>   .metric .estimator .estimate
#>   <chr>   <chr>          <dbl>
#> 1 recall  binary         0.688
```

We can also compute the recall for each resample using group_by().

```
nb_rs_predictions %>%
  group_by(id) %>%
  recall(product, .pred_class)
```

```
#> # A tibble: 10 x 4
#>    id      .metric .estimator .estimate
#>    <chr>   <chr>   <chr>          <dbl>
#> 1 Fold01  recall  binary         0.694
#> 2 Fold02  recall  binary         0.725
#> 3 Fold03  recall  binary         0.673
#> 4 Fold04  recall  binary         0.660
```

```
#>  5 Fold05 recall  binary        0.705
#>  6 Fold06 recall  binary        0.602
#>  7 Fold07 recall  binary        0.741
#>  8 Fold08 recall  binary        0.702
#>  9 Fold09 recall  binary        0.775
#> 10 Fold10 recall  binary        0.601
```

Many of the metrics used for classification are functions of the true positive, true negative, false positive, and false negative rates. The confusion matrix, a contingency table of observed classes and predicted classes, gives us information on these rates directly.

```
conf_mat_resampled(nb_rs, tidy = FALSE)
```

```
#>          Credit   Other
#> Credit  2865.6   440.4
#> Other   1301.2  4183.8
```

It is possible with many data sets to achieve high accuracy just by predicting the majority class all the time, but such a model is not useful in the real world. Accuracy alone is often not a good way to assess the performance of classification models.

For the full set of classification metric options, see the yardstick documentation[3].

7.11   The full game: classification

We have come a long way from our first classification model in Section 7.1.1, and it is time to see how we can use what we have learned to improve it. We started this chapter with a simple naive Bayes model and token counts. Since then have we looked at different models, preprocessing techniques, and domain-specific feature engineering. For our final model, let's use some of

---

[3] https://yardstick.tidymodels.org/reference/

the domain-specific features we developed in Section 7.9 along with our lasso regularized classification model and tune both the regularization penalty, as well as the number of tokens to include. For this final model we will:

- train on the same set of cross-validation resamples used throughout this chapter,

- include text (but not `tags` or date features, since those did not result in better performance),

- tune the number of tokens used in the model,

- include unigrams only,

- include custom-engineered features,

- finally evaluate on the testing set, which we have not touched at all yet.

7.11.1 Feature selection

We start by creating a new preprocessing recipe, using only the text of the complaints for feature engineering.

```
complaints_rec_v2 <-
  recipe(product ~ consumer_complaint_narrative, data = complaints_train)
```

After exploring this text data more in Section 7.9, we want to add these custom features to our final model. To do this, we use `step_textfeature()` to compute custom text features. We create a list of the custom text features and pass this list to `step_textfeature()` via the `extract_functions` argument. Note how we have to take a copy of `consumer_complaint_narrative` using `step_mutate()` as `step_textfeature()` consumes the column.

```
extract_funs <- list(creditcard_count = creditcard_count,
                     percent_censoring = percent_censoring,
                     max_money = max_money)

complaints_rec_v2 <- complaints_rec_v2 %>%
  step_mutate(narrative_copy = consumer_complaint_narrative) %>%
  step_textfeature(narrative_copy, extract_functions = extract_funs)
```

The tokenization will be similar to the other models in this chapter. In our original model, we only included 1000 tokens; for our final model, let's treat the number of tokens as a hyperparameter that we vary when we tune the final model. Let's also set the min_times argument to 100, to throw away tokens that appear less than 100 times in the entire corpus. We want our model to be robust and a token needs to appear enough times before we include it.

This data set has many more than 100 of even the most common 5000 or more tokens, but it can still be good practice to specify min_times to be safe. Your choice for min_times should depend on your data and how robust you need your model to be.

```
complaints_rec_v2 <- complaints_rec_v2 %>%
  step_tokenize(consumer_complaint_narrative) %>%
  step_tokenfilter(consumer_complaint_narrative,
                   max_tokens = tune(), min_times = 100) %>%
  step_tfidf(consumer_complaint_narrative)
```

7.11.2 Specify the model

We use a lasso regularized classifier since it performed well throughout this chapter. We can reuse parts of the old workflow sparse_wf from Section 7.5 and update the recipe specification.

```
sparse_wf_v2 <- sparse_wf %>%
  update_recipe(complaints_rec_v2, blueprint = sparse_bp)

sparse_wf_v2
```

```
#> == Workflow ====================================================================
#> Preprocessor: Recipe
#> Model: logistic_reg()
#>
#> -- Preprocessor ----------------------------------------------------------------
#> 5 Recipe Steps
#>
#> * step_mutate()
```

```
#> * step_textfeature()
#> * step_tokenize()
#> * step_tokenfilter()
#> * step_tfidf()
#>
#> -- Model ------------------------------------------------------------------
#> Logistic Regression Model Specification (classification)
#>
#> Main Arguments:
#>    penalty = tune()
#>    mixture = 1
#>
#> Computational engine: glmnet
```

Before we tune the model, we need to set up a set of possible parameter values to try.

There are *two* tunable parameters in this model, the regularization parameter and the maximum number of tokens included in the model.

Let's include different possible values for each parameter, for a combination of 60 models.

```
final_grid <- grid_regular(
  penalty(range = c(-4, 0)),
  max_tokens(range = c(1e3, 3e3)),
  levels = c(penalty = 20, max_tokens = 3)
)

final_grid
```

```
#> # A tibble: 60 x 2
#>      penalty max_tokens
#>        <dbl>      <int>
#>  1 0.0001          1000
#>  2 0.000162        1000
#>  3 0.000264        1000
#>  4 0.000428        1000
#>  5 0.000695        1000
#>  6 0.00113         1000
#>  7 0.00183         1000
#>  8 0.00298         1000
#>  9 0.00483         1000
#> 10 0.00785         1000
#> # ... with 50 more rows
```

 We used `grid_regular()` here where we fit a model at every combination of parameters, but if you have a model with many tuning parameters, you may wish to try a space-filling grid instead, such as `grid_max_entropy()` or `grid_latin_hypercube()`. The **tidymodels** package for creating and handling tuning parameters and parameter grids is **dials** (Kuhn 2020).

Now it's time to set up our tuning grid. Let's save the predictions so we can explore them in more detail, and let's also set custom metrics instead of using the defaults. Let's compute accuracy, sensitivity, and specificity during tuning. Sensitivity and specificity are closely related to recall and precision.

```
set.seed(2020)
tune_rs <- tune_grid(
  sparse_wf_v2,
  complaints_folds,
  grid = final_grid,
  metrics = metric_set(accuracy, sensitivity, specificity)
)
```

We have fitted these classification models!

7.11.3 Evaluate the modeling

Now that all of the models with possible parameter values have been trained, we can compare their performance. Figure 7.11 shows us the relationship between performance (as measured by the metrics we chose), the number of tokens, and regularization.

```
autoplot(tune_rs) +
  labs(
    color = "Number of tokens",
    title = "Model performance across regularization penalties and tokens",
    subtitle = paste("We can choose a simpler model with higher regularization")
  )
```

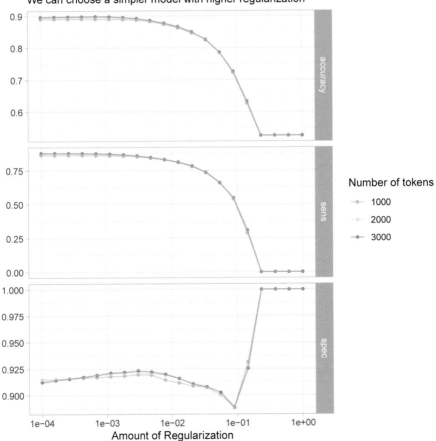

FIGURE 7.11: Model performance is similar for the higher token options so we can choose a simpler model. Note the logarithmic scale on the x-axis for the regularization penalty.

Since this is our final version of this model, we want to choose final parameters and update our model object so we can use it with new data. We have several options for choosing our final parameters, such as selecting the numerically best model. Instead, let's choose a simpler model within some limit around that numerically best result, with more regularization that gives close-to-best performance. Let's choose by percent loss compared to the best model (the default choice is 2% loss), and let's say we care most about overall accuracy (rather than sensitivity or specificity).

```
choose_acc <- tune_rs %>%
  select_by_pct_loss(metric = "accuracy", -penalty)

choose_acc
```

```
#> # A tibble: 1 x 10
#>   penalty max_tokens .metric .estimator  mean     n std_err .config .best .loss
#>     <dbl>      <int> <chr>   <chr>      <dbl> <int>   <dbl> <chr>    <dbl> <dbl>
#> 1 0.00483       1000 accuracy binary    0.882    10 0.00101 Prepro~ 0.898  1.75
```

After we have those parameters, `penalty` and `max_tokens`, we can finalize our earlier tunable workflow, by updating it with this value.

```
final_wf <- finalize_workflow(sparse_wf_v2, choose_acc)
final_wf
```

```
#> == Workflow ========================================================
#> Preprocessor: Recipe
#> Model: logistic_reg()
#>
#> -- Preprocessor ----------------------------------------------------
#> 5 Recipe Steps
#>
#> * step_mutate()
#> * step_textfeature()
#> * step_tokenize()
#> * step_tokenfilter()
#> * step_tfidf()
#>
#> -- Model -----------------------------------------------------------
#> Logistic Regression Model Specification (classification)
#>
#> Main Arguments:
```

```
#>    penalty = 0.00483293023857175
#>    mixture = 1
#>
#> Computational engine: glmnet
```

The `final_wf` workflow now has finalized values for `max_tokens` and `penalty`.

We can now fit this finalized workflow on training data and *finally* return to our testing data.

> Notice that this is the first time we have used our testing data during this entire chapter; we tuned and compared models using resampled data sets instead of touching the testing set.

We can use the function `last_fit()` to **fit** our model one last time on our training data and **evaluate** it on our testing data. We only have to pass this function our finalized model/workflow and our data split.

```
final_fitted <- last_fit(final_wf, complaints_split)

collect_metrics(final_fitted)
```

```
#> # A tibble: 2 x 4
#>    .metric  .estimator .estimate .config
#>    <chr>    <chr>          <dbl> <chr>
#> 1 accuracy binary         0.882 Preprocessor1_Model1
#> 2 roc_auc  binary         0.949 Preprocessor1_Model1
```

The metrics for the test set look about the same as the resampled training data and indicate we did not overfit during tuning. The accuracy of our final model has improved compared to our earlier models, both because we are combining multiple preprocessing steps and because we have tuned the number of tokens.

The confusion matrix on the testing data in Figure 7.12 also yields pleasing results. It appears symmetric with a strong presence on the diagonal, showing that there isn't any strong bias towards either of the classes.

```
collect_predictions(final_fitted) %>%
  conf_mat(truth = product, estimate = .pred_class) %>%
  autoplot(type = "heatmap")
```

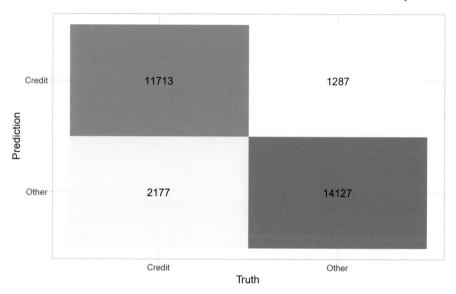

FIGURE 7.12: Confusion matrix on the test set for final lasso regularized classifier

Figure 7.13 shows the ROC curve for the testing set, to demonstrate how well this final classification model can distinguish between the two classes.

```
collect_predictions(final_fitted)  %>%
  roc_curve(truth = product, .pred_Credit) %>%
  autoplot() +
  labs(
    color = NULL,
    title = "ROC curve for US Consumer Finance Complaints",
    subtitle = "With final tuned lasso regularized classifier on the test set"
  )
```

The output of last_fit() also contains a fitted model (a workflow, to be more specific) that has been trained on the *training* data. We can use the vip package to understand what the most important variables are in the predictions, shown in Figure 7.14.

```
library(vip)

complaints_imp <- pull_workflow_fit(final_fitted$.workflow[[1]]) %>%
  vi(lambda = choose_acc$penalty)
```

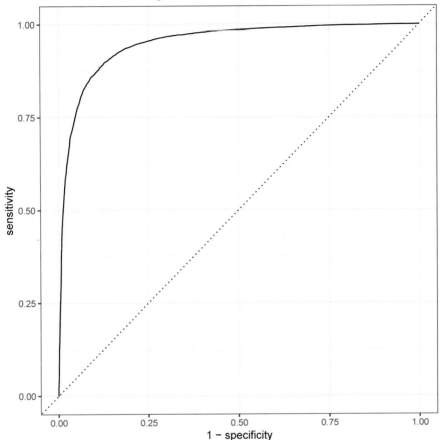

FIGURE 7.13: ROC curve with the test set for final lasso regularized classifier

```
complaints_imp %>%
  mutate(
    Sign = case_when(Sign == "POS" ~ "Less about credit reporting",
                     Sign == "NEG" ~ "More about credit reporting"),
    Importance = abs(Importance),
    Variable = str_remove_all(Variable, "tfidf_consumer_complaint_narrative_"),
    Variable = str_remove_all(Variable, "textfeature_narrative_copy_")
  ) %>%
  group_by(Sign) %>%
```

```
top_n(20, Importance) %>%
ungroup %>%
ggplot(aes(x = Importance,
           y = fct_reorder(Variable, Importance),
           fill = Sign)) +
geom_col(show.legend = FALSE) +
scale_x_continuous(expand = c(0, 0)) +
facet_wrap(~Sign, scales = "free") +
labs(
  y = NULL,
  title = "Variable importance for predicting the topic of a CFPB complaint",
  subtitle = paste0("These features are the most important in predicting\n",
                    "whether a complaint is about credit or not")
)
```

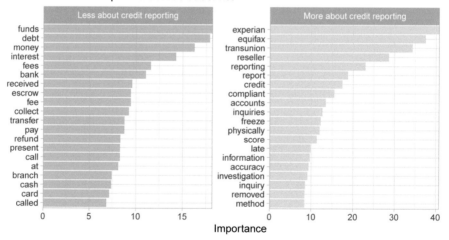

FIGURE 7.14: Some words increase a CFPB complaint's probability of being about credit reporting while some decrease that probability

Tokens like "interest," "bank," and "escrow" contribute in this model away from a classification as about credit reporting, while tokens like the names of the credit reporting agencies, "reporting," and "report" contribute in this model *toward* classification as about credit reporting.

The top features we see here are all tokens learned directly from the text. None of our hand-crafted custom features, like `percent_censoring` or `max_money` are top features in terms of variable importance. In many cases, it can be difficult to create features from text that perform better than the tokens themselves.

We can gain some final insight into our model by looking at observations from the test set that it *misclassified*. Let's bind together the predictions on the test set with the original `complaints_test` data. Then let's look at complaints that were labeled as about credit reporting in the original data but that our final model thought had a low probability of being about credit reporting.

```
complaints_bind <- collect_predictions(final_fitted) %>%
  bind_cols(complaints_test %>% select(-product))
```

```
complaints_bind %>%
  filter(product == "Credit", .pred_Credit < 0.2) %>%
  select(consumer_complaint_narrative) %>%
  slice_sample(n = 10)
```

```
#> # A tibble: 10 x 1
#>    consumer_complaint_narrative
#>    <chr>
#>  1 "Bank of America took more than 30 days to send me documents to validate a d~
#>  2 "My account was on auto pay. Mohela says they stopped taking payments from m~
#>  3 "Received a cancellation of debt form from Cavalry SPV I LLC. The address li~
#>  4 "A certified letter was sent to AAS Debt recovery Inc for debt validation. I~
#>  5 "I have indicated to the credit bureau as well as the creditor the medical b~
#>  6 "ftc violations was sent to XXXX XXXX and all the credit company please have~
#>  7 "This was open without my knowledge, I have been trying to get this remove f~
#>  8 ". They keep on putting this account on my credit report they called many ti~
#>  9 "I sent a debt validation request letter to XXXX in early XX/XX/2019 about t~
#> 10 "I had a divorce and my husband kept the home because it was in his name.. h~
```

We can see why some of these would be difficult for our model to classify as about credit reporting, since some are about other topics as well. The original label may also be incorrect in some cases.

What about misclassifications in the other direction, observations in the test set that were *not* labeled as about credit reporting but that our final model gave a high probability of being about credit reporting?

```
complaints_bind %>%
  filter(product == "Other", .pred_Credit > 0.8) %>%
  select(consumer_complaint_narrative) %>%
  slice_sample(n = 10)
```

```
#> # A tibble: 10 x 1
#>    consumer_complaint_narrative
#>    <chr>
#>  1 "Please review the attachment. Remove the inquiries and place an extended fr~
#>  2 "USAA continue using old accounts that are including and discharged in Chapt~
#>  3 "To Whom It May Concern, This letter is a formal complaint that Experian is ~
#>  4 "I submitted a dispute through Transunion for a supposed medical debt that I~
#>  5 "I paid XXXX XXXX XXXX directly and by law, they must recall the account fro~
#>  6 "Suntrust Bank # XXXX XXXX XXXX # XXXX, and XXXX # XXXX, XXXX XXXX XXXX # XX~
#>  7 "Billing amount is not accurate - Correct amount XXXX Billing date is not ac~
#>  8 "In response to a denial of an extension of credit this consumer checked wit~
#>  9 "Navient Is reporting delinquent history. They are purging which is the same~
#> 10 "This account is coming from XXXX and it is showing up more then once on my ~
```

Again, these are "mistakes" on the part of the model that we can understand based on the content of these complaints. The original labeling on the complaints looks to be not entirely correct or consistent, typical of real data from the real world.

7.12 Summary

You can use classification modeling to predict labels or categorical variables from a data set, including data sets that include text. Naive Bayes models can perform well with text data since each feature is handled independently and thus large numbers of features are computational feasible. This is important as bag-of-word text models can involve thousands of tokens. We also saw that regularized linear models, such as lasso, often work well for text data sets. Your own domain knowledge about your text data is valuable, and using that knowledge in careful engineering of custom features can improve your model in some cases.

7.12.1 In this chapter, you learned:

- how text data can be used in a classification model

- to tune hyperparameters of a model

- how to compare different model types

- that models can combine both text and non-text predictors

- about engineering custom features for machine learning

- about performance metrics for classification models

Part III

Deep Learning Methods

Overview

In Chapters 6 and 7, we use algorithms such as regularized linear models, support vector machines, and naive Bayes models to predict outcomes from predictors including text data. Deep learning models approach the same tasks and have the same goals, but the algorithms involved are different. Deep learning models are "deep" in the sense that they use multiple layers to learn how to map from input features to output outcomes; this is in contrast to the kinds of models we used in the previous two chapters, which use a shallow (single) mapping.

> Deep learning models can be effective for text prediction problems because they use these multiple layers to capture complex relationships in language.

The layers in a deep learning model are connected in a network, and these models are called **neural networks**, although they do not work much like a human brain. The layers can be connected in different configurations called network architectures, which sometimes incorporate word embeddings, as described in Chapter 5. We will cover three network architectures in the following chapters:

- Chapter 8 starts our exploration of deep learning for text with a densely connected neural network. Think of this more straightforward architecture as a bridge between the "shallow" learning approaches of Chapters 6 and 7 that treated text as a bag of words and the more complex architectures to come.

- Chapter 9 continues by walking through how to train and evaluate a more advanced architecture, a long short-term memory (LSTM) network. LSTMs are among the most common architectures used for text data because they model text as a long sequence of words or characters.

- Chapter 10 wraps up our treatment of deep learning for text with the convolutional neural network (CNN) architecture. CNNs are another advanced architecture appropriate for text data because they can capture specific local patterns.

Our discussion of network architectures is fairly specific to text data; in other situations you may do best using a different architecture, for example, when working with dense, tabular data.

For the following chapters, we will use tidymodels packages along with Tensorflow[4] and the R interface to Keras (Allaire and Chollet 2021) for preprocessing, modeling, and evaluation.

The **keras** R package provides an interface for R users to Keras, a high-level API for building neural networks.

The following table presents some key differences between deep learning and what, in this book, we call machine learning methods.

Machine learning	Deep learning
Faster to train	Takes more time to train
Software is typically easier to install	Software can be more challenging to install
Can achieve good performance with less data	Requires more data for good performance
Depends on preprocessing to model more than very simple relationships	Can model highly complex relationships

Deep learning and more traditional machine learning algorithms are different, but the structure of the modeling process is largely the same, no matter what the specific details of prediction or algorithm are.

Spending your data budget

A limited amount of data is available for any given modeling project, and this data must be allocated to different tasks to balance competing priorities. We

---

[4] https://www.tensorflow.org/

espouse an approach of first splitting data in testing and training sets, holding the testing set back until all modeling tasks are completed, including feature engineering and tuning. This testing set is then used as a final check on model performance, to estimate how the final model will perform on new data.

The training data is available for tasks from model parameter estimation to determining which features are important and more. To compare or tune model options or parameters, this training set can be further split so that models can be evaluated on a validation set, or it can be resampled as described in Section 6.1.2 to create new simulated data sets for the purpose of evaluation.

Feature engineering

Text data requires extensive processing to be appropriate for modeling, whether via an algorithm like regularized regression or a neural network. Chapters 1 through 5 covered several of the most important techniques that are used to transform language into a representation appropriate for computation. This feature engineering part of the modeling process can be intensive for text, sometimes more computationally expensive than fitting a model algorithm.

We espouse an approach of implementing feature engineering on training data only, typically using resampled data sets, to avoid obtaining an overly optimistic estimate of model performance. Feature engineering can sometimes be a part of the machine learning process where subtle *data leakage* occurs, when practitioners use information (say, to preprocess data or engineer features) that will not be available at prediction time. One example of this is tf-idf, which we introduced in Chapter 5 and used in both Chapters 6 and 7. As a reminder, the term frequency of a word is how frequently a word occurs in a document, and the inverse document frequency of a word is a weight, typically defined as:

$$idf(\text{term}) = \ln \left(\frac{n_{\text{documents}}}{n_{\text{documents containing term}}} \right)$$

These two quantities are multiplied together to compute a term's tf-idf, a statistic that measures the frequency of a term adjusted for how rarely it is used. Computing inverse document frequency involves the whole corpus or collection of documents. When you are fitting a model, how should that corpus be defined? We strongly advise that you should use your *training data only* in such a situation. Using all the data available to you (training plus testing) involves leakage of information from the testing set to the model, and any

estimates you may make of how your model may perform on new data may
be overly optimistic.

> This specific example focused on tf-idf, but data leakage is a serious chal-
> lenge in general for building machine learning models and systems. The
> tidymodels framework is designed to encourage good statistical practice,
> such as learning feature engineering transformations from training data
> and then applying those transformation to othe data sets.

Fitting and tuning

Many different kinds of models are appropriate for text data, from more
straightforward models like the linear models explored deeply in Chapter 6
to the neural network models we cover in Chapters 10 and 9. Some of these
models have hyperparameters that cannot be learned from data during fitting,
like the regularization parameter of the models in Chapter 6; these hyperparameters can be tuned using resampled data sets.

Model evaluation

Once models are trained and perhaps tuned, we can evaluate their performance
quantitatively using metrics appropriate for the kind of practical problem
being dealt with. Model explanation analysis, such as feature importance,
also helps us understand how well and why models are behaving the way they
do.

Putting the model process in context

This outline of the model process depends on us as data practitioners coming
prepared for modeling with a healthy understanding of our data sets from

exploratory data analysis. Silge and Robinson (2017) provide a guide for exploratory data analysis for text.

Also, in practice, the structure of a real modeling project is iterative. After fitting and tuning a first model or set of a models, a practitioner will often return to build more or better features, then refit models, and evaluate in a more detailed way. Notice that we take this approach in each chapter, both for more straightforward machine learning and deep learning; we start with a simpler model and then go back again and again to improve it in several ways. This iterative approach is healthy and appropriate, as long as good practices in data "spending" are observed. The testing set cannot be used during this iterative back-and-forth, and using resampled data sets can set us up as practitioners for more accurate estimates of performance.

8

Dense neural networks

Like we discussed in the previous overview, these three chapters on deep learning for text are organized by network architecture, rather than by outcome type as we did in Chapters 6 and 7. We'll use Keras with its Tensorflow backend for these deep learning models; Keras is a well-established framework for deep learning with bindings in Python and, via reticulate (Ushey, Allaire, and Tang 2021), R. Keras provides an extensive, high-level API for creating and training many kinds of neural networks, but less support for resampling and preprocessing. Throughout this and the next chapters, we will demonstrate how to use tidymodels packages together with Keras to address these tasks.

> The **tidymodels** framework of R packages is modular, so we can use it for certain parts of our modeling analysis without committing to it entirely, when appropriate.

This chapter explores one of the most straightforward configurations for a deep learning model, a **densely connected neural network**. This is typically not a model that will achieve the highest performance on text data, but it is a good place to start to understand the process of building and evaluating deep learning models for text. We can also use this type of network architecture as a bridge between the bag-of-words approaches we explored in detail in Chapters 6 and 7 to the approaches beyond bag-of-words we will use in Chapters 9 and 10. Deep learning allows us to incorporate not just word counts but also word sequences and positions.

Figure 8.1 depicts a densely-connected neural network architecture *feed-forward*. The input comes in to the network all at once and is densely (in this case, fully) connected to the first hidden layer. A layer is "hidden" in the sense that it doesn't connect to the outside world; the input and output layers take care of this. The neurons in any given layer are only connected to the next layer. The numbers of layers and nodes within each layer are variable and are hyperparameters of the model selected by the practitioner.

Figure 8.1 shows the input units with words, but this is not an entirely accurate

DOI: 10.1201/9781003093459-8

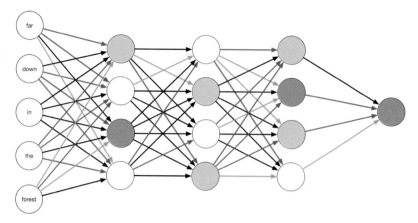

FIGURE 8.1: A high-level diagram of a feed-forward neural network. The lines connecting the nodes are shaded differently to illustrate the different weights connecting units.

representation of a neural network. These words will in practice be represented by embedding vectors because these networks can only work with numeric variables.

8.1 Kickstarter data

For all our chapters on deep learning, we will build binary classification models, much like we did in Chapter 7, but we will use neural networks instead of shallow learning models. As we discussed in the overview to these deep learning chapters, much of the overall model process will look the same, but we will use a different kind of algorithm. We will use a data set of descriptions or "blurbs" for campaigns from the crowdfunding platform Kickstarter[1].

```
library(tidyverse)

kickstarter <- read_csv("data/kickstarter.csv.gz")
kickstarter
```

---

[1] https://www.kickstarter.com/

```
#> # A tibble: 269,790 x 3
#>    blurb                                              state created_at
#>    <chr>                                              <dbl> <date>
#>  1 Exploring paint and its place in a digital world.      0 2015-03-17
#>  2 Mike Fassio wants a side-by-side photo of me and Hazel eati~  0 2014-07-11
#>  3 I need your help to get a nice graphics tablet and Photosho~  0 2014-07-30
#>  4 I want to create a Nature Photograph Series of photos of wi~  0 2015-05-08
#>  5 I want to bring colour to the world in my own artistic skil~  0 2015-02-01
#>  6 We start from some lovely pictures made by us and we decide~  0 2015-11-18
#>  7 Help me raise money to get a drawing tablet              0 2015-04-03
#>  8 I would like to share my art with the world and to do that ~  0 2014-10-15
#>  9 Post Card don' t set out to simply decorate stories. Our goa~  0 2015-06-25
#> 10 My name is Siu Lon Liu and I am an illustrator seeking fund~  0 2014-07-19
#> # ... with 269,780 more rows
```

The state of each observation records whether the campaign was successful in its crowdfunding goal; a value of 1 means it was successful and a value of 0 means it was not successful. The texts for the campaign descriptions, contained in blurb, are short, less than a few hundred characters. What is the distribution of characters?

```
kickstarter %>%
  ggplot(aes(nchar(blurb))) +
  geom_histogram(binwidth = 1, alpha = 0.8) +
  labs(x = "Number of characters per campaign blurb",
       y = "Number of campaign blurbs")
```

Figure 8.2 shows that the distribution of characters per blurb is right-skewed, with two thresholds. Individuals creating campaigns don't have much space to make an impression, so most people choose to use most of it! There is an oddity in this chart, a steep drop somewhere between 130 and 140 with another threshold around 150 characters. Let's investigate to see if we can find the reason.

We can use count() to find the most common blurb length.

```
kickstarter %>%
  count(nchar(blurb), sort = TRUE)
```

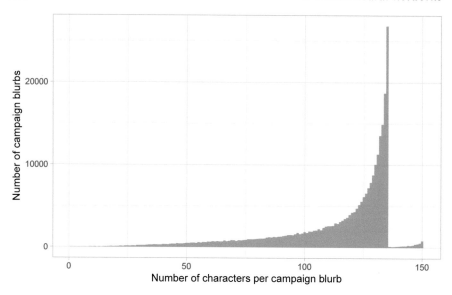

FIGURE 8.2: Distribution of character count for Kickstarter campaign blurbs

```
#> # A tibble: 151 x 2
#>     `nchar(blurb)`      n
#>             <int> <int>
#> 1             135 26827
#> 2             134 18726
#> 3             133 14913
#> 4             132 13559
#> 5             131 11320
#> 6             130 10085
#> 7             129  8786
#> 8             128  7874
#> 9             127  7239
#> 10            126  6590
#> # ... with 141 more rows
```

Let's use our own eyes to see what happens around this cutoff point. We can use slice_sample() to draw a few random blurbs.

Were the blurbs truncated at 135 characters? Let's look at some blurbs with exactly 135 characters.

```
set.seed(1)
kickstarter %>%
```

```
filter(nchar(blurb) == 135) %>%
slice_sample(n = 5) %>%
pull(blurb)
```

```
#> [1] "A science fiction/drama about a young man and woman encountering beings
not of this earth. Armed with only their minds to confront this"
#> [2] "No, not my virginity. That was taken by a girl named Ramona the night
of my senior prom. I'm talking about my novel, THE USE OF REGRET."
#> [3] "In a city where the sun has stopped rising, the music never stops. Now
only a man and his guitar can free the people from the Red King."
#> [4] "First Interfaith & Community FM Radio Station needs transmitter in
Menifee, CA Programs online, too CLICK PHOTO ABOVE FOR OUR CAT VIDEO"
#> [5] "This documentary asks if the twenty-four hour news cycle has altered
people's opinions of one another. We explore unity in one another."
```

All of these blurbs appear coherent and some of them even end with a period to end the sentence. Let's now look at blurbs with more than 135 characters to see if they are different.

```
set.seed(1)
kickstarter %>%
  filter(nchar(blurb) > 135) %>%
  slice_sample(n = 5) %>%
  pull(blurb)
```

```
#> [1] "This is a puzzle game for the Atari 2600. The unique thing about this
is that (some) of the cartridge cases will be made out of real wood, hand
carved"
#> [2] "Art supplies for 10 girls on the east side of Detroit to make drawings
of their neighborhood, which is also home to LOVELAND's Plymouth microhood"
#> [3] "Help us make a video for 'Never', one of the most popular songs on
Songs To Wear Pants To and the lead single from Your Heart's upcoming album
Autumn."
#> [4] "Pyramid Cocoon is an interactive sculpture to be installed during the
Burning Man Festival 2010. Users can rest, commune or cocoon in the piece"
#> [5] "Back us to own, wear, or see a show of great student art we've
collected from Artloop partner schools in NYC. The $ goes right back to art
programs!"
```

All of these blurbs also look fine so the strange distribution doesn't seem like a data collection issue.

The `kickstarter` data set also includes a `created_at` variable; let's explore that next. Figure 8.3 is a heatmap of the lengths of blurbs and the time the campaign was posted.

```
kickstarter %>%
  ggplot(aes(created_at, nchar(blurb))) +
  geom_bin2d() +
  labs(x = NULL,
       y = "Number of characters per campaign blurb")
```

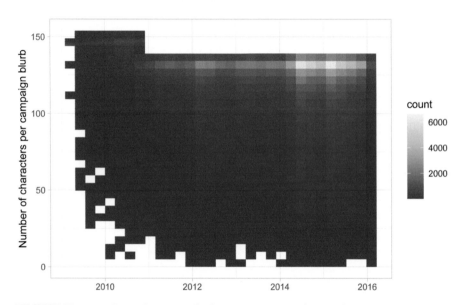

FIGURE 8.3: Distribution of character count for Kickstarter campaign blurbs over time

That looks like the explanation! It appears that at the end of 2010 there was a policy change in the blurb length, shortening from 150 characters to 135 characters.

```
kickstarter %>%
  filter(nchar(blurb) > 135) %>%
  summarise(max(created_at))
```

```
#> # A tibble: 1 x 1
#>   `max(created_at)`
#>   <date>
#> 1 2010-10-20
```

We can't say for sure if the change happened on 2010-10-20, but that is the last day a campaign was launched with more than 135 characters.

8.2 A first deep learning model

Like all our previous modeling, our first step is to split our data into training and testing sets. We will still use our training set to build models and save the testing set for a final estimate of how our model will perform on new data.

> It is very easy to overfit deep learning models, so an unbiased estimate of future performance from a test set is more important than ever.

We use `initial_split()` to define the training and testing splits. We will focus on modeling the blurb alone in these deep learning chapters. Also, we will restrict our modeling analysis to only include blurbs with more than 15 characters, because the shortest blurbs tend to consist of uninformative single words.

```
library(tidymodels)
set.seed(1234)
kickstarter_split <- kickstarter %>%
  filter(nchar(blurb) >= 15) %>%
  initial_split()

kickstarter_train <- training(kickstarter_split)
kickstarter_test <- testing(kickstarter_split)
```

There are 202,092 blurbs in the training set and 67,365 in the testing set.

8.2.1 Preprocessing for deep learning

Preprocessing for deep learning models is different from preprocessing for most other text models. These neural networks model *sequences*, so we have to choose the length of sequences we would like to include. Documents that are longer than this length are truncated (information is thrown away), and documents that are shorter than this length are padded with zeroes (an empty, non-informative value) to get to the chosen sequence length. This sequence length is a hyperparameter of the model, and we need to select this value such that we don't:

- overshoot and introduce a lot of padded zeroes, which would make the model hard to train, or

- undershoot and cut off too much informative text from our documents.

We can use the `count_words()` function from the tokenizers package to calculate the number of words and generate a histogram in Figure 8.4. Notice how we are only using the training data set to avoid data leakage when selecting this value.

```
kickstarter_train %>%
  mutate(n_words = tokenizers::count_words(blurb)) %>%
  ggplot(aes(n_words)) +
  geom_bar() +
  labs(x = "Number of words per campaign blurb",
       y = "Number of campaign blurbs")
```

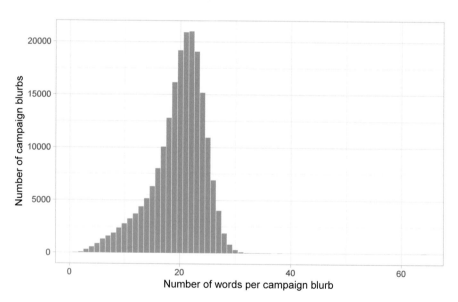

FIGURE 8.4: Distribution of word count for Kickstarter campaign blurbs

Given that we don't have many words for this particular data set to begin with, let's err on the side of longer sequences so we don't lose valuable data.

Let's try 30 words for our threshold `max_length`, and let's include 20,000 words in our vocabulary.

> We will use the **recipes** and **textrecipes** packages for data preprocessing and feature engineering for our deep learning models, just like we did for our models in Chapters 6 and 7. To use a recipe, we first specify it with the variables we want to include and the steps we want to use in feature engineering.

```r
library(textrecipes)

max_words <- 2e4
max_length <- 30

kick_rec <- recipe(~ blurb, data = kickstarter_train) %>%
  step_tokenize(blurb) %>%
  step_tokenfilter(blurb, max_tokens = max_words) %>%
  step_sequence_onehot(blurb, sequence_length = max_length)

kick_rec
```

```
#> Data Recipe
#>
#> Inputs:
#>
#>        role #variables
#>   predictor          1
#>
#> Operations:
#>
#> Tokenization for blurb
#> Text filtering for blurb
#> Sequence 1 hot encoding for blurb
```

The formula used to specify this recipe ~ `blurb` does not have an outcome, because we are using **recipes** and **textrecipes** functions on their own, outside of the rest of the tidymodels framework; we don't need to know about the outcome here. This preprocessing recipe tokenizes our text (Chapter 2) and filters to keep only the top 20,000 words, but then it transforms the tokenized text in a new way to prepare for deep learning that we have not used in this book before, using `step_sequence_onehot()`.

8.2.2   One-hot sequence embedding of text

The function `step_sequence_onehot()` transforms tokens into a numeric format appropriate for modeling, like `step_tf()` and `step_tfidf()`. However, it is different in that it takes into account the order of the tokens, unlike `step_tf()` and `step_tfidf()`, which do not take order into account.

Steps like `step_tf()` and `step_tfidf()` are used for approaches called "bag of words", meaning the words are treated like they are just thrown in a bag without attention paid to their order.

Let's take a closer look at how `step_sequence_onehot()` works and how its parameters will change the output.

When we use `step_sequence_onehot()`, two things happen. First, each word is assigned an *integer index*. You can think of this as a key-value pair of the vocabulary. Next, the sequence of tokens is replaced with the corresponding indices; this sequence of integers makes up the final numeric representation. Let's illustrate with a small example:

```
small_data <- tibble(
  text = c("Adventure Dice Game",
           "Spooky Dice Game",
           "Illustrated Book of Monsters",
           "Monsters, Ghosts, Goblins, Me, Myself and I")
)

small_spec <- recipe(~ text, data = small_data) %>%
  step_tokenize(text) %>%
  step_sequence_onehot(text, sequence_length = 6, prefix = "")

prep(small_spec)
```

```
#> Data Recipe
#>
#> Inputs:
#>
#>        role #variables
#> predictor          1
#>
```

```
#> Training data contained 4 data points and no missing data.
#>
#> Operations:
#>
#> Tokenization for text [trained]
#> Sequence 1 hot encoding for text [trained]
```

What does the function `prep()` do? Before when we have used recipes, we put them in a `workflow()` that handles low-level processing. The `prep()` function will compute or estimate statistics from the training set; the output of `prep()` is a prepped recipe.

Once we have the prepped recipe, we can `tidy()` it to extract the vocabulary, represented in the `vocabulary` and `token` columns[2].

```
prep(small_spec) %>%
    tidy(2)
```

```
#> # A tibble: 14 x 4
#>     terms vocabulary token        id
#>     <chr>      <int> <chr>        <chr>
#>  1 text           1 adventure    sequence_onehot_9p9uj
#>  2 text           2 and          sequence_onehot_9p9uj
#>  3 text           3 book         sequence_onehot_9p9uj
#>  4 text           4 dice         sequence_onehot_9p9uj
#>  5 text           5 game         sequence_onehot_9p9uj
#>  6 text           6 ghosts       sequence_onehot_9p9uj
#>  7 text           7 goblins      sequence_onehot_9p9uj
#>  8 text           8 i            sequence_onehot_9p9uj
#>  9 text           9 illustrated  sequence_onehot_9p9uj
#> 10 text          10 me           sequence_onehot_9p9uj
#> 11 text          11 monsters     sequence_onehot_9p9uj
#> 12 text          12 myself       sequence_onehot_9p9uj
#> 13 text          13 of           sequence_onehot_9p9uj
#> 14 text          14 spooky       sequence_onehot_9p9uj
```

---

[2]The `terms` column refers to the column we have applied `step_sequence_onehot()` to and `id` is its unique identifier. Note that **textrecipes** allows `step_sequence_onehot()` to be applied to multiple text variables independently, and they will have their own vocabularies.

If we take a look at the resulting matrix, we have one row per observation. The first row starts with some padded zeroes but then contains 1, 4, and 5, which we can use together with the vocabulary to construct the original sentence.

```
prep(small_spec) %>%
  bake(new_data = NULL, composition = "matrix")
```

```
#>        _text_1 _text_2 _text_3 _text_4 _text_5 _text_6
#> [1,]        0       0       0       1       4       5
#> [2,]        0       0       0      14       4       5
#> [3,]        0       0       9       3      13      11
#> [4,]        6       7      10      12       2       8
```

When we `bake()` a prepped recipe, we apply the preprocessing to a data set. We can get out the training set that we started with by specifying `new_data = NULL` or apply it to another set via `new_data = my_other_data_set`. The output of `bake()` is a data set like a tibble or a matrix, depending on the `composition` argument.

But wait, the 4th line should have started with an 11 since the sentence starts with "monsters!" The entry in `_text_1` is 6 instead. This is happening because the sentence is too long to fit inside the specified sequence length. We must answer three questions before using `step_sequence_onehot()`:

1. How long should the output sequence be?
2. What happens to sequences that are too long?
3. What happens to sequences that are too short?

Choosing the right sequence length is a balancing act. You want the length to be long enough such that you don't truncate too much of your text data, but still short enough to keep the size of the data manageable and to avoid excessive padding. Truncating, having large training data, and excessive padding all lead to worse model performance. This parameter is controlled by the `sequence_length` argument in `step_sequence_onehot()`.

If the sequence is too long, then it must be truncated. This can be done by removing values from the beginning (`"pre"`) or the end (`"post"`) of the sequence. This choice is mostly influenced by the data, and you need to evaluate where most of the useful information of the text is located. News articles typically start with the main points and then go into detail. If your goal is to detect the broad category, then you may want to keep the beginning of the texts, whereas if you are working with speeches or conversational text, then you might find that the last thing to be said carries more information.

Lastly, we need to decide how to pad a document that is too short. Pre-padding tends to be more popular, especially when working with RNN and LSTM models (Chapter 9) since having post-padding could result in the hidden states getting flushed out by the zeroes before getting to the text itself (Section 9.5).

The defaults for `step_sequence_onehot()` are `sequence_length = 100`, `padding = "pre"`, and `truncating = "pre"`. If we change the truncation to happen at the end with:

```
recipe(~ text, data = small_data) %>%
  step_tokenize(text) %>%
  step_sequence_onehot(text, sequence_length = 6, prefix = "",
                       padding = "pre", truncating = "post") %>%
  prep() %>%
  bake(new_data = NULL, composition = "matrix")
```

```
#>      _text_1 _text_2 _text_3 _text_4 _text_5 _text_6
#> [1,]       0       0       0       1       4       5
#> [2,]       0       0       0      14       4       5
#> [3,]       0       0       9       3      13      11
#> [4,]      11       6       7      10      12       2
```

then we see the 11 at the beginning of the last row representing the "monsters." The starting points are not aligned since we are still padding on the left side. We can left-align all the sequences by setting `padding = "post"`.

```
recipe(~ text, data = small_data) %>%
  step_tokenize(text) %>%
  step_sequence_onehot(text, sequence_length = 6, prefix = "",
                       padding = "post", truncating = "post") %>%
  prep() %>%
  bake(new_data = NULL, composition = "matrix")
```

```
#>      _text_1 _text_2 _text_3 _text_4 _text_5 _text_6
#> [1,]       1       4       5       0       0       0
#> [2,]      14       4       5       0       0       0
#> [3,]       9       3      13      11       0       0
#> [4,]      11       6       7      10      12       2
```

Now we have all digits representing the first characters neatly aligned in the first column.

Let's now prepare and apply our feature engineering recipe `kick_rec` so we can use it in for our deep learning model.

```
kick_prep <- prep(kick_rec)
kick_train <- bake(kick_prep, new_data = NULL, composition = "matrix")
dim(kick_train)
```

```
#> [1] 202092     30
```

The matrix `kick_train` has 202,092 rows, corresponding to the rows of the training data, and 30 columns, corresponding to our chosen sequence length.

8.2.3   Simple flattened dense network

Our first deep learning model embeds these Kickstarter blurbs in sequences of vectors, flattens them, and then trains a dense network layer to predict whether the campaign was successful or not.

```
library(keras)
```

```
dense_model <- keras_model_sequential() %>%
  layer_embedding(input_dim = max_words + 1,
                  output_dim = 12,
                  input_length = max_length) %>%
  layer_flatten() %>%
  layer_dense(units = 32, activation = "relu") %>%
  layer_dense(units = 1, activation = "sigmoid")
```

```
dense_model
```

```
#> Model
#> Model: "sequential"
#> _____
#> Layer (type)                    Output Shape                 Param #
#> ============================================================================
#> embedding (Embedding)           (None, 30, 12)               240012
#> _____
#> flatten (Flatten)               (None, 360)                  0
```

```
#> _____
#> dense_1 (Dense)                    (None, 32)                    11552
#> _____
#> dense (Dense)                      (None, 1)                     33
#> =======================================================================
#> Total params: 251,597
#> Trainable params: 251,597
#> Non-trainable params: 0
#> _____
```

Let us step through this model specification one layer at a time.

- We initiate the Keras model by using `keras_model_sequential()` to indicate that we want to compose a linear stack of layers.

- Our first `layer_embedding()` is equipped to handle the preprocessed data we have in `kick_train`. It will take each observation/row in `kick_train` and make dense vectors from our word sequences. This turns each observation into an `embedding_dim` × `sequence_length` matrix, 12×30 matrix in our case. In total, we will create a `number_of_observations` × `embedding_dim` × `sequence_length` data cube.

- The next `layer_flatten()` layer takes the matrix for each observation and flattens them into one dimension. This will create a `30 * 12 = 360` long vector for each observation.

- Lastly, we have 2 densely connected layers. The last layer has a sigmoid activation function to give us an output between 0 and 1, since we want to model a probability for a binary classification problem.

We still have a few things left to add to this model before we can fit it to the data. A Keras model requires an *optimizer* and a *loss function* to be able to compile.

When the neural network finishes passing a batch of data through the network, it needs a way to use the difference between the predicted values and true values to update the network's weights. The algorithm that determines those weights is known as the optimization algorithm. Many optimizers are available within Keras itself[3]; you can even create custom optimizers if what you need isn't on the list. We will start by using the Adam optimizer, a good default optimizer for many problems.

---

[3] https://keras.io/api/optimizers/

An optimizer can either be set with the name of the optimizer as a character or by supplying the function `optimizer_foo()` where `foo` is the name of the optimizer. If you use the function then you can specify parameters for the optimizer.

During training of a neural network, there must be some quantity that we want to have minimized; this is called the loss function. Again, many loss functions are available within Keras[4]. These loss functions typically have two arguments, the true value and the predicted value, and return a measure of how close they are. Since we are working on a binary classification task and the final layer of the network returns a probability, binary cross-entropy is an appropriate loss function. Binary cross-entropy does well at dealing with probabilities because it measures the "distance" between probability distributions. In our case, this would be the ground-truth distribution and the predictions.

We can also add any number of metrics[5] to be calculated and reported during training. These metrics will not affect the training loop, which is controlled by the optimizer and loss function. The metrics' only job is to report back a single number that will inform you how well the model is performing. We will select accuracy as a reported metric for now.

Let's set these three options (`optimizer`, `loss`, and `metrics`) using the `compile()` function:

```
dense_model %>% compile(
  optimizer = "adam",
  loss = "binary_crossentropy",
  metrics = c("accuracy")
)
```

Notice how the `compile()` function modifies the model *in place*. This is different from how objects are conventionally handled in R so be vigilant about model definition and modification in your code. This is a conscious decision[6] that was made when creating the **keras** R package to match the data structures and behavior of the underlying Keras library.

---

[4] https://keras.io/api/losses/

[5] https://keras.io/api/metrics/

Finally, we can fit this model! We need to supply the data for training as a matrix of predictors x and a numeric vector of labels y. This is sufficient information to get started training the model, but we are going to specify a few more arguments to get better control of the training loop. First, we set the number of observations to pass through at a time with batch_size, and we set epochs = 20 to tell the model to pass all the training data through the training loop 20 times. Lastly, we set validation_split = 0.25 to specify an internal validation split; this will keep 25% of the data for validation.

```
dense_history <- dense_model %>%
  fit(
    x = kick_train,
    y = kickstarter_train$state,
    batch_size = 512,
    epochs = 20,
    validation_split = 0.25,
    verbose = FALSE
  )
```

We can visualize the results of the training loop by plotting the dense_history in Figure 8.5.

```
plot(dense_history)
```

We have dealt with accuracy in other chapters; remember that a higher value (a value near one) is better. Loss is new in these deep learning chapters, and a lower value is better.

The loss and accuracy both improve with more training epochs on the training data; this dense network more and more closely learns the characteristics of the training data as its trains longer. The same is not true of the validation data, the held-out 25% specified by validation_split = 0.25. The performance is worse on the validation data than the testing data, and *degrades* somewhat as training continues. If we wanted to use this model, we would want to only train it about 7 or 8 epochs.

---

[6]https://keras.rstudio.com/articles/faq.html#why-are-keras-objects-modified-in-place-

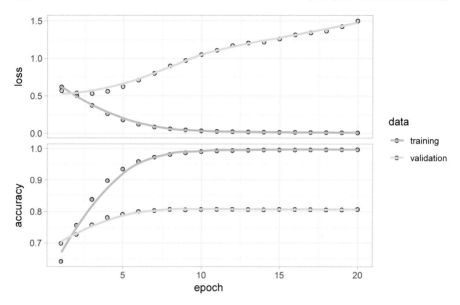

FIGURE 8.5: Training and validation metrics for dense network

8.2.4   Evaluation

For our first deep learning model, we used the Keras defaults for creating a
validation split and tracking metrics, but we can use tidymodels functions to
be more specific about these model characteristics. Instead of using the val-
idation_split argument to fit(), we can create our own validation set using
tidymodels and use validation_data argument for fit(). We create our validation split from the *training* set.

```
set.seed(234)
kick_val <- validation_split(kickstarter_train, strata = state)
kick_val
```

```
#> # Validation Set Split (0.75/0.25)  using stratification
#> # A tibble: 1 x 2
#>   splits                id
#>   <list>                <chr>
#> 1 <split [151568/50524]> validation
```

The split object contains the information necessary to extract the data we will
use for training/analysis and the data we will use for validation/assessment.
We can extract these data sets in their raw, unprocessed form from the split

using the helper functions `analysis()` and `assessment()`. Then, we can apply our prepped preprocessing recipe `kick_prep` to both to transform this data to the appropriate format for our neural network architecture.

```
kick_analysis <- bake(kick_prep, new_data = analysis(kick_val$splits[[1]]),
                      composition = "matrix")
dim(kick_analysis)
```

```
#> [1] 151568     30
```

```
kick_assess <- bake(kick_prep, new_data = assessment(kick_val$splits[[1]]),
                    composition = "matrix")
dim(kick_assess)
```

```
#> [1] 50524     30
```

These are each matrices now appropriate for a deep learning model like the one we trained in the previous section. We will also need the outcome variables for both sets.

```
state_analysis <- analysis(kick_val$splits[[1]]) %>% pull(state)
state_assess <- assessment(kick_val$splits[[1]]) %>% pull(state)
```

Let's set up our same dense neural network architecture.

```
dense_model <- keras_model_sequential() %>%
  layer_embedding(input_dim = max_words + 1,
                  output_dim = 12,
                  input_length = max_length) %>%
  layer_flatten() %>%
  layer_dense(units = 32, activation = "relu") %>%
  layer_dense(units = 1, activation = "sigmoid")

dense_model %>% compile(
  optimizer = "adam",
  loss = "binary_crossentropy",
  metrics = c("accuracy")
)
```

Now we can fit this model to `kick_analysis` and validate on `kick_assess`. Let's only fit for 10 epochs this time.

```
val_history <- dense_model %>%
  fit(
    x = kick_analysis,
    y = state_analysis,
    batch_size = 512,
    epochs = 10,
    validation_data = list(kick_assess, state_assess),
    verbose = FALSE
  )

val_history
```

```
#>
#> Final epoch (plot to see history):
#>          loss: 0.03639
#>      accuracy: 0.9914
#>      val_loss: 1.062
#> val_accuracy: 0.8056
```

Figure 8.6 still shows significant overfitting at 10 epochs.

```
plot(val_history)
```

Using our own validation set also allows us to flexibly measure performance using tidymodels functions from the **yardstick** package. We do need to set up a few transformations between Keras and tidymodels to make this work. The following function `keras_predict()` creates a little bridge between the two frameworks, combining a Keras model with baked (i.e., preprocessed) data and returning the predictions in a tibble format.

```
library(dplyr)

keras_predict <- function(model, baked_data, response) {
  predictions <- predict(model, baked_data)[, 1]
  tibble(
    .pred_1 = predictions,
    .pred_class = if_else(.pred_1 < 0.5, 0, 1),
```

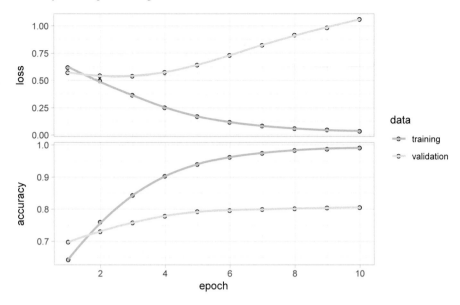

FIGURE 8.6: Training and validation metrics for dense network with validation set

```
    state = response
) %>%
    mutate(across(c(state, .pred_class),        ## create factors
                ~ factor(.x, levels = c(1, 0)))) ## with matching levels
}
```

This function only works with binary classification models that take a preprocessed matrix as input and return a single probability for each observation. It returns both the predicted probability as well as the predicted class, using a 50% probability threshold.

This function creates prediction results that seamlessly connect with tidymodels and **yardstick** functions.

```
val_res <- keras_predict(dense_model, kick_assess, state_assess)
val_res
```

```
#> # A tibble: 50,524 x 3
#>        .pred_1 .pred_class state
#>          <dbl> <fct>       <fct>
#>  1 0.00119     0           0
#>  2 0.00592     0           0
#>  3 0.000280    0           0
#>  4 0.000224    0           0
#>  5 1.00        1           1
#>  6 0.997       1           1
#>  7 0.00000507  0           0
#>  8 0.00153     0           0
#>  9 0.000177    0           1
#> 10 1.00        1           1
#> # ... with 50,514 more rows
```

We can calculate the standard metrics with metrics().

```
metrics(val_res, state, .pred_class)
```

```
#> # A tibble: 2 x 3
#>   .metric  .estimator .estimate
#>   <chr>    <chr>          <dbl>
#> 1 accuracy binary         0.806
#> 2 kap      binary         0.610
```

This matches what we saw when we looked at the output of val_history.

Since we have access to tidymodels' full capacity for model evaluation, we can also compute confusion matrices and ROC curves. The heatmap in Figure 8.7 shows that there isn't any dramatic bias in how the model performs for the two classes, success and failure for the crowdfunding campaigns. The model certainly isn't perfect; its accuracy is a little over 80%, but at least it is more or less evenly good at predicting both classes.

```
val_res %>%
  conf_mat(state, .pred_class) %>%
  autoplot(type = "heatmap")
```

The ROC curve in Figure 8.8 shows how the model performs at different thresholds.

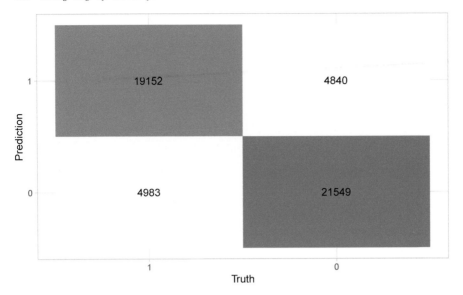

FIGURE 8.7: Confusion matrix for first DNN model predictions of Kickstarter campaign success

```
val_res %>%
  roc_curve(truth = state, .pred_1) %>%
  autoplot() +
  labs(
    title = "Receiver operator curve for Kickstarter blurbs"
  )
```

8.3 Using bag-of-words features

Before we move on with neural networks and this new way to represent the text sequences, let's explore what happens if we use the *same* preprocessing as in Chapters 6 and 7. We will employ a bag-of-words preprocessing and input word counts only to the neural network. This model will not use any location-based information about the tokens, just the counts.

For this, we need to create a new recipe to transform the data into counts.

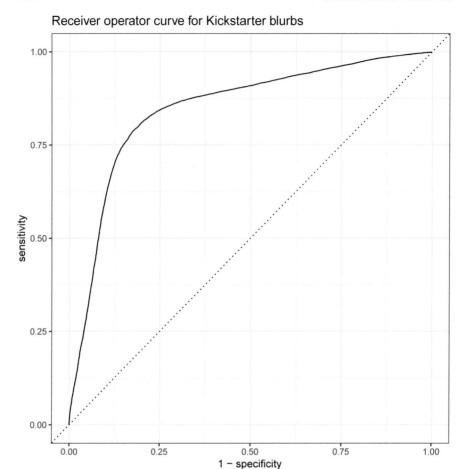

FIGURE 8.8: ROC curve for first DNN model predictions of Kickstarter campaign success

 The objects in this chapter are named using bow to indicate that they are using **bag of w**ord data.

```
kick_bow_rec <- recipe(~ blurb, data = kickstarter_train) %>%
  step_tokenize(blurb) %>%
  step_stopwords(blurb) %>%
```

```
step_tokenfilter(blurb, max_tokens = 1e3) %>%
step_tf(blurb)
```

We will prep() and bake() this recipe to get out our processed data. The result will be quite sparse, since the blurbs are short, and we are counting only the most frequent 1000 tokens after removing the Snowball stop word list.

```
kick_bow_prep <-  prep(kick_bow_rec)

kick_bow_analysis <- bake(kick_bow_prep,
                     new_data = analysis(kick_val$splits[[1]]),
                     composition = "matrix")

kick_bow_assess <- bake(kick_bow_prep,
                     new_data = assessment(kick_val$splits[[1]]),
                     composition = "matrix")
```

Now that we have the analysis and assessment data sets calculated, we can define the neural network architecture. We won't be using an embedding layer this time; we will input the word count data directly into the first dense layer. This dense layer is followed by another hidden layer and then a final layer with a sigmoid activation to leave us with a value between 0 and 1 that we treat as the probability.

```
bow_model <- keras_model_sequential() %>%
  layer_dense(units = 64, activation = "relu", input_shape = c(1e3)) %>%
  layer_dense(units = 64, activation = "relu") %>%
  layer_dense(units = 1, activation = "sigmoid")

bow_model %>% compile(
  optimizer = "adam",
  loss = "binary_crossentropy",
  metrics = c("accuracy")
)
```

In many ways, this model architecture is not that different from the model we used in Section 8.2. The main difference here is the *preprocessing*; the shape and information of the data from kick_bow_prep are different from what we saw before since the matrix elements represent counts (something that Keras can handle directly) and not indicators for words in the vocabulary. Keras handles the indicators with `layer_embedding()`, by mapping them through an embedding layer.

The fitting procedure remains unchanged.

```
bow_history <- bow_model %>%
  fit(
    x = kick_bow_analysis,
    y = state_analysis,
    batch_size = 512,
    epochs = 10,
    validation_data = list(kick_bow_assess, state_assess),
    verbose = FALSE
  )

bow_history
```

```
#>
#> Final epoch (plot to see history):
#>         loss: 0.3197
#>     accuracy: 0.864
#>     val_loss: 0.6766
#> val_accuracy: 0.7246
```

We use `keras_predict()` again to get predictions, and calculate the standard metrics with `metrics()`.

```
bow_res <- keras_predict(bow_model, kick_bow_assess, state_assess)

metrics(bow_res, state, .pred_class)
```

```
#> # A tibble: 2 x 3
#>   .metric  .estimator .estimate
#>   <chr>    <chr>          <dbl>
#> 1 accuracy binary         0.725
#> 2 kap      binary         0.449
```

This model does not perform as well as the model we used in Section 8.2. This suggests that a model incorporating more than word counts alone is useful here. This model did outperform a baseline linear model (shown in Appendix C), which achieved an accuracy of 0.686; that linear baseline is a regularized linear model trained on the same data set, using tf-idf weights and 5000 tokens.

This simpler model does not outperform our initial model in this chapter, but it is typically worthwhile to investigate if a simpler model can rival or beat a model we are working with.

8.4 Using pre-trained word embeddings

The models in Section 8.2 included an embedding layer to make dense vectors from our word sequences that the model learned, along with the rest of the model as a whole. This is not the only way to handle this task. In Chapter 5, we examined how word embeddings are created and how they are used. Instead of having the embedding layer start randomly and be trained alongside the other parameters, let's try to *provide* the embeddings.

This section serves to show how to use pre-trained word embeddings, but in most realistic situations, your data and pre-trained embeddings may not match well. The main takeaways from this section should be that this approach is possible and how you can get started with it. Keep in mind that it may not be appropriate for your data and problem.

We start by obtaining pre-trained embeddings. The GloVe embeddings that we used in Section 5.4 are a good place to start. Setting `dimensions = 50` and only selecting the first 12 dimensions will make it easier for us to compare to our previous models directly.

```
library(textdata)

glove6b <- embedding_glove6b(dimensions = 50) %>% select(1:13)
glove6b
```

```
#> # A tibble: 400,000 x 13
#>    token     d1     d2     d3     d4     d5      d6     d7      d8        d9
#>    <chr>  <dbl>  <dbl>  <dbl>  <dbl>  <dbl>   <dbl>  <dbl>   <dbl>     <dbl>
#> 1 "the"  0.418  0.250 -0.412  0.122  0.345 -0.0445 -0.497 -0.179 -0.000660
```

```
#>  2 ","    0.0134   0.237  -0.169   0.410   0.638    0.477  -0.429  -0.556   -0.364
#>  3 "."     0.152   0.302  -0.168   0.177   0.317    0.340  -0.435  -0.311   -0.450
#>  4 "of"    0.709   0.571  -0.472   0.180   0.544    0.726   0.182  -0.524    0.104
#>  5 "to"    0.680  -0.0393  0.302  -0.178   0.430   0.0322  -0.414   0.132   -0.298
#>  6 "and"   0.268   0.143  -0.279  0.0163  0.114    0.699  -0.513  -0.474   -0.331
#>  7 "in"    0.330   0.250  -0.609   0.109  0.0364    0.151  -0.551 -0.0742  -0.0923
#>  8 "a"     0.217   0.465  -0.468   0.101   1.01     0.748  -0.531  -0.263    0.168
#>  9 "\""    0.258   0.456  -0.770  -0.377   0.593  -0.0635   0.205  -0.574   -0.290
#> 10 "'s"    0.237   0.405  -0.205   0.588   0.655    0.329  -0.820  -0.232    0.274
#> # ... with 399,990 more rows, and 3 more variables: d10 <dbl>, d11 <dbl>,
#> #   d12 <dbl>
```

The `embedding_glove6b()` function returns a tibble; this isn't the right format for
Keras. Also, notice how many rows are present in this embedding, far more
than what the trained recipe is expecting. The vocabulary can be extracted
from the trained recipe using `tidy()`. Let's apply `tidy()` to `kick_prep` to get the
list of steps that the recipe contains.

```
tidy(kick_prep)
```

```
#> # A tibble: 3 x 6
#>    number operation type             trained skip  id
#>     <int> <chr>     <chr>            <lgl>   <lgl> <chr>
#> 1       1 step      tokenize         TRUE    FALSE tokenize_nHrhX
#> 2       2 step      tokenfilter      TRUE    FALSE tokenfilter_2TrDo
#> 3       3 step      sequence_onehot  TRUE    FALSE sequence_onehot_H16cB
```

We see that the third step is the `sequence_onehot` step, so by setting `number = 3`
we can extract the embedding vocabulary.

```
tidy(kick_prep, number = 3)
```

```
#> # A tibble: 20,000 x 4
#>    terms vocabulary token id
#>    <chr>      <int> <chr> <chr>
#> 1 blurb          1 0     sequence_onehot_H16cB
#> 2 blurb          2 00    sequence_onehot_H16cB
#> 3 blurb          3 000   sequence_onehot_H16cB
#> 4 blurb          4 00pm  sequence_onehot_H16cB
#> 5 blurb          5 01    sequence_onehot_H16cB
#> 6 blurb          6 02    sequence_onehot_H16cB
```

```
#>  7 blurb           7 03      sequence_onehot_H16cB
#>  8 blurb           8 05      sequence_onehot_H16cB
#>  9 blurb           9 07      sequence_onehot_H16cB
#> 10 blurb          10 09      sequence_onehot_H16cB
#> # ... with 19,990 more rows
```

We can then use `left_join()` to combine these tokens to the `glove6b` embedding tibble and only keep the tokens of interest. We replace any tokens from the vocabulary not found in `glove6b` with 0 using `mutate_all()` and `replace_na()`. We can transform the results into a matrix, and add a row of zeroes at the top of the matrix to account for the out-of-vocabulary words.

```
glove6b_matrix <- tidy(kick_prep, 3) %>%
  select(token) %>%
  left_join(glove6b, by = "token") %>%
  mutate_all(replace_na, 0) %>%
  select(-token) %>%
  as.matrix() %>%
  rbind(0, .)
```

We'll keep the model architecture itself as unchanged as possible. The `output_dim` argument is set equal to `ncol(glove6b_matrix)` to make sure that all the dimensions line up correctly, but everything else stays the same.

```
dense_model_pte <- keras_model_sequential() %>%
  layer_embedding(input_dim = max_words + 1,
                  output_dim = ncol(glove6b_matrix),
                  input_length = max_length) %>%
  layer_flatten() %>%
  layer_dense(units = 32, activation = "relu") %>%
  layer_dense(units = 1, activation = "sigmoid")
```

Now we use `get_layer()` to access the first layer (which is the embedding layer), set the weights with `set_weights()`, and then freeze the weights with `freeze_weights()`.

Freezing the weights stops them from being updated during the training loop.

```
dense_model_pte %>%
  get_layer(index = 1) %>%
  set_weights(list(glove6b_matrix)) %>%
  freeze_weights()
```

Now we compile and fit the model just like the last one we looked at.

```
dense_model_pte %>% compile(
  optimizer = "adam",
  loss = "binary_crossentropy",
  metrics = c("accuracy")
)
```

```
dense_pte_history <- dense_model_pte %>%
  fit(
    x = kick_analysis,
    y = state_analysis,
    batch_size = 512,
    epochs = 20,
    validation_data = list(kick_assess, state_assess),
    verbose = FALSE
  )
```

```
dense_pte_history
```

```
#>
#> Final epoch (plot to see history):
#>         loss: 0.5967
#>     accuracy: 0.6771
#>     val_loss: 0.6698
#> val_accuracy: 0.6111
```

This model is not performing well at all! We can confirm by computing metrics on our validation set.

```
pte_res <- keras_predict(dense_model_pte, kick_assess, state_assess)
metrics(pte_res, state, .pred_class)
```

```
#> # A tibble: 2 x 3
#>   .metric  .estimator .estimate
#>   <chr>    <chr>          <dbl>
#> 1 accuracy binary         0.611
#> 2 kap      binary         0.221
```

Why did this happen? Part of the training loop for a model like this one typically *adjusts* the weights in the network. When we froze the weights in this network, we froze them at values that did not perform very well. These pre-trained GloVe embeddings (Pennington, Socher, and Manning 2014) are trained on a Wikipedia dump and Gigaword 5[7], a comprehensive archive of newswire text. The text contained on Wikipedia and in news articles both follow certain styles and semantics. Both will tend to be written formally and in the past tense, with longer and complete sentences. There are many more distinct features of both Wikipedia text and news articles, but the relevant aspect here is how similar they are to the data we are trying to model. These Kickstarter blurbs are very short, lack punctuation, stop words, narrative, and tense. Many of the blurbs simply try to pack as many buzz words as possible into the allowed character count while keeping the sentence readable. Perhaps it should not surprise us that these word embeddings don't perform well in this model, since the text used to train the embeddings is so different from the text is it being applied to (Section 5.4).

Although this approach didn't work well with our data set, that doesn't mean that using pre-trained word embeddings is always a bad idea.

The key point is how well the embeddings match the data you are modeling. Also, there is another way we can use these particular embeddings in our network architecture; we can load them in as a starting point as before but *not* freeze the weights. This allows the model to adjust the weights to better fit the data. The intention here is that we as the modeling practitioners think these pre-trained embeddings offer a better starting point than the randomly generated embedding we get if we don't set the weights at all.

We specify a new model to get started on this approach.

---

[7] https://catalog.ldc.upenn.edu/LDC2011T07

```
dense_model_pte2 <- keras_model_sequential() %>%
  layer_embedding(input_dim = max_words + 1,
                  output_dim = ncol(glove6b_matrix),
                  input_length = max_length) %>%
  layer_flatten() %>%
  layer_dense(units = 32, activation = "relu") %>%
  layer_dense(units = 1, activation = "sigmoid")
```

Now, we set the weights with set_weights(), but we *don't* freeze them.

```
dense_model_pte2 %>%
  get_layer(index = 1) %>%
  set_weights(list(glove6b_matrix))
```

We compile and fit the model as before.

```
dense_model_pte2 %>% compile(
  optimizer = "adam",
  loss = "binary_crossentropy",
  metrics = c("accuracy")
)
```

```
dense_pte2_history <- dense_model_pte2 %>% fit(
  x = kick_analysis,
  y = state_analysis,
  batch_size = 512,
  epochs = 20,
  validation_data = list(kick_assess, state_assess),
  verbose = FALSE
)
```

How did this version of using pre-trained embeddings do?

```
pte2_res <- keras_predict(dense_model_pte2, kick_assess, state_assess)
metrics(pte2_res, state, .pred_class)
```

```
#> # A tibble: 2 x 3
#>   .metric  .estimator .estimate
#>   <chr>    <chr>          <dbl>
#> 1 accuracy binary         0.764
#> 2 kap      binary         0.527
```

This performs quite a bit better than when we froze the weights, although not as well as when we did not use pre-trained embeddings at all.

> If you have enough text data in the field you are working in, then it is worth considering training a word embedding yourself that better captures the structure of the domain you are trying to work with, both for the reasons laid out here and for the issues highlighted in Section 5.5.

8.5   Cross-validation for deep learning models

The Kickstarter data set we are using is big enough that we have adequate data to use a single training set, validation set, and testing set that all contain enough observations in them to give reliable performance metrics. In some situations, you may not have that much data or you may want to compute more precise performance metrics. In those cases, it is time to turn to resampling. For example, we can create cross-validation folds.

```
set.seed(345)
kick_folds <- vfold_cv(kickstarter_train, v = 5)
kick_folds
```

```
#> #   5-fold cross-validation
#> # A tibble: 5 x 2
#>    splits               id
#>    <list>               <chr>
#> 1 <split [161673/40419]> Fold1
#> 2 <split [161673/40419]> Fold2
#> 3 <split [161674/40418]> Fold3
#> 4 <split [161674/40418]> Fold4
#> 5 <split [161674/40418]> Fold5
```

Each of these folds has an analysis/training set and an assessment/validation set. Instead of training our model one time and getting one measure of performance, we can train our model v times and get v measures, for more reliability.

In our previous chapters, we used models with full tidymodels support and functions like `add_recipe()` and `workflow()`. Deep learning models are more modular and unique, so we will need to create our own function to handle preprocessing, fitting, and evaluation.

```r
fit_split <- function(split, prepped_rec) {
  ## preprocessing
  x_train <- bake(prepped_rec, new_data = analysis(split),
                  composition = "matrix")
  x_val   <- bake(prepped_rec, new_data = assessment(split),
                  composition = "matrix")

  ## create model
  y_train <- analysis(split) %>% pull(state)
  y_val   <- assessment(split) %>% pull(state)

  mod <- keras_model_sequential() %>%
    layer_embedding(input_dim = max_words + 1,
                    output_dim = 12,
                    input_length = max_length) %>%
    layer_flatten() %>%
    layer_dense(units = 32, activation = "relu") %>%
    layer_dense(units = 1, activation = "sigmoid") %>% compile(
      optimizer = "adam",
      loss = "binary_crossentropy",
      metrics = c("accuracy")
    )

  ## fit model
  mod %>%
    fit(
      x_train,
      y_train,
      epochs = 10,
      validation_data = list(x_val, y_val),
      batch_size = 512,
      verbose = FALSE
    )

  ## evaluate model
  keras_predict(mod, x_val, y_val) %>%
    metrics(state, .pred_class, .pred_1)
}
```

We can `map()` this function across all our cross-validation folds. This takes longer than our previous models to train, since we are training for 10 epochs each on 5 folds.

```
cv_fitted <- kick_folds %>%
  mutate(validation = map(splits, fit_split, kick_prep))

cv_fitted
```

```
#> # 5-fold cross-validation
#> # A tibble: 5 x 3
#>   splits                id     validation
#>   <list>                <chr>  <list>
#> 1 <split [161673/40419]> Fold1 <tibble [4 x 3]>
#> 2 <split [161673/40419]> Fold2 <tibble [4 x 3]>
#> 3 <split [161674/40418]> Fold3 <tibble [4 x 3]>
#> 4 <split [161674/40418]> Fold4 <tibble [4 x 3]>
#> 5 <split [161674/40418]> Fold5 <tibble [4 x 3]>
```

Now we can use `unnest()` to find the metrics we computed.

```
cv_fitted %>%
  unnest(validation)
```

```
#> # A tibble: 20 x 5
#>    splits                id     .metric      .estimator .estimate
#>    <list>                <chr>  <chr>        <chr>          <dbl>
#>  1 <split [161673/40419]> Fold1 accuracy     binary         0.819
#>  2 <split [161673/40419]> Fold1 kap          binary         0.638
#>  3 <split [161673/40419]> Fold1 mn_log_loss  binary         1.00
#>  4 <split [161673/40419]> Fold1 roc_auc      binary         0.857
#>  5 <split [161673/40419]> Fold2 accuracy     binary         0.817
#>  6 <split [161673/40419]> Fold2 kap          binary         0.633
#>  7 <split [161673/40419]> Fold2 mn_log_loss  binary         1.06
#>  8 <split [161673/40419]> Fold2 roc_auc      binary         0.854
#>  9 <split [161674/40418]> Fold3 accuracy     binary         0.820
#> 10 <split [161674/40418]> Fold3 kap          binary         0.639
#> 11 <split [161674/40418]> Fold3 mn_log_loss  binary         1.04
#> 12 <split [161674/40418]> Fold3 roc_auc      binary         0.857
#> 13 <split [161674/40418]> Fold4 accuracy     binary         0.815
#> 14 <split [161674/40418]> Fold4 kap          binary         0.629
#> 15 <split [161674/40418]> Fold4 mn_log_loss  binary         1.02
```

```
#> 16 <split [161674/40418]> Fold4 roc_auc      binary        0.853
#> 17 <split [161674/40418]> Fold5 accuracy     binary        0.821
#> 18 <split [161674/40418]> Fold5 kap          binary        0.641
#> 19 <split [161674/40418]> Fold5 mn_log_loss binary         1.00
#> 20 <split [161674/40418]> Fold5 roc_auc      binary        0.860
```

We can summarize the unnested results to match what we normally would get from collect_metrics()

```
cv_fitted %>%
  unnest(validation) %>%
  group_by(.metric) %>%
  summarize(
    mean = mean(.estimate),
    n = n(),
    std_err = sd(.estimate) / sqrt(n)
  )
```

```
#> # A tibble: 4 x 4
#>    .metric      mean      n std_err
#>    <chr>       <dbl> <int>   <dbl>
#> 1 accuracy    0.818     5 0.00103
#> 2 kap         0.636     5 0.00204
#> 3 mn_log_loss 1.02      5 0.0108
#> 4 roc_auc     0.856     5 0.00115
```

This data set is large enough that we probably wouldn't need to take this approach, and the fold-to-fold metrics have little variance. However, resampling can, at times, be an important piece of the modeling toolkit even for deep learning models.

Training deep learning models typically takes more time than other kinds of machine learning, so resampling may be an unfeasible choice. There is special hardware available that speeds up deep learning because it is particularly well-suited to fitting such models. GPUs (graphics processing units) are used for displaying graphics (as indicated in their name) and gaming, but also for deep learning because of their highly parallel computational ability. GPUs can make solving deep learning problems faster, or even tractable to start with. Be aware, though, that you might not need a GPU for even real-world deep learning modeling. All the models in this book were trained on a CPU only.

8.6 Compare and evaluate DNN models

Let's return to the results we evaluated on a single validation set. We can combine all the predictions on these last three models to more easily compare the results between them.

```
all_dense_model_res <- bind_rows(
  val_res %>% mutate(model = "dense"),
  pte_res %>% mutate(model = "pte (locked weights)"),
  pte2_res %>% mutate(model = "pte (not locked weights)")
)
```

Now that the results are combined in `all_dense_model_res`, we can calculate group-wise evaluation statistics by grouping by the `model` variable.

```
all_dense_model_res %>%
  group_by(model) %>%
  metrics(state, .pred_class)
```

```
#> # A tibble: 6 x 4
#>   model                    .metric  .estimator .estimate
#>   <chr>                    <chr>    <chr>          <dbl>
#> 1 dense                    accuracy binary         0.806
#> 2 pte (locked weights)     accuracy binary         0.611
#> 3 pte (not locked weights) accuracy binary         0.764
#> 4 dense                    kap      binary         0.610
#> 5 pte (locked weights)     kap      binary         0.221
#> 6 pte (not locked weights) kap      binary         0.527
```

We can also do this for ROC curves. Figure 8.9 shows the three different ROC curves together in one chart. As we know, the model using pre-trained word embeddings with locked weights didn't perform very well at all and its ROC curve is the lowest of the three. The other two models perform more similarly but the model using an embedding learned from scratch ends up being the best.

```
all_dense_model_res %>%
  group_by(model) %>%
  roc_curve(truth = state, .pred_1) %>%
  autoplot() +
  labs(
    title = "Receiver operator curve for Kickstarter blurbs"
  )
```

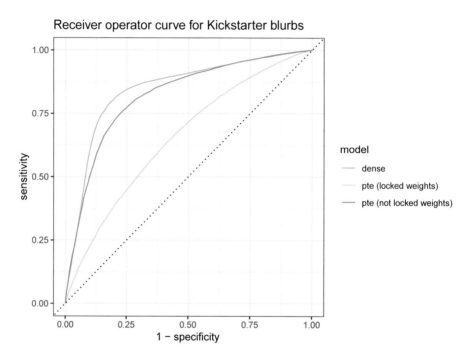

FIGURE 8.9: ROC curve for all DNN models' predictions of Kickstarter campaign success

Using pre-trained embeddings is not the only way to take advantage of ready-to-use, state-of-the-art deep learning models. You can also use whole pre-trained models in your analyses, such as the transformers models available from Hugging Face. Check out this blog post for a tutorial[8] on how to use Hugging Face transfomers in R with Keras. Large language models like these are subject to many of the same concerns as embeddings discussed in Section 5.5.

We compared these three model options using the validation set we created. Let's return to the testing set now that we know which model we expect to perform best and obtain a final estimate for how we expect it to perform on new data. For this final evaluation, we will:

- preprocess the test data using the feature engineering recipe kick_prep so it is in the correct format for our deep learning model,

- find the predictions for the processed testing data, and

- compute metrics for these results.

```
kick_test <- bake(kick_prep, new_data = kickstarter_test,
                  composition = "matrix")
final_res <- keras_predict(dense_model, kick_test, kickstarter_test$state)
final_res %>% metrics(state, .pred_class, .pred_1)
```

```
#> # A tibble: 4 x 3
#>    .metric      .estimator .estimate
#>    <chr>        <chr>          <dbl>
#> 1 accuracy     binary         0.808
#> 2 kap          binary         0.616
#> 3 mn_log_loss  binary         1.06
#> 4 roc_auc      binary         0.849
```

The metrics we see here are about the same as what we achieved in Section 8.2.4 on the validation data, so we can be confident that we have not overfit during our training or model choosing process.

Just like we did toward the end of both Sections 6.9.4 and 7.11.3, we can look at some examples of test set observations that our model did a bad job at predicting. Let's bind together the predictions on the test set with the original kickstarter_test data. Then let's look at blurbs that were successful but that our final model thought had a low probability of being successful.

```
kickstarter_bind <- final_res %>%
  bind_cols(kickstarter_test %>% select(-state))

kickstarter_bind %>%
```

---

[8] https://blogs.rstudio.com/ai/posts/2020-07-30-state-of-the-art-nlp-models-from-r/

```
  filter(state == 1, .pred_1 < 0.2) %>%
  select(blurb) %>%
  slice_sample(n = 10)
```

```
#> # A tibble: 10 x 1
#>     blurb
#>     <chr>
#>  1 Living and working with Peruvian farmers in remote regions, bringing the hig~
#>  2 Arduino-compatible board that includes a prototyping area and rechargeable b~
#>  3 Wyoming based Americana singer/songwriter Doug Balmain is ready to record hi~
#>  4 The purpose of this EP, titled FURY, is to spark a flame in the hearts of to~
#>  5 A new generation of creators tell stories set in the universe of the cult cl~
#>  6 I am learning to create Mobile games but I need some mental support not to g~
#>  7 Boss Betties Photo Company by Amanda is a mobile photography company that sp~
#>  8 LED dog collars w/ eight full color RGB LEDs. Use our free iOS/Android app t~
#>  9 This new font feels like writing quickly with an inked brush, fast and full ~
#> 10 Help me on an ambitious project to write & publish 5 ebooks about the journe~
```

What about misclassifications in the other direction, observations in the test set that were *not* successful but that our final model gave a high probability of being successful?

```
kickstarter_bind %>%
  filter(state == 0, .pred_1 > 0.8) %>%
  select(blurb) %>%
  slice_sample(n = 10)
```

```
#> # A tibble: 10 x 1
#>     blurb
#>     <chr>
#>  1 Purchase the new CD in advance, get great deals on other merch, and help Moo~
#>  2 Coolest cocktails poster ever! Meticulously researched and designed. Beautif~
#>  3 I will hike through the entire western United States and Canada and document~
#>  4 The life of Black Panther Party co-founder and Minister of Self Defense Huey~
#>  5 Antroid is an Android strategy game similar to Command and Conquer. The only~
#>  6 inkman is a new superhero that has the ability to use his art powers to draw~
#>  7 After having  success with our first album in April 2013, Vagablondes aim to~
#>  8 Distracted driving caused 3,328 deaths and 421,000 injuries in 2012. The w8 ~
#>  9 I've been in a female music group since the 8th grade and have finally decid~
#> 10 Epic Abraham tells the tale of one mans journey into supernatural madness an~
```

Notice that although some steps for model fitting are different now that we are using deep learning, model evaluation is much the same as it was in Chapters 6 and 7.

8.7 Limitations of deep learning

Deep learning models achieve excellent performance on many tasks; the flexibility and potential complexity of their architecture is part of the reason why. One of the main downsides of deep learning models is that the interpretability of the models themselves is poor.

> Notice that we have not talked about which words are more associated with success or failure for the Kickstarter campaigns in this whole chapter!

This means that practitioners who work in fields where interpretability is vital, such as some parts of health care, shy away from deep learning models since they are hard to understand and interpret.

Another limitation of deep learning models is that they do not facilitate a comprehensive theoretical understanding or learning of their inner organization (Shwartz-Ziv and Tishby 2017). These two points together lead to deep learning models often being called "black box" models (Shrikumar, Greenside, and Kundaje 2017), models where is it hard to peek into the inner workings to understand what they are doing. Not being able to reason about the inner workings of a model means that we will have a hard time explaining why a model is working well. It also means it will be hard to remedy a biased model that performs well in some settings but badly in other settings. This is a problem since it can hide biases from the training set that may lead to unfair, wrong, or even illegal decisions based on protected classes (Guidotti et al. 2018).

Practitioners have built approaches to understand local feature importance for deep learning models, which we demonstrate in Section 10.5, but these are limited tools compared to the interpretability of other kinds of models. Lastly, deep learning models tend to require more training data than traditional statistical machine learning methods. This means that it can be hard to train a deep learning model if you have a very small data set (Lampinen and McClelland 2018).

8.8   Summary

You can use deep learning to build classification models to predict labels or categorical variables from a data set, including data sets that include text. Dense neural networks are the most straightforward network architecture that can be used to fit classification models for text features and are a good bridge for understanding the more complex model architectures that are used more often in practice for text modeling. These models have many parameters compared to the models we trained in earlier chapters, and require different preprocessing than those models. We can tokenize and create features for modeling that capture the order of the tokens in the original text. Doing this can allow a model to learn from patterns in sequences and order, something not possible in the models we saw in Chapters 6 and 7. We gave up some of the fine control over feature engineering, such as hand-crafting features using domain knowledge, in the hope that the network could learn important features on its own. However, feature engineering is not completely out of our hands as practitioners, since we still make decisions about tokenization and normalization before the tokens are passed into the network.

8.8.1   In this chapter, you learned:

- that you can tokenize and preprocess text to retain the order of the tokens

- how to build and train a dense neural network with Keras

- that you can evaluate deep learning models with the same approaches used for other types of models

- how to train word embeddings alongside your model

- how to use pre-trained word embeddings in a neural network

- about resampling strategies for deep learning models

- about the low interpretability of deep learning models

9

Long short-term memory (LSTM) networks

In Chapter 8, we trained our first deep learning models with straightforward dense network architectures that provide a bridge for our understanding as we move from shallow learning algorithms to more complex network architectures. Those first neural network architectures are not simple compared to the kinds of models we used in Chapters 6 and 7, but it is possible to build many more different and more complex kinds of networks for prediction with text data. This chapter will focus on the family of **long short-term memory** networks (LSTMs) (Hochreiter and Schmidhuber 1997).

9.1 A first LSTM model

We will be using the same data from the previous chapter, described in Sections 8.1 and B.4. This data contains short text blurbs for prospective crowdfunding campaigns and whether those campaigns were successful. Our modeling goal is to predict whether a Kickstarter crowdfunding campaign was successful or not, based on the text blurb describing the campaign. Let's start by splitting our data into training and testing sets.

```
library(tidyverse)
```

```
kickstarter <- read_csv("data/kickstarter.csv.gz")
kickstarter
```

```
#> # A tibble: 269,790 x 3
#>    blurb                                                state created_at
#>    <chr>                                                <dbl> <date>
#> 1 Exploring paint and its place in a digital world.        0 2015-03-17
#> 2 Mike Fassio wants a side-by-side photo of me and Hazel eati~    0 2014-07-11
#> 3 I need your help to get a nice graphics tablet and Photosho~    0 2014-07-30
#> 4 I want to create a Nature Photograph Series of photos of wi~    0 2015-05-08
```

DOI: 10.1201/9781003093459-9

```
#>  5 I want to bring colour to the world in my own artistic skil~     0 2015-02-01
#>  6 We start from some lovely pictures made by us and we decide~     0 2015-11-18
#>  7 Help me raise money to get a drawing tablet                      0 2015-04-03
#>  8 I would like to share my art with the world and to do that ~     0 2014-10-15
#>  9 Post Card don' t set out to simply decorate stories. Our goa~    0 2015-06-25
#> 10 My name is Siu Lon Liu and I am an illustrator seeking fund~     0 2014-07-19
#> # ... with 269,780 more rows
```

```
library(tidymodels)
set.seed(1234)
kickstarter_split <- kickstarter %>%
  filter(nchar(blurb) >= 15) %>%
  mutate(state = as.integer(state)) %>%
  initial_split()

kickstarter_train <- training(kickstarter_split)
kickstarter_test <- testing(kickstarter_split)
```

Just as described in Chapter 8, the preprocessing needed for deep learning network architectures is somewhat different than for the models we used in Chapters 6 and 7. The first step is still to tokenize the text, as described in Chapter 2. After we tokenize, we filter to keep only how many words we'll include in the analysis; step_tokenfilter() keeps the top tokens based on frequency in this data set.

```
library(textrecipes)

max_words <- 2e4
max_length <- 30

kick_rec <- recipe(~ blurb, data = kickstarter_train) %>%
  step_tokenize(blurb) %>%
  step_tokenfilter(blurb, max_tokens = max_words) %>%
  step_sequence_onehot(blurb, sequence_length = max_length)
```

After tokenizing, the preprocessing is different. We use step_sequence_onehot() to encode the sequences of words as integers representing each token in the vocabulary of 20,000 words, as described in detail in Section 8.2.2. This is different than the representations we used in Chapters 6 and 7, mainly because information about word sequence is encoded in this representation.

Using `step_sequence_onehot()` to preprocess text data records and encodes *sequence* information, unlike the document-term matrix and/or bag-of-tokens approaches we used in Chapters 7 and 6.

There are 202,092 blurbs in the training set and 67,365 in the testing set.

Like we discussed in the last chapter, we are using **recipes** and **text-recipes** for preprocessing before modeling. When we `prep()` a recipe, we compute or estimate statistics from the training set; the output of `prep()` is a recipe. When we `bake()` a recipe, we apply the preprocessing to a data set, either the training set that we started with or another set like the testing data or new data. The output of `bake()` is a data set like a tibble or a matrix.

We could have applied these `prep()` and `bake()` functions to any preprocessing recipes throughout this book, but we typically didn't need to because our modeling workflows automated these steps.

```
kick_prep <- prep(kick_rec)
kick_train <- bake(kick_prep, new_data = NULL, composition = "matrix")

dim(kick_train)
```

```
#> [1] 202092      30
```

Here we use `composition = "matrix"` because the Keras modeling functions operate on matrices, rather than a dataframe or tibble.

9.1.1 Building an LSTM

An LSTM is a specific kind of network architecture with feedback loops that allow information to persist through steps[1] and memory cells that can learn

---

[1] Vanilla neural networks do not have this ability for information to persist at all; they start learning from scratch at every step.

to "remember" and "forget" information through sequences. LSTMs are well-suited for text because of this ability to process text as a long sequence of words or characters, and can model structures within text like word dependencies. LSTMs are useful in text modeling because of this memory through long sequences; they are also used for time series, machine translation, and similar problems.

Figure 9.1 depicts a high-level diagram of how the LSTM unit of a network works. In the diagram, part of the neural network, A, operates on some of the input and outputs a value. During this process, some information is held inside A to make the network "remember" this updated network. Network A is then applied to the next input where it predicts new output and its memory is updated.

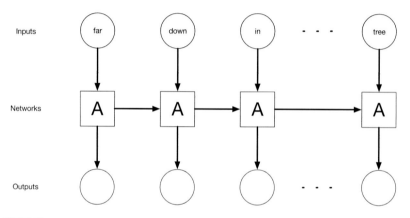

FIGURE 9.1: High-level diagram of an unrolled recurrent neural network. The recurrent neural network is the backbone of LSTM networks.

The exact shape and function of network A are beyond the reach of this book. For further study, Christopher Olah's blog post "Understanding LSTM Networks"[2] gives a more technical overview of how LSTM networks work.

The Keras library has convenient functions for broadly-used architectures like LSTMs so we don't have to build it from scratch using layers; we can instead use `layer_lstm()`. This comes *after* an embedding layer that makes dense vectors from our word sequences and *before* a densely-connected layer for output.

```
library(keras)

lstm_mod <- keras_model_sequential() %>%
  layer_embedding(input_dim = max_words + 1, output_dim = 32) %>%
```

---

[2]https://colah.github.io/posts/2015-08-Understanding-LSTMs/

```
  layer_lstm(units = 32) %>%
  layer_dense(units = 1, activation = "sigmoid")

lstm_mod
```

```
#> Model
#> Model: "sequential"
#>  _____
#>  Layer (type)                    Output Shape                 Param #
#>  ==================================================================
#>  embedding (Embedding)           (None, None, 32)             640032
#>  _____
#>  lstm (LSTM)                     (None, 32)                   8320
#>  _____
#>  dense (Dense)                   (None, 1)                    33
#>  ==================================================================
#>  Total params: 648,385
#>  Trainable params: 648,385
#>  Non-trainable params: 0
#>  _____
```

Notice the number of parameters in this LSTM model, about twice as many as the dense neural networks in Chapter 8. It is easier to overfit an LSTM model, and it takes more time and memory to train, because of the large number of parameters.

Because we are training a binary classification model, we use activation = "sigmoid" for the last layer; we want to fit and predict to class probabilities.

Next we compile() the model, which configures the model for training with a specific optimizer and set of metrics.

A good default optimizer for many problems is "adam" (Kingma and Ba 2017), and a good loss function for binary classification is "binary_crossentropy".

```
lstm_mod %>%
  compile(
    optimizer = "adam",
    loss = "binary_crossentropy",
    metrics = c("accuracy")
  )
```

As we noted in Chapter 8, the neural network model is modified **in place**; the object lstm_mod is different after we compile it, even though we didn't assign the object to anything. This is different from how most objects in R work, so pay special attention to the state of your model objects.

After the model is compiled, we can fit it. The fit() method for Keras models has an argument validation_split that will set apart a fraction of the training data for evaluation and assessment. The performance metrics are evaluated on the validation set at the *end* of each epoch.

```
lstm_history <- lstm_mod %>%
  fit(
    kick_train,
    kickstarter_train$state,
    epochs = 10,
    validation_split = 0.25,
    batch_size = 512,
    verbose = FALSE
  )

lstm_history
```

```
#>
#> Final epoch (plot to see history):
#>         loss: 0.257
#>     accuracy: 0.8786
#>     val_loss: 0.7729
#> val_accuracy: 0.7555
```

The loss on the training data (called loss here) is much better than the loss on the validation data (val_loss), indicating that we are overfitting pretty dramatically. We can see this by plotting the history as well in Figure 9.2.

```
plot(lstm_history)
```

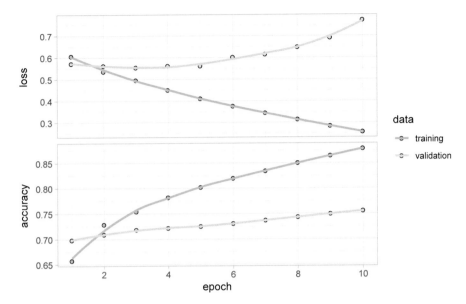

FIGURE 9.2: Training and validation metrics for LSTM

Remember that lower loss indicates a better fitting model, and higher accuracy (closer to 1) indicates a better model.

This model continues to improve epoch after epoch on the training data, but performs worse on the validation set than the training set after the first few epochs and eventually starts to exhibit *worsening* performance on the validation set as epochs pass, demonstrating how extremely it is overfitting to the training data. This is very common for powerful deep learning models, including LSTMs.

9.1.2   Evaluation

We used some Keras defaults for model evaluation in the previous section, but just like we demonstrated in Section 8.2.4, we can take more control if we want or need to. Instead of using the `validation_split` argument, we can use the validation_data argument and send in our own validation set creating with rsample.

```
set.seed(234)
kick_val <- validation_split(kickstarter_train, strata = state)
kick_val
```

```
#> # Validation Set Split (0.75/0.25)  using stratification
#> # A tibble: 1 x 2
#>   splits              id
#>   <list>              <chr>
#> 1 <split [151568/50524]> validation
```

We can access the two data sets specified by this split via the functions analysis() (the analog to training) and assessment() (the analog to testing). We need to apply our prepped preprocessing recipe kick_prep to both to transform this data to the appropriate format for our neural network architecture.

```
kick_analysis <- bake(kick_prep, new_data = analysis(kick_val$splits[[1]]),
                      composition = "matrix")
dim(kick_analysis)
```

```
#> [1] 151568      30
```

```
kick_assess <- bake(kick_prep, new_data = assessment(kick_val$splits[[1]]),
                    composition = "matrix")
dim(kick_assess)
```

```
#> [1] 50524      30
```

These are each matrices appropriate for a Keras model. We will also need the outcome variables for both sets.

```
state_analysis <- analysis(kick_val$splits[[1]]) %>% pull(state)
state_assess <- assessment(kick_val$splits[[1]]) %>% pull(state)
```

Let's also think about our LSTM model architecture. We saw evidence for significant overfitting with our first LSTM, and we can counteract that by including dropout, both in the regular sense (`dropout`) and in the feedback loops (`recurrent_dropout`).

When we include some dropout, we temporarily remove some units together with their connections from the network. The purpose of this is typically to reduce overfitting (Srivastava et al. 2014). Dropout is not exclusive to LSTM models, and can also be used in many other kinds of network architectures. Another way to add dropout to a network is with `layer_dropout()`.

```r
lstm_mod <- keras_model_sequential() %>%
  layer_embedding(input_dim = max_words + 1, output_dim = 32) %>%
  layer_lstm(units = 32, dropout = 0.4, recurrent_dropout = 0.4) %>%
  layer_dense(units = 1, activation = "sigmoid")

lstm_mod %>%
  compile(
    optimizer = "adam",
    loss = "binary_crossentropy",
    metrics = c("accuracy")
  )

val_history <- lstm_mod %>%
  fit(
    kick_analysis,
    state_analysis,
    epochs = 10,
    validation_data = list(kick_assess, state_assess),
    batch_size = 512,
    verbose = FALSE
  )

val_history
```

```
#>
#> Final epoch (plot to see history):
#>          loss: 0.3756
```

```
#>      accuracy: 0.8245
#>      val_loss: 0.6247
#> val_accuracy: 0.7325
```

The overfitting has been reduced, and Figure 9.3 shows that the difference between our model's performance on training and validation data is now smaller.

```
plot(val_history)
```

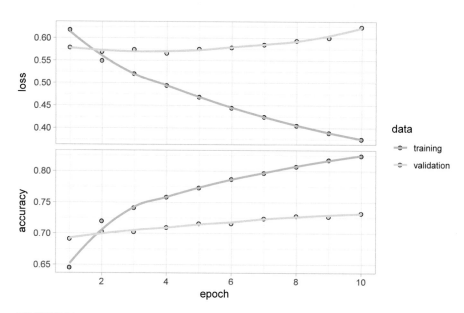

FIGURE 9.3: Training and validation metrics for LSTM with dropout

Remember that this is specific validation data that we have chosen ahead of
time, so we can evaluate metrics flexibly in any way we need to, for example,
using yardstick functions. We can create a tibble with the true and predicted
values for the validation set.

```
val_res <- keras_predict(lstm_mod, kick_assess, state_assess)
val_res %>% metrics(state, .pred_class, .pred_1)
```

```
#> # A tibble: 4 x 3
#>   .metric    .estimator .estimate
#>   <chr>      <chr>          <dbl>
#> 1 accuracy   binary         0.733
```

```
#> 2 kap          binary          0.461
#> 3 mn_log_loss binary          0.625
#> 4 roc_auc      binary          0.803
```

A regularized linear model trained on this data set achieved results of accuracy of 0.686 and an AUC for the ROC curve of 0.752 (Appendix C). This first LSTM with dropout is already performing better than such a linear model. We can plot the ROC curve in Figure 9.4 to evaluate the performance across the range of thresholds.

```
val_res %>%
  roc_curve(state, .pred_1) %>%
  autoplot()
```

9.2 Compare to a recurrent neural network

An LSTM is actually a specific kind of recurrent neural network (RNN) (Elman 1990). Simple RNNs have feedback loops and hidden state that allow information to persist through steps but do not have memory cells like LSTMs. This difference between RNNs and LSTMs amounts to what happens in network *A* in Figure 9.1. RNNs tend to have a very simple structure, typically just a single tanh() layer, much simpler than what happens in LSTMs.

Simple RNNs can only connect very recent information and structure in sequences, but LSTMS can learn long-range dependencies and broader context.

Let's train an RNN to see how it compares to the LSTM.

```
rnn_mod <- keras_model_sequential() %>%
  layer_embedding(input_dim = max_words + 1, output_dim = 32) %>%
  layer_simple_rnn(units = 32, dropout = 0.4, recurrent_dropout = 0.4) %>%
  layer_dense(units = 1, activation = "sigmoid")
```

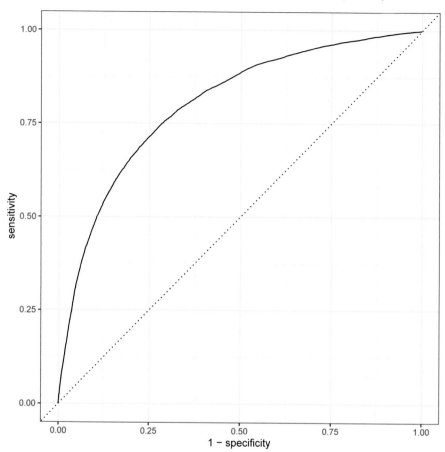

FIGURE 9.4: ROC curve for LSTM with dropout predictions of Kickstarter campaign success

```
rnn_mod %>%
  compile(
    optimizer = "adam",
    loss = "binary_crossentropy",
    metrics = c("accuracy")
  )

rnn_history <- rnn_mod %>%
  fit(
    kick_analysis,
    state_analysis,
    epochs = 10,
```

```
    validation_data = list(kick_assess, state_assess),
    batch_size = 512,
    verbose = FALSE
)

rnn_history
```

```
#>
#> Final epoch (plot to see history):
#>          loss: 0.4955
#>      accuracy: 0.7684
#>      val_loss: 0.5963
#> val_accuracy: 0.7116
```

Looks like more overfitting! We can see this by plotting the history as well in Figure 9.5.

```
plot(rnn_history)
```

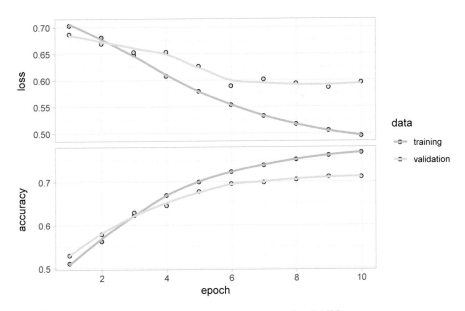

FIGURE 9.5: Training and validation metrics for RNN

These results are pretty disappointing overall, with worse performance than our first LSTM. Simple RNNs like the ones in this section can be challenging to train well, and just cranking up the number of embedding dimensions, units, or other network characteristics usually does not fix the problem. Often, RNNs just don't work well compared to simpler deep learning architectures like the dense network introduced in Section 8.2 (Minaee et al. 2021), or even other machine learning approaches like regularized linear models with good preprocessing.

Fortunately, we can build on the ideas of a simple RNN with more complex architectures like LSTMs to build better-performing models.

9.3   Case study: bidirectional LSTM

The RNNs and LSTMs that we have fit so far have modeled text as sequences, specifically sequences where information and memory persists moving forward. These kinds of models can learn structures and dependencies moving forward *only*. In language, the structures move both directions, though; the words that come *after* a given structure or word can be just as important for understanding it as the ones that come before it.

We can build this into our neural network architecture with a **bidirectional** wrapper for RNNs or LSTMs.

A bidirectional LSTM allows the network to have both the forward and backward information about the sequences at each step.

The input sequences are passed through the network in two directions, both forward and backward, allowing the network to learn more context, structures, and dependencies.

```
bilstm_mod <- keras_model_sequential() %>%
  layer_embedding(input_dim = max_words + 1, output_dim = 32) %>%
  bidirectional(layer_lstm(units = 32, dropout = 0.4,
                           recurrent_dropout = 0.4)) %>%
  layer_dense(units = 1, activation = "sigmoid")

bilstm_mod %>%
  compile(
```

```
  optimizer = "adam",
  loss = "binary_crossentropy",
  metrics = c("accuracy")
)

bilstm_history <- bilstm_mod %>%
  fit(
    kick_analysis,
    state_analysis,
    epochs = 10,
    validation_data = list(kick_assess, state_assess),
    batch_size = 512,
    verbose = FALSE
  )

bilstm_history
```

```
#>
#> Final epoch (plot to see history):
#>         loss: 0.3629
#>     accuracy: 0.832
#>     val_loss: 0.6208
#> val_accuracy: 0.7384
```

The bidirectional LSTM is more able to represent the data well, but with the same amount of dropout, we do see more dramatic overfitting. Still, there is some improvement on the validation set as well.

```
bilstm_res <- keras_predict(bilstm_mod, kick_assess, state_assess)
bilstm_res %>% metrics(state, .pred_class, .pred_1)
```

```
#> # A tibble: 4 x 3
#>   .metric     .estimator .estimate
#>   <chr>       <chr>          <dbl>
#> 1 accuracy    binary         0.738
#> 2 kap         binary         0.476
#> 3 mn_log_loss binary         0.621
#> 4 roc_auc     binary         0.805
```

This bidirectional LSTM, able to learn both forward and backward text structures, provides some improvement over the regular LSTM on the validation set (which had an accuracy of 0.733).

9.4 Case study: stacking LSTM layers

Deep learning architectures can be built up to create extremely complex networks. For example, RNN and/or LSTM layers can be stacked on top of each other, or together with other kinds of layers. The idea of this stacking is to increase the ability of a network to represent the data well.

Intermediate layers must be set up to return sequences (with `return_sequences = TRUE`) instead of the last output for each sequence.

Let's start by adding one single additional layer.

```r
stacked_mod <- keras_model_sequential() %>%
  layer_embedding(input_dim = max_words + 1, output_dim = 32) %>%
  layer_lstm(units = 32, dropout = 0.4, recurrent_dropout = 0.4,
             return_sequences = TRUE) %>%
  layer_lstm(units = 32, dropout = 0.4, recurrent_dropout = 0.4) %>%
  layer_dense(units = 1, activation = "sigmoid")

stacked_mod %>%
  compile(
    optimizer = "adam",
    loss = "binary_crossentropy",
    metrics = c("accuracy")
  )

stacked_history <- stacked_mod %>%
  fit(
    kick_analysis,
    state_analysis,
    epochs = 10,
    validation_data = list(kick_assess, state_assess),
    batch_size = 512,
    verbose = FALSE
  )

stacked_history
```

```
#>
#> Final epoch (plot to see history):
#>          loss: 0.3771
#>      accuracy: 0.826
#>      val_loss: 0.6079
#> val_accuracy: 0.7357
```

Adding another separate layer in the forward direction appears to have improved the network, about as much as extending the LSTM layer to handle information in the backward direction via the bidirectional LSTM.

```
stacked_res <- keras_predict(stacked_mod, kick_assess, state_assess)
stacked_res %>% metrics(state, .pred_class, .pred_1)
```

```
#> # A tibble: 4 x 3
#>   .metric     .estimator .estimate
#>   <chr>       <chr>          <dbl>
#> 1 accuracy    binary         0.736
#> 2 kap         binary         0.470
#> 3 mn_log_loss binary         0.608
#> 4 roc_auc     binary         0.804
```

We can gradually improve a model by changing and adding to its architecture.

9.5 Case study: padding

One of the most important themes of this book is that text must be heavily preprocessed in order to be useful for machine learning algorithms, and these preprocessing decisions have big effects on model results. One decision that seems like it may not be all that important is how sequences are *padded* for a deep learning model. The matrix that is used as input for a neural network must be rectangular, but the training data documents are typically all different lengths. Sometimes, like in the case of the Supreme Court opinions, the lengths vary a lot; sometimes, like with the Kickstarter data, the lengths vary a little bit.

Either way, the sequences that are too long must be truncated and the sequences that are too short must be padded, typically with zeroes. This does literally mean that words or tokens are thrown away for the long documents and zeroes are added to the shorter documents, with the goal of creating a rectangular matrix that can be used for computation.

It is possible to set up an LSTM network that works with sequences of varied length; this can sometimes improve performance but takes more work to set up and is outside the scope of this book.

The default in textrecipes, as well as most deep learning for text, is `padding = "pre"`, where zeroes are added at the beginning, and `truncating = "pre"`, where values at the beginning are removed. What happens if we change one of these defaults?

```
padding_rec <- recipe(~ blurb, data = kickstarter_train) %>%
  step_tokenize(blurb) %>%
  step_tokenfilter(blurb, max_tokens = max_words) %>%
  step_sequence_onehot(blurb, sequence_length = max_length, padding = "post")

padding_prep <- prep(padding_rec)
padding_matrix <- bake(padding_prep, new_data = NULL, composition = "matrix")
dim(padding_matrix)
```

```
#> [1] 202092     30
```

This matrix has the same dimensions as `kick_train` but instead of padding with zeroes at the beginning of these Kickstarter blurbs, this matrix is padded with zeroes at the end. (This preprocessing strategy still truncates longer sequences in the same way.)

```
pad_analysis <- bake(padding_prep, new_data = analysis(kick_val$splits[[1]]),
                     composition = "matrix")
pad_assess <- bake(padding_prep, new_data = assessment(kick_val$splits[[1]]),
                   composition = "matrix")
```

Now, let's create and fit an LSTM to this preprocessed data.

```
padding_mod <- keras_model_sequential() %>%
  layer_embedding(input_dim = max_words + 1, output_dim = 32) %>%
  layer_lstm(units = 32, dropout = 0.4, recurrent_dropout = 0.4) %>%
  layer_dense(units = 1, activation = "sigmoid")

padding_mod %>%
  compile(
    optimizer = "adam",
    loss = "binary_crossentropy",
    metrics = c("accuracy")
  )

padding_history <- padding_mod %>%
  fit(
    pad_analysis,
    state_analysis,
    epochs = 10,
    validation_data = list(pad_assess, state_assess),
    batch_size = 512,
    verbose = FALSE
  )

padding_history
```

```
#>
#> Final epoch (plot to see history):
#>         loss: 0.4303
#>     accuracy: 0.7905
#>     val_loss: 0.5949
#> val_accuracy: 0.7155
```

This padding strategy results in noticeably worse performance than the default
option!

```
padding_res <- keras_predict(padding_mod, pad_assess, state_assess)
padding_res %>% metrics(state, .pred_class, .pred_1)
```

```
#> # A tibble: 4 x 3
#>   .metric    .estimator .estimate
#>   <chr>      <chr>          <dbl>
#> 1 accuracy   binary         0.715
#> 2 kap        binary         0.430
```

```
#> 3 mn_log_loss binary          0.595
#> 4 roc_auc      binary          0.789
```

The same model architecture with default padding preprocessing resulted in an accuracy of 0.733 and an AUC of 0.803; changing to `padding = "post"` has resulted in a remarkable degrading of predictive capacity. This result is typically attributed to the RNN/LSTM's hidden states being flushed out by the added zeroes, before getting to the text itself.

Different preprocessing strategies have a huge impact on deep learning results.

9.6   Case study: training a regression model

All our deep learning models for text so far have used the Kickstarter crowd-funding blurbs to predict whether the campaigns were successful or not, a classification problem. In our experience, classification is more common than regression tasks with text data, but these techniques can be used for either kind of supervised machine learning question. Let's return to the regression problem of Chapter 6 and predict the year of United States Supreme Court decisions, starting out by splitting into training and testing sets.

```
library(scotus)
set.seed(1234)
scotus_split <- scotus_filtered %>%
  mutate(
    year = (as.numeric(year) - 1920) / 50,
    text = str_remove_all(text, "'")
  ) %>%
  initial_split(strata = year)

scotus_train <- training(scotus_split)
scotus_test <- testing(scotus_split)
```

Notice that we also shifted (subtracted) and scaled (divided) the year outcome by constant factors so all the values are centered around zero and not too large. Neural networks for regression problems typically behave better when dealing with outcomes that are roughly between −1 and 1.

Next, let's build a preprocessing recipe for these Supreme Court decisions. These documents are much longer than the Kickstarter blurbs, many thousands of words long instead of just a handful. Let's try keeping the size of our vocabulary the same (max_words) but we will need to increase the sequence length information we store (max_length) by a great deal.

```
max_words <- 2e4
max_length <- 1e3

scotus_rec <- recipe(~ text, data = scotus_train) %>%
  step_tokenize(text) %>%
  step_tokenfilter(text, max_tokens = max_words) %>%
  step_sequence_onehot(text, sequence_length = max_length)

scotus_prep <- prep(scotus_rec)
scotus_train_baked <- bake(scotus_prep,
                           new_data = scotus_train,
                           composition = "matrix")
scotus_test_baked <- bake(scotus_prep,
                          new_data = scotus_test,
                          composition = "matrix")
```

What does our training data look like now?

```
dim(scotus_train_baked)
```

```
#> [1] 7498 1000
```

We only have 7498 rows of training data, and because these documents are so long and we want to keep more of each sequence, the training data has 1000 columns. You are probably starting to guess that we are going to run into problems.

Let's create an LSTM and see what we can do. We will need to use higher-dimensional embeddings, since our sequences are much longer (we may want to increase the number of units as well, but will leave that out for the time being). Because we are training a regression model, there is no activation function for the last layer; we want to fit and predict to arbitrary values for the year.

A good default loss function for regression is mean squared error, "mse".

```
scotus_mod <- keras_model_sequential() %>%
  layer_embedding(input_dim = max_words + 1, output_dim = 64) %>%
  layer_lstm(units = 32, dropout = 0.4, recurrent_dropout = 0.4) %>%
  layer_dense(units = 1)

scotus_mod %>%
  compile(
    optimizer = "adam",
    loss = "mse",
    metrics = c("mean_squared_error")
  )

scotus_history <- scotus_mod %>%
  fit(
    scotus_train_baked,
    scotus_train$year,
    epochs = 10,
    validation_split = 0.25,
    verbose = FALSE
  )
```

How does this model perform on the test data? Let's transform back to real values for year so our metrics will be on the same scale as in Chapter 6.

```
scotus_res <- tibble(year = scotus_test$year,
                     .pred = predict(scotus_mod, scotus_test_baked)[, 1]) %>%
  mutate(across(everything(), ~ . * 50 + 1920))

scotus_res %>% metrics(year, .pred)
```

```
#> # A tibble: 3 x 3
#>   .metric .estimator .estimate
#>   <chr>   <chr>          <dbl>
#> 1 rmse    standard       27.1
#> 2 rsq     standard        0.758
#> 3 mae     standard       19.6
```

This is much worse than the final regularized linear model trained in Section 6.9, with an RMSE almost a decade worth of years worse. It's possible we may be able to do a little better than this simple LSTM, but as this chapter has demonstrated, our improvements will likely not be enormous compared to the first LSTM baseline.

> The main problem with this regression model is that there isn't that much data to start with; this is an example where a deep learning model is *not* a good choice and we should stick with a different machine learning algorithm like regularized regression.

9.7 Case study: vocabulary size

In this chapter so far, we've worked with a vocabulary of 20,000 words or tokens. This is a *hyperparameter* of the model, and could be tuned, as we show in detail in Section 10.6. Instead of tuning in this chapter, let's try a smaller value, corresponding to faster preprocessing and model fitting but a less powerful model, and explore whether and how much it affects model performance.

```
max_words <- 1e4
max_length <- 30

smaller_rec <- recipe(~ blurb, data = kickstarter_train) %>%
  step_tokenize(blurb) %>%
  step_tokenfilter(blurb, max_tokens = max_words) %>%
  step_sequence_onehot(blurb, sequence_length = max_length)

kick_prep <- prep(smaller_rec)
```

```
kick_analysis <- bake(kick_prep, new_data = analysis(kick_val$splits[[1]]),
                        composition = "matrix")
kick_assess <- bake(kick_prep, new_data = assessment(kick_val$splits[[1]]),
                        composition = "matrix")
```

Once our preprocessing is done and applied to our validation split kick_val, we can set up our model, another straightforward LSTM neural network.

```
smaller_mod <- keras_model_sequential() %>%
  layer_embedding(input_dim = max_words + 1, output_dim = 32) %>%
  layer_lstm(units = 32, dropout = 0.4, recurrent_dropout = 0.4) %>%
  layer_dense(units = 1, activation = "sigmoid")

smaller_mod %>%
  compile(
    optimizer = "adam",
    loss = "binary_crossentropy",
    metrics = c("accuracy")
  )

smaller_history <- smaller_mod %>%
  fit(
    kick_analysis,
    state_analysis,
    epochs = 10,
    validation_data = list(kick_assess, state_assess),
    batch_size = 512,
    verbose = FALSE
  )

smaller_history
```

```
#>
#> Final epoch (plot to see history):
#>          loss: 0.468
#>      accuracy: 0.7712
#>      val_loss: 0.5879
#> val_accuracy: 0.7084
```

How did this smaller model, based on a smaller vocabulary in the model, perform?

```
smaller_res <- keras_predict(smaller_mod, kick_assess, state_assess)
smaller_res %>% metrics(state, .pred_class, .pred_1)
```

```
#> # A tibble: 4 x 3
#>   .metric      .estimator .estimate
#>   <chr>        <chr>          <dbl>
#> 1 accuracy     binary         0.708
#> 2 kap          binary         0.414
#> 3 mn_log_loss  binary         0.588
#> 4 roc_auc      binary         0.780
```

The original LSTM model with the larger vocabulary had an accuracy of 0.733 and an AUC of 0.803. Reducing the model's capacity to capture and learn text meaning by restricting its access to vocabulary does result in a corresponding reduction in model performance, but a small one.

The relationship between this hyperparameter and model performance is weak over this range. Notice that we cut the vocabulary in half, and saw only modest reductions in accuracy.

9.8 The full game: LSTM

We've come a long way in this chapter, even though we've focused on a very specific kind of recurrent neural network, the LSTM. Let's step back and build one final model, incorporating what we have been able to learn.

9.8.1 Preprocess the data

We know that we want to stick with the defaults for padding, and to use a larger vocabulary for our final model. For this final model, we are not going to use our validation split again, so we only need to preprocess the training data.

```
max_words <- 2e4
max_length <- 30

kick_rec <- recipe(~ blurb, data = kickstarter_train) %>%
  step_tokenize(blurb) %>%
  step_tokenfilter(blurb, max_tokens = max_words) %>%
  step_sequence_onehot(blurb, sequence_length = max_length)

kick_prep <- prep(kick_rec)
kick_train <- bake(kick_prep, new_data = NULL, composition = "matrix")

dim(kick_train)
```

```
#> [1] 202092      30
```

9.8.2   Specify the model

We've learned a lot about how to model this data set over the course of this chapter.

- We can use `dropout` to reduce overfitting.

- Let's stack several layers together, and in fact increase the number of LSTM layers to three.

- The bidirectional LSTM performed better than the regular LSTM, so let's set up each LSTM layer to be able to learn sequences in both directions.

Instead of using specific validation data that we can then compute performance metrics for, let's go back to specifying `validation_split = 0.1` and let the Keras model choose the validation set.

```
final_mod <- keras_model_sequential() %>%
  layer_embedding(input_dim = max_words + 1, output_dim = 32) %>%
  bidirectional(layer_lstm(
    units = 32, dropout = 0.4, recurrent_dropout = 0.4,
    return_sequences = TRUE
  )) %>%
  bidirectional(layer_lstm(
    units = 32, dropout = 0.4, recurrent_dropout = 0.4,
```

```
    return_sequences = TRUE
  )) %>%
  bidirectional(layer_lstm(
    units = 32, dropout = 0.4, recurrent_dropout = 0.4
  )) %>%
  layer_dense(units = 1, activation = "sigmoid")

final_mod %>%
  compile(
    optimizer = "adam",
    loss = "binary_crossentropy",
    metrics = c("accuracy")
  )

final_history <- final_mod %>%
  fit(
    kick_train,
    kickstarter_train$state,
    epochs = 10,
    validation_split = 0.1,
    batch_size = 512,
    verbose = FALSE
  )

final_history
```

```
#>
#> Final epoch (plot to see history):
#>         loss: 0.3341
#>     accuracy: 0.8492
#>     val_loss: 0.5484
#> val_accuracy: 0.774
```

This looks promising! Let's finally turn to the testing set, for the first time during this chapter, to evaluate this last model on data that has never been touched as part of the fitting process.

```
kick_test <- bake(kick_prep, new_data = kickstarter_test,
                  composition = "matrix")
final_res <- keras_predict(final_mod, kick_test, kickstarter_test$state)
final_res %>% metrics(state, .pred_class, .pred_1)
```

```
#> # A tibble: 4 x 3
#>   .metric     .estimator .estimate
#>   <chr>       <chr>          <dbl>
#> 1 accuracy    binary         0.764
#> 2 kap         binary         0.527
#> 3 mn_log_loss binary         0.561
#> 4 roc_auc     binary         0.834
```

This is our best-performing model in this chapter on LSTM models, although not by much. We can again create an ROC curve, this time using the test data in Figure 9.6.

```
final_res %>%
  roc_curve(state, .pred_1) %>%
  autoplot()
```

We have been able to incrementally improve our model by adding to the structure and making good choices about preprocessing. We can visualize this final LSTM model's performance using a confusion matrix as well, in Figure 9.7.

```
final_res %>%
  conf_mat(state, .pred_class) %>%
  autoplot(type = "heatmap")
```

Notice that this final model still does not perform as well as any of the best models of Chapter 8.

For this data set of Kickstarter campaign blurbs, an LSTM architecture is not turning out to give a great result compared to other options. However, LSTMs typically perform very well for text data and are an important piece of the text modeling toolkit.

For the Kickstarter data, these less-than-spectacular results are likely due to the documents' short lengths. LSTMs often work well for text data, but this is not universally true for all kinds of text. Also, keep in mind that LSTMs take both more time and memory to train, compared to the simpler models discussed in Chapter 8.

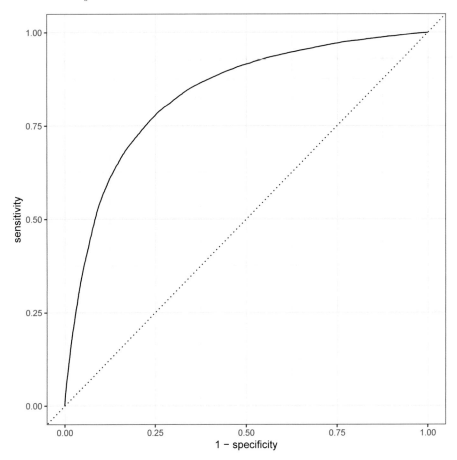

FIGURE 9.6: ROC curve for final LSTM model predictions on testing set of Kickstarter campaign success

9.9 Summary

LSTMs are a specific kind of recurrent neural network that are capable of learning long-range dependencies and broader context. They are often an excellent choice for building supervised models for text because of this ability to model sequences and structures within text like word dependencies. Text must be heavily preprocessed for LSTMs in much the same way it needs to be preprocessed for dense neural networks, with tokenization and one-hot encoding of sequences. A major characteristic of LSTMs, like other deep learning architectures, is their tendency to memorize the features of training data; we

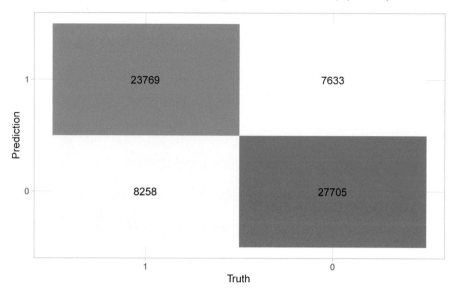

FIGURE 9.7: Confusion matrix for final LSTM model predictions on testing set of Kickstarter campaign success

can use strategies like dropout and ensuring that the batch size is large enough to reduce overfitting.

9.9.1   In this chapter, you learned:

- how to preprocess text data for LSTM models

- about RNN, LSTM, and bidirectional LSTM network architectures

- how to use dropout to reduce overfitting for deep learning models

- that network layers (including RNNs and LSTMs) can be stacked for greater model capacity

- about the importance of centering and scaling regression outcomes for neural networks

- how to evaluate LSTM models for text

10

Convolutional neural networks

The first neural networks we built in Chapter 8 did not have the capacity to learn much about structure, sequences, or long-range dependencies in our text data. The LSTM networks we trained in Chapter 9 were especially suited to learning long-range dependencies. In this final chapter, we will focus on **convolutional neural network** (CNN) architecture (Yoon Kim 2014), which can learn local, spatial structure within data.

CNNs can be well-suited for modeling text data because text often contains quite a lot of local structure. A CNN does not learn long-range structure within a sequence like an LSTM, but instead detects local patterns. A CNN network layer takes data (like text) as input and then hopefully produces output that represents specific structures in the data.

> Let's take more time with CNNs in this chapter to explore their construction, different features, and the hyperparameters we can tune.

10.1 What are CNNs?

CNNs can work with data of different dimensions (like two-dimensional images or three-dimensional video), but for text modeling, we typically work in one dimension. The illustrations and explanations in this chapter use only one dimension to match the text use case. Figure 10.1 illustrates a typical CNN architecture. A convolutional filter slides along the sequence to produce a new, smaller sequence. This is repeated multiple times, typically with different parameters for each layer, until we are left with a small data cube that we can transform into our required output shape, a value between 0 and 1 in the case of binary classification.

This figure isn't entirely accurate because we technically don't feed characters

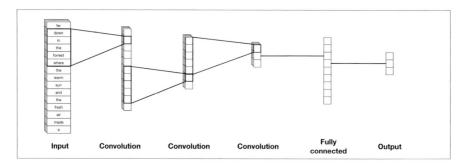

FIGURE 10.1: A template CNN architecture for one-dimensional input data. A sequence of consecutive CNN layers incremently reduces the size, ending with single output value.

into a CNN, but instead use one-hot sequence encoding (Section 8.2.2) with a possible word embedding. Let's talk about two of the most important CNN concepts, **kernels** and **kernel size**.

10.1.1   Kernel

The kernel is a small vector that slides along the input. When it is sliding, it performs element-wise multiplication of the values in the input and its own weights, and then sums up the values to get a single value. Sometimes an activation function is applied as well. It is these weights that are trained via gradient descent to find the best fit. In Keras, the `filters` represent how many different kernels are trained in each layer. You typically start with fewer `filters` at the beginning of your network and then increase them as you go along.

10.1.2   Kernel size

The most prominent hyperparameter is the kernel size. The kernel size is the length of the vector that contains the weights. A kernel of size 5 will have 5 weights. These kernels can capture local information similarly to how n-grams capture location patterns. Increasing the size of the kernel decreases the size of the output, as shown in Figure 10.2.

Larger kernels learn larger and less frequent patterns, while smaller kernels will find fine-grained features. Notice how the choice of token affects how we think about kernel size. For character tokenization, a kernel size of 5 will (in early layers) find patterns in subwords more often than patterns across words, since 5 characters will typically not span multiple words. By contrast, a kernel size of 5 with word tokenization will learn patterns within sentences instead.

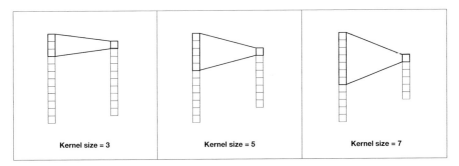

FIGURE 10.2: The kernel size affects the size of the output. A kernel size of 3 uses the information from 3 values to compute 1 value.

10.2 A first CNN model

We will be using the same data, which we examine in Sections 8.1 and B.4 and use throughout Chapters 8 and 9. This data set contains short text blurbs for prospective crowdfunding campaigns on Kickstarter, along with if they were successful. Our goal of this modeling is to predict successful campaigns from the text contained in the blurb. We will also use the same preprocessing and feature engineering recipe that we created and described in Sections 8.2.1 and 9.1.

Our first CNN will look a lot like what is shown in Figure 10.1. We start with an embedding layer, followed by a single one-dimensional convolution layer `layer_conv_1d()`, then a global max pooling layer `layer_global_max_pooling_1d()`, a densely connected layer, and end with a dense layer with a sigmoid activation function to give us one value between 0 and 1 to use in our binary classification task.

```
library(keras)

simple_cnn_model <- keras_model_sequential() %>%
  layer_embedding(input_dim = max_words + 1, output_dim = 16,
                  input_length = max_length) %>%
  layer_conv_1d(filter = 32, kernel_size = 5, activation = "relu") %>%
  layer_global_max_pooling_1d() %>%
  layer_dense(units = 64, activation = "relu") %>%
  layer_dense(units = 1, activation = "sigmoid")

simple_cnn_model
```

```
#> Model
#> Model: "sequential"
#> _____
#> Layer (type)                    Output Shape                    Param #
#> ===========================================================================
#> embedding (Embedding)           (None, 30, 16)                   320016
#>
#> _____
#> conv1d (Conv1D)                 (None, 26, 32)                   2592
#>
#> _____
#> global_max_pooling1d (GlobalMaxPool (None, 32)                   0
#>
#> _____
#> dense_1 (Dense)                 (None, 64)                       2112
#>
#> _____
#> dense (Dense)                   (None, 1)                        65
#> ===========================================================================
#> Total params: 324,785
#> Trainable params: 324,785
#> Non-trainable params: 0
#> _____
```

We are using the same embedding layer with the same `max_length` as in the previous networks so there is nothing new there. The `layer_global_max_pooling_1d()` layer collapses the remaining CNN output into one dimension so we can finish it off with a densely connected layer and the sigmoid activation function.

This might not end up being the best CNN configuration, but it is a good starting point. One of the challenges when working with CNNs is to ensure that we manage the dimensionality correctly. The length of the sequence decreases by (`kernel_size` - 1) for each layer. For this input, we have a sequence of length `max_length = 30`, which is decreased by (5 - 1) = 4 resulting in a sequence of 26, as shown in the printed output of `simple_cnn_model`. We could create seven layers with `kernel_size = 5`, since we would end with 30 - 4 - 4 - 4 - 4 - 4 - 4 - 4 = 2 elements in the resulting sequence. However, we would not be able to do a network with 3 layers of `kernel_size = 7` followed by 3 layers of `kernel_size = 5` since the resulting sequence would be 30 - 6 - 6 - 6 - 4 - 4 - 4 = 0 and we must have a positive length for our sequence. Remember that `kernel_size` is not the only argument that will change the length of the resulting sequence.

Constructing a sequence layer by layer and using the print method from **keras** to check the configuration is a great way to make sure your architecture is valid.

The compilation and fitting are the same as we have seen before, using a validation split created with tidymodels as shown in Sections 8.2.4 and 9.1.2.

```
simple_cnn_model %>% compile(
  optimizer = "adam",
  loss = "binary_crossentropy",
  metrics = c("accuracy")
)

cnn_history <- simple_cnn_model %>% fit(
  x = kick_analysis,
  y = state_analysis,
  batch_size = 512,
  epochs = 10,
  validation_data = list(kick_assess, state_assess)
)
```

We are using the `"adam"` optimizer since it performs well for many kinds of models. You may have to experiment to find the optimizer that works best for your model and data.

Now that the model is done fitting, we can evaluate it on the validation data set using the same `keras_predict()` function we created in Section 8.2.4 and used throughout Chapters 8 and 9.

```
val_res <- keras_predict(simple_cnn_model, kick_assess, state_assess)
val_res
```

```
#> # A tibble: 50,524 x 3
#>        .pred_1 .pred_class state
#>          <dbl> <fct>       <fct>
#> 1 0.00000331 0           0
#> 2 0.0000570  0           0
#> 3 0.000785   0           0
#> 4 0.000134   0           0
#> 5 0.967      1           1
#> 6 0.999      1           1
#> 7 0.00000238 0           0
```

```
#>  8 0.000199   0           0
#>  9 0.0841     0           1
#> 10 0.998      1           1
#> # ... with 50,514 more rows
```

We can calculate some standard metrics with `metrics()`.

```
metrics(val_res, state, .pred_class, .pred_1)
```

```
#> # A tibble: 4 x 3
#>    .metric     .estimator .estimate
#>    <chr>       <chr>          <dbl>
#> 1 accuracy    binary         0.812
#> 2 kap         binary         0.624
#> 3 mn_log_loss binary         0.956
#> 4 roc_auc     binary         0.862
```

We already see improvement over the densely connected network from Chapter 8, our best performing model on the Kickstarter data so far.

The heatmap in Figure 10.3 shows that the model performs about the same for the two classes, success and failure for the crowdfunding campaigns; we are getting fairly good results from a baseline CNN model!

```
val_res %>%
  conf_mat(state, .pred_class) %>%
  autoplot(type = "heatmap")
```

The ROC curve in Figure 10.4 shows how the model performs at different thresholds.

```
val_res %>%
  roc_curve(truth = state, .pred_1) %>%
  autoplot() +
  labs(
    title = "Receiver operator curve for Kickstarter blurbs"
  )
```

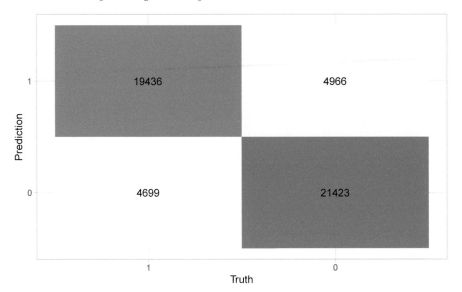

FIGURE 10.3: Confusion matrix for first CNN model predictions of Kickstarter campaign success

10.3 Case study: adding more layers

Now that we know how our basic CNN performs, we can see what happens when we apply some common modifications to it. This case study will examine:

- how we can add additional *convolutional* layers to our base model and

- how additional *dense* layers can be added.

Let's start by adding another fully connected layer. We take the architecture we used in `simple_cnn_model` and add another `layer_dense()` after the first `layer_dense()` in the model. Increasing the depth of the model via the fully connected layers allows the model to find more complex patterns. There is, however, a trade-off. Adding more layers adds more weights to the model, making it more complex and harder to train. If you don't have enough data or the patterns you are trying to classify aren't that complex, then model performance will suffer since the model will start overfitting as it starts memorizing patterns in the training data that don't generalize to new data.

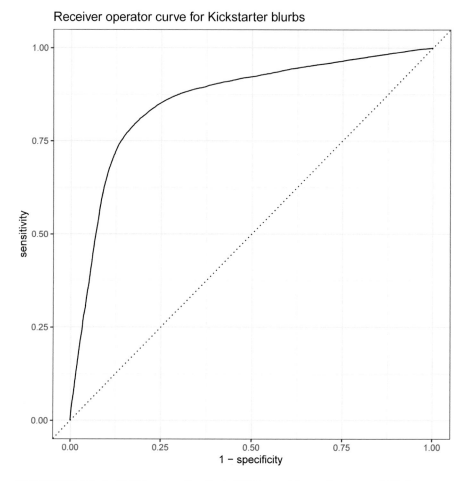

FIGURE 10.4: ROC curve for first CNN model predictions of Kickstarter campaign success

When working with CNNs, the different layers perform different tasks. A convolutional layer extracts local patterns as it slides along the sequences, while a fully connected layer finds global patterns.

We can think of the convolutional layers as doing preprocessing on the text, which is then fed into the dense neural network that tries to fit the best curve. Adding more fully connected layers allows the network to create more intricate curves, and adding more convolutional layers creates richer features that are used when fitting the curves. Your job when constructing a CNN is to make the architecture just complex enough to match the data without overfitting. One ad-hoc rule to follow when refining your network architecture is to start small and keep adding layers until the validation error does not improve anymore.

```
cnn_double_dense <- keras_model_sequential() %>%
  layer_embedding(input_dim = max_words + 1, output_dim = 16,
                  input_length = max_length) %>%
  layer_conv_1d(filter = 32, kernel_size = 5, activation = "relu") %>%
  layer_global_max_pooling_1d() %>%
  layer_dense(units = 64, activation = "relu") %>%
  layer_dense(units = 64, activation = "relu") %>%
  layer_dense(units = 1, activation = "sigmoid")

cnn_double_dense
```

```
#> Model
#> Model: "sequential_1"
#> _____
#> Layer (type)                       Output Shape              Param #
#> ========================================================================
#> embedding_1 (Embedding)            (None, 30, 16)            320016
#> _____
#> conv1d_1 (Conv1D)                  (None, 26, 32)            2592
#> _____
#> global_max_pooling1d_1 (GlobalMaxPo (None, 32)               0
#> _____
#> dense_4 (Dense)                    (None, 64)                2112
#> _____
#> dense_3 (Dense)                    (None, 64)                4160
#> _____
#> dense_2 (Dense)                    (None, 1)                 65
#> ========================================================================
#> Total params: 328,945
#> Trainable params: 328,945
#> Non-trainable params: 0
#> _____
```

We can compile and fit this new model. We will try to keep as much as we can constant as we compare the different models.

```
cnn_double_dense %>% compile(
  optimizer = "adam",
  loss = "binary_crossentropy",
  metrics = c("accuracy")
)

history <- cnn_double_dense %>% fit(
  x = kick_analysis,
  y = state_analysis,
  batch_size = 512,
  epochs = 10,
  validation_data = list(kick_assess, state_assess)
)



val_res_double_dense <- keras_predict(
  cnn_double_dense,
  kick_assess,
  state_assess
)

metrics(val_res_double_dense, state, .pred_class, .pred_1)


#> # A tibble: 4 x 3
#>   .metric     .estimator .estimate
#>   <chr>       <chr>          <dbl>
#> 1 accuracy    binary         0.801
#> 2 kap         binary         0.602
#> 3 mn_log_loss binary         1.01
#> 4 roc_auc     binary         0.858
```

This model performs well, but it is not entirely clear that it is working much better than the first CNN model we tried. This could be an indication that the original model had enough fully connected layers for the amount of training data we have available.

If we have two models with nearly identical performance, we should choose the less complex of the two, since it will have faster performance.

We can also change the number of convolutional layers, by adding more such layers.

```
cnn_double_conv <- keras_model_sequential() %>%
  layer_embedding(input_dim = max_words + 1, output_dim = 16,
                  input_length = max_length) %>%
  layer_conv_1d(filter = 32, kernel_size = 5, activation = "relu") %>%
  layer_max_pooling_1d(pool_size = 2) %>%
  layer_conv_1d(filter = 64, kernel_size = 3, activation = "relu") %>%
  layer_global_max_pooling_1d() %>%
  layer_dense(units = 64, activation = "relu") %>%
  layer_dense(units = 1, activation = "sigmoid")


cnn_double_conv
```

```
#> Model
#> Model: "sequential_2"
#> _____
#> Layer (type)                     Output Shape                   Param #
#> ========================================================================
#> embedding_2 (Embedding)          (None, 30, 16)                 320016
#> _____
#> conv1d_3 (Conv1D)                (None, 26, 32)                 2592
#> _____
#> max_pooling1d (MaxPooling1D)     (None, 13, 32)                 0
#> _____
#> conv1d_2 (Conv1D)                (None, 11, 64)                 6208
#> _____
#> global_max_pooling1d_2 (GlobalMaxPo (None, 64)                  0
#> _____
#> dense_6 (Dense)                  (None, 64)                     4160
#> _____
#> dense_5 (Dense)                  (None, 1)                      65
#> ========================================================================
#> Total params: 333,041
#> Trainable params: 333,041
#> Non-trainable params: 0
#> _____
```

There are a lot of different ways we can extend the network by adding convolutional layers with `layer_conv_1d()`. We must consider the individual characteristics of each layer, with respect to kernel size, as well as other CNN parameters we have not discussed in detail yet like stride, padding, and dilation rate. We also have to consider the progression of these layers within the network itself. The model is using an increasing number of filters in each layer, doubling the number of filters for each layer. This is to ensure that there are more filters later on to capture enough of the global information.

This model is using a kernel size of 5 twice. There aren't any hard rules about how you structure kernel sizes, but the sizes you choose will change what features the model can detect.

The early layers extract general or low-level features while the later layers learn finer detail or high-level features in the data. The choice of kernel size determines the size of these features.

Having a small kernel size in the first layer will let the model detect low-level features locally.

We are also including a max-pooling layer with `layer_max_pooling_1d()` between the convolutional layers. This layer performs a pooling operation that calculates the maximum values in its pooling window; in this model, that is set to 2. This is done in the hope that the pooled features will be able to perform better by weeding out the small weights. This is another parameter you can tinker with when you are designing the network.

We compile this model like the others, again trying to keep as much as we can constant. The only thing that changed in this model compared to the first is the addition of a `layer_max_pooling_1d()` and a `layer_conv_1d()`.

```
cnn_double_conv %>% compile(
    optimizer = "adam",
    loss = "binary_crossentropy",
    metrics = c("accuracy")
)

history <- cnn_double_conv %>% fit(
    x = kick_analysis,
    y = state_analysis,
    batch_size = 512,
    epochs = 10,
    validation_data = list(kick_assess, state_assess)
)
```

```
val_res_double_conv <- keras_predict(
  cnn_double_conv,
  kick_assess,
  state_assess
)

metrics(val_res_double_conv, state, .pred_class, .pred_1)
```

```
#> # A tibble: 4 x 3
#>   .metric     .estimator .estimate
#>   <chr>       <chr>          <dbl>
#> 1 accuracy    binary         0.805
#> 2 kap         binary         0.610
#> 3 mn_log_loss binary         1.04
#> 4 roc_auc     binary         0.854
```

This model also performs well compared to earlier results. Let us extract the the prediction using `keras_predict()` we defined in Section 8.2.4.

```
all_cnn_model_predictions <- bind_rows(
  mutate(val_res, model = "Basic CNN"),
  mutate(val_res_double_dense, model = "Double Dense"),
  mutate(val_res_double_conv, model = "Double Conv")
)

all_cnn_model_predictions
```

```
#> # A tibble: 151,572 x 4
#>        .pred_1 .pred_class state model
#>          <dbl> <fct>       <fct> <chr>
#>  1 0.00000331 0               0     Basic CNN
#>  2 0.0000570  0               0     Basic CNN
#>  3 0.000785   0               0     Basic CNN
#>  4 0.000134   0               0     Basic CNN
#>  5 0.967      1               1     Basic CNN
#>  6 0.999      1               1     Basic CNN
#>  7 0.00000238 0               0     Basic CNN
#>  8 0.000199   0               0     Basic CNN
#>  9 0.0841     0               1     Basic CNN
#> 10 0.998      1               1     Basic CNN
#> # ... with 151,562 more rows
```

Now that the results are combined in `all_cnn_model_predictions` we can calculate group-wise evaluation statistics by grouping them by the `model` variable.

```
all_cnn_model_predictions %>%
  group_by(model) %>%
  metrics(state, .pred_class, .pred_1)
```

```
#> # A tibble: 12 x 4
#>    model        .metric     .estimator .estimate
#>    <chr>        <chr>       <chr>          <dbl>
#>  1 Basic CNN    accuracy    binary         0.812
#>  2 Double Conv  accuracy    binary         0.805
#>  3 Double Dense accuracy    binary         0.801
#>  4 Basic CNN    kap         binary         0.624
#>  5 Double Conv  kap         binary         0.610
#>  6 Double Dense kap         binary         0.602
#>  7 Basic CNN    mn_log_loss binary         0.956
#>  8 Double Conv  mn_log_loss binary         1.04
#>  9 Double Dense mn_log_loss binary         1.01
#> 10 Basic CNN    roc_auc     binary         0.862
#> 11 Double Conv  roc_auc     binary         0.854
#> 12 Double Dense roc_auc     binary         0.858
```

We can also compute ROC curves for all our models so far. Figure 10.5 shows the three different ROC curves together in one chart.

```
all_cnn_model_predictions %>%
  group_by(model) %>%
  roc_curve(truth = state, .pred_1) %>%
  autoplot() +
  labs(
    title = "Receiver operator curve for Kickstarter blurbs"
  )
```

The curves are *very* close in this chart, indicating that we don't have much to gain by adding more layers and that they don't improve performance substantively. This doesn't mean that we are done with CNNs! There are still many things we can explore, like different tokenization approaches and hyperparameters that can be trained.

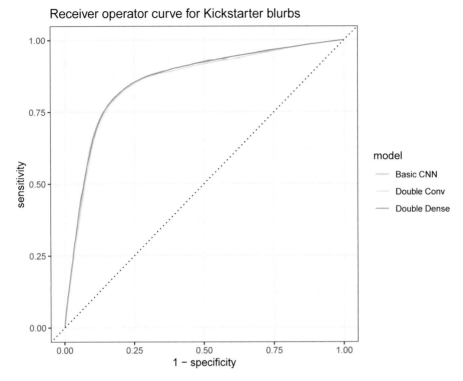

FIGURE 10.5: ROC curve for three CNN variants' predictions of Kickstarter campaign success

10.4 Case study: byte pair encoding

In our models in this chapter so far we have used words as the token of interest. We saw in Section 6.5 how n-grams can be used in modeling as well. One of the reasons why the Kickstarter data set is hard to work with is because the text is quite short so we don't have that many individual tokens to work with in a given blurb. Another choice of token is *subwords*, where we split the text into smaller units than words; longer words especially will be broken into multiple subword units. One way to tokenize text into subword units is *byte pair encoding* (Gage 1994). This algorithm has been repurposed to work on text by iteratively merging frequently occurring subword pairs. Methods such as BERT[1] and GPT-2[2] use subword units for text with great success. The byte pair encoding algorithm has a hyperparameter controlling the size of the

---

[1] https://github.com/google-research/bert
[2] https://openai.com/blog/better-language-models/

vocabulary. Setting it to higher values allows the models to find more rarely used character sequences in the text.

Byte pair encoding offers a good trade-off between character-level and word-level information, and can also encode unknown words. For example, suppose that the model is aware of the word "woman." A simple tokenizer would have to put a word such as "womanhood" into an unknown bucket or ignore it completely, whereas byte pair encoding should be able to pick up on the subwords "woman" and "hood" (or "woman," "h," and "ood," depending on whether the model found "hood" as a common enough subword). Using a subword tokenizer such as byte pair encoding should let us see the text with more granularity since we will have more and smaller tokens for each observation.

Character-level CNNs have also proven successful in some contexts. They have been explored by Zhang, Zhao, and LeCun (2015) and work quite well on some shorter texts such as headlines and tweets (Vosoughi, Vijayaraghavan, and Roy 2016).

We need to remind ourselves that these models don't contain any linguistic knowledge at all; they only "learn" the morphological patterns of sequences of characters (Section 1.2) in the training set. This does not make the models useless, but it should set our expectations about what any given model is capable of.

Since we are using a completely different preprocessing approach, we need to specify a new feature engineering recipe.

The **textrecipes** package has a tokenization engine to perform byte pair encoding, but we need to determine the vocabulary size and the appropriate sequence length.

Let's write a function that takes a character vector and a vocabulary size and returns a dataframe with the number of tokens in each observation.

```
library(textrecipes)

get_bpe_token_dist <- function(vocab_size, x) {
```

```
recipe(~text, data = tibble(text = x)) %>%
  step_mutate(text = tolower(text)) %>%
  step_tokenize(text,
                engine = "tokenizers.bpe",
                training_options = list(vocab_size = vocab_size)) %>%
  prep() %>%
  bake(new_data = NULL) %>%
  transmute(n_tokens = lengths(textrecipes:::get_tokens(text)),
            vocab_size = vocab_size)
}
```

We can use `map()` to try a handful of different vocabulary sizes.

```
bpe_token_dist <- map_dfr(
  c(2500, 5000, 10000, 20000),
  get_bpe_token_dist,
  kickstarter_train$blurb
)
bpe_token_dist
```

```
#> # A tibble: 808,368 x 2
#>    n_tokens vocab_size
#>       <int>      <dbl>
#> 1        16       2500
#> 2        34       2500
#> 3        22       2500
#> 4        26       2500
#> 5        13       2500
#> 6        19       2500
#> 7        33       2500
#> 8        24       2500
#> 9        35       2500
#> 10       37       2500
#> # ... with 808,358 more rows
```

If we compare with the word count distribution we saw in Figure 8.4, then we see in Figure 10.6 that any of these choices for vocabulary size will result in more tokens overall.

```
bpe_token_dist %>%
  ggplot(aes(n_tokens)) +
  geom_bar() +
  facet_wrap(~vocab_size) +
  labs(x = "Number of subwords per campaign blurb",
       y = "Number of campaign blurbs")
```

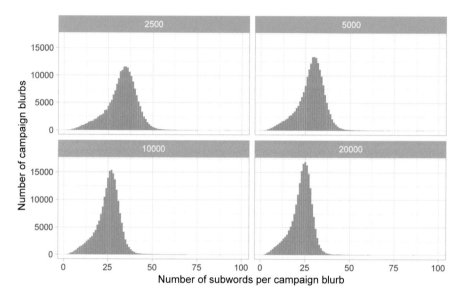

FIGURE 10.6: Distribution of subword count for Kickstarter campaign blurbs for different vocabulary sizes

Let's pick a vocabulary size of 10,000 and a corresponding sequence length of 40. To use byte pair encoding as a tokenizer in textrecipes set `engine = "tokenizers.bpe"`; the vocabulary size can be denoted using the `training_options` argument. Everything else in the recipe stays the same.

```
max_subwords <- 10000
bpe_max_length <- 40

bpe_rec <- recipe(~blurb, data = kickstarter_train) %>%
  step_mutate(blurb = tolower(blurb)) %>%
  step_tokenize(blurb,
                engine = "tokenizers.bpe",
                training_options = list(vocab_size = max_subwords)) %>%
  step_sequence_onehot(blurb, sequence_length = bpe_max_length)
```

```
bpe_prep <- prep(bpe_rec)

bpe_analysis <- bake(bpe_prep, new_data = analysis(kick_val$splits[[1]]),
                     composition = "matrix")
bpe_assess <- bake(bpe_prep, new_data = assessment(kick_val$splits[[1]]),
                     composition = "matrix")
```

Our model will be very similar to the baseline CNN model from Section 10.2;
we'll use a larger kernel size of 7 to account for the finer detail in the tokens.

```
cnn_bpe <- keras_model_sequential() %>%
  layer_embedding(input_dim = max_words + 1, output_dim = 16,
                  input_length = bpe_max_length) %>%
  layer_conv_1d(filter = 32, kernel_size = 7, activation = "relu") %>%
  layer_global_max_pooling_1d() %>%
  layer_dense(units = 64, activation = "relu") %>%
  layer_dense(units = 1, activation = "sigmoid")

cnn_bpe
```

```
#> Model
#> Model: "sequential_3"
#> _____
#> Layer (type)                      Output Shape                  Param #
#> ========================================================================
#> embedding_3 (Embedding)           (None, 40, 16)                320016
#> _____
#> conv1d_4 (Conv1D)                 (None, 34, 32)                3616
#> _____
#> global_max_pooling1d_3 (GlobalMaxPo (None, 32)                  0
#> _____
#> dense_8 (Dense)                   (None, 64)                    2112
#> _____
#> dense_7 (Dense)                   (None, 1)                     65
#> ========================================================================
#> Total params: 325,809
#> Trainable params: 325,809
#> Non-trainable params: 0
#> _____
```

We can compile and train like we have done so many times now.

```
cnn_bpe %>% compile(
  optimizer = "adam",
  loss = "binary_crossentropy",
  metrics = c("accuracy")
)

bpe_history <- cnn_bpe %>% fit(
  bpe_analysis,
  state_analysis,
  epochs = 10,
  validation_data = list(bpe_assess, state_assess),
  batch_size = 512
)

bpe_history
```

```
#>
#> Final epoch (plot to see history):
#>          loss: 0.03372
#>      accuracy: 0.9941
#>      val_loss: 0.9678
#> val_accuracy: 0.8117
```

The performance is doing quite well, which is a pleasant surprise! This is what we hoped would happen if we switched to a higher-detail tokenizer.

The confusion matrix in Figure 10.7 also clearly shows that there isn't much bias between the two classes with this new tokenizer.

```
val_res_bpe <- keras_predict(cnn_bpe, bpe_assess, state_assess)

val_res_bpe %>%
  conf_mat(state, .pred_class) %>%
  autoplot(type = "heatmap")
```

What are the subwords being used in this model? We can extract them from `step_sequence_onehot()` using `tidy()` on the prepped recipe. All the tokens that start with an `"h"` are seen here.

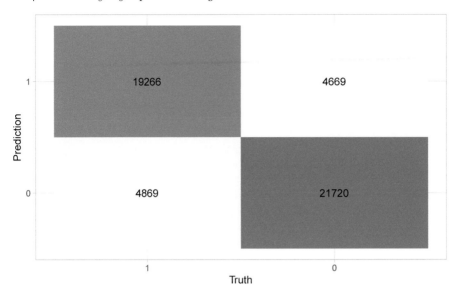

FIGURE 10.7: Confusion matrix for CNN model using byte pair encoding tokenization

```
bpe_rec %>%
  prep() %>%
  tidy(3) %>%
  filter(str_detect(token, "^h")) %>%
  pull(token)
```

```
#>  [1] "h"       "ha"      "hab"      "hal"     "ham"     "hand"    "he"
#>  [8] "head"    "heart"   "hearted"  "heast"   "hed"     "hedul"   "heim"
#> [15] "hel"     "help"    "hem"      "hen"     "hent"    "her"     "here"
#> [22] "hern"    "hero"    "hes"      "hes,"    "hes."    "hest"    "het"
#> [29] "hetic"   "hett"    "hib"      "hic"     "hing"    "hing."   "hip"
#> [36] "hist"    "hn"      "hol"      "hold"    "hood"    "hop"     "hor"
#> [43] "hous"    "house"   "how"      "hr"      "hs"      "hu"
```

Notice how some of these subword tokens are full words, and some are parts of words. This is what allows the model to be able to "read" long unknown words by combining many smaller subwords. We can also look at common long words.

```
bpe_rec %>%
  prep() %>%
```

```
tidy(3) %>%
arrange(desc(nchar(token))) %>%
slice_head(n = 25) %>%
pull(token)
```

```
#>  [1] "_singer-songwriter" "_singer/songwriter" "_post-apocalyptic"
#>  [4] "_interchangeable"   "_singer/songwrit"   "_entertainment."
#>  [7] "_feature-length"    "_groundbreaking"    "_illustrations."
#> [10] "_professionally"    "_relationships."    "_self-published"
#> [13] "_sustainability"    "_transformation"    "_unconventional"
#> [16] "_architectural"     "_automatically"     "_award-winning"
#> [19] "_collaborating"     "_collaboration"     "_collaborative"
#> [22] "_coming-of-age"     "_communication"     "_comprehensive"
#> [25] "_consciousness"
```

These 25 words were common enough to get their own subword token, and helps us understand the nature of these Kickstarter crowdfunding campaigns.

Examining the longest subword tokens gives you a good sense of the data you are working with!

10.5   Case study: explainability with LIME

We noted in Section 8.7 that one of the significant limitations of deep learning models is that they are hard to reason about. One of the ways to understand a predictive model, even a "black box" one, is using an algorithm for observation-level variable importance like the *Local Interpretable Model-Agnostic Explanations* (Ribeiro, Singh, and Guestrin 2016) algorithm, or **LIME** for short.

As indicated by its name, LIME is an approach to compute local feature importance, or explainability at the individual observation level. It does not offer global feature importance, or explainability for the model as a whole.

The **lime** package in R (Pedersen and Benesty 2021) implements the LIME algorithm; it can take a prediction from a model and determine a small set of features in the original data that drives the outcome of the prediction.

To use this package we need to write a helper function to get the data in the format we want. The `lime()` function takes two mandatory arguments, x and model. The model argument is the trained model we are trying to explain. The `lime()` function works out of the box with Keras models so we should be good to go there. The x argument is the training data used for training the model. This is where we need to to create a helper function; the lime package is expecting x to be a character vector so we'll need a function that takes a character vector as input and returns the matrix the Keras model is expecting.

```
kick_prepped_rec <- prep(kick_rec)

text_to_matrix <- function(x) {
  bake(
    kick_prepped_rec,
    new_data = tibble(blurb = x),
    composition = "matrix"
  )
}
```

Since the function needs to be able to work with just the x parameter alone, we need to put `prepped_recipe` inside the function rather than passing it in as an argument. This will work with R's scoping rules but does require you to create a new function for each recipe.

Let's select a couple of training observations to explain.

```
sentence_to_explain <- kickstarter_train %>%
  slice(c(1, 5)) %>%
  pull(blurb)

sentence_to_explain
```

```
#> [1] "The new way of learning English made simple, interesting and practical!"
#> [2] "Happiness in a jar has finally been reached."
```

We now load the lime package and pass observations into `lime()` along with the model we are trying to explain and the preprocess function.

> Be sure that the preprocessing function *matches* the preprocessing that was used to train the model.

```
library(lime)

explainer <- lime(
  x = sentence_to_explain,
  model = simple_cnn_model,
  preprocess = text_to_matrix
)
```

This `explainer` object can now be used with `explain()` to generate explanations for the sentences. We set `n_labels = 1` to only get explanations for the first label, since we are working with a binary classification model[3]. We set `n_features = 12` to return the 12 most important features. If we were dealing with longer text, we might want to change `n_features` to return more features (tokens).

```
explanation <- explain(
  x = sentence_to_explain,
  explainer = explainer,
  n_labels = 1,
  n_features = 12
)

explanation
```

```
#> # A tibble: 19 x 13
#>    model_type    case label label_prob model_r2 model_intercept model_prediction
#>  * <chr>        <int> <chr>      <dbl>    <dbl>           <dbl>            <dbl>
```

---

[3]The explanations of the second label would just be the inverse of the first label. If you have more than two labels, it makes sense to explore some or all of them.

```
#>  1 classification    1 1      0.999    0.319      0.701        1.02
#>  2 classification    1 1      0.999    0.319      0.701        1.02
#>  3 classification    1 1      0.999    0.319      0.701        1.02
#>  4 classification    1 1      0.999    0.319      0.701        1.02
#>  5 classification    1 1      0.999    0.319      0.701        1.02
#>  6 classification    1 1      0.999    0.319      0.701        1.02
#>  7 classification    1 1      0.999    0.319      0.701        1.02
#>  8 classification    1 1      0.999    0.319      0.701        1.02
#>  9 classification    1 1      0.999    0.319      0.701        1.02
#> 10 classification    1 1      0.999    0.319      0.701        1.02
#> 11 classification    1 1      0.999    0.319      0.701        1.02
#> 12 classification    2 1      0.999    0.391      0.124        0.683
#> 13 classification    2 1      0.999    0.391      0.124        0.683
#> 14 classification    2 1      0.999    0.391      0.124        0.683
#> 15 classification    2 1      0.999    0.391      0.124        0.683
#> 16 classification    2 1      0.999    0.391      0.124        0.683
#> 17 classification    2 1      0.999    0.391      0.124        0.683
#> 18 classification    2 1      0.999    0.391      0.124        0.683
#> 19 classification    2 1      0.999    0.391      0.124        0.683
#> # ... with 6 more variables: feature <chr>, feature_value <chr>,
#> #    feature_weight <dbl>, feature_desc <chr>, data <chr>, prediction <list>
```

The output comes in a tibble format where feature and feature_weight are included, but fortunately lime contains some functions to visualize these weights. Figure 10.8 shows the result of using plot_features(), with each facet containing an observation-label pair and the bars showing the weight of the different tokens. Bars in the positive direction (darker) indicate that the weights *support* the prediction and bars in the negative direction (lighter) indicate *contradictions*. This chart is great for finding the most prominent features in an observation.

```
plot_features(explanation)
```

Figure 10.9 shows the weights by highlighting the words directly in the text. This gives us a way to see if any local patterns contain a lot of weight.

```
plot_text_explanations(explanation)
```

The interactive_text_explanations() function can be used to launch an interactive Shiny app where you can explore the model weights.

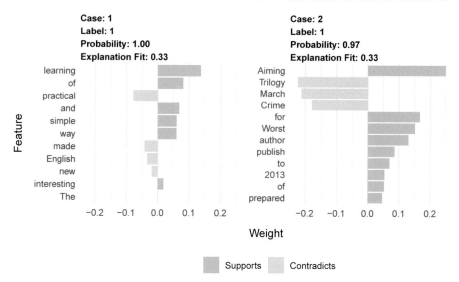

FIGURE 10.8: Plot of most important features for a CNN model predicting two observations.

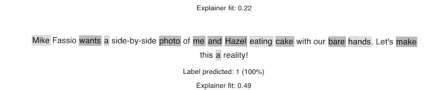

FIGURE 10.9: Feature highlighting of words for two examples explained by a CNN model.

One of the ways a deep learning model is hard to explain is that changes to a part of the input can affect how the input is being used as a whole. Remember that in bag-of-words models adding another token when predicting would just add another unit in the weight; this is not always the case when using deep learning models. The following example shows this effect. We have created two very similar sentences in `fake_sentences`.

```
fake_sentences <- c(
  "Fun and exciting dice game for the whole family",
  "Fun and exciting dice game for the family"
)
```

```
explainer <- lime(
  x = fake_sentences,
  model = simple_cnn_model,
  preprocess = text_to_matrix
)

explanation <- explain(
  x = fake_sentences,
  explainer = explainer,
  n_labels = 1,
  n_features = 12
)
```

Explanations based on these two sentences are fairly similar as we can see in Figure 10.10. However, notice how the removal of the word "whole" affects the weights of the other words in the examples, in some cases switching the sign from supporting to contradicting.

```
plot_text_explanations(explanation)
```

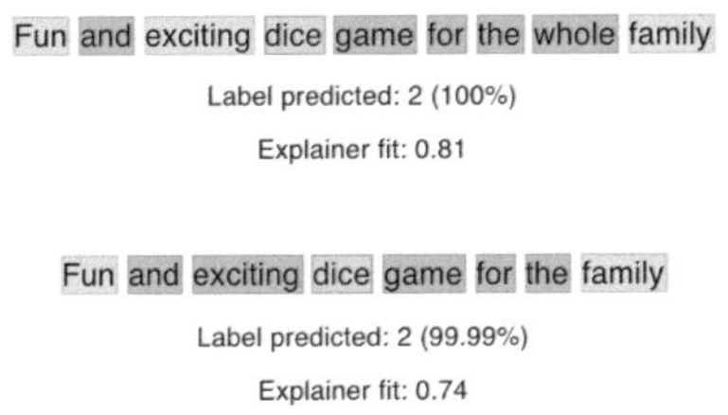

FIGURE 10.10: Feature highlighting of words in two examples explained by a CNN model.

It is these kinds of correlated patterns that can make deep learning models hard to reason about and can deliver surprising results.

The LIME algorithm and **lime** R package are not limited to explaining CNNs. This approach can be used with any of the models we have used in this book, even the ones trained with **parsnip**.

10.6   Case study: hyperparameter search

So far in all our deep learning models, we have only used one configuration of hyperparameters. Sometimes we want to try different hyperparameters out and find what works best for our model like we did in Sections 6.9 and 7.11 using the **tune** package. We can use the **tfruns**[4] package to run multiple Keras models and compare the results.

This workflow will be a little different than what we have seen in the book so far since we will have to create a .R file that contains the necessary modeling steps and then use that file to fit multiple models. Such an example file named cnn-spec.R used for the following models is available on GitHub[5]. The first thing we need to do is specify what hyperparameters we want to vary. By convention, this object is named FLAGS and it is created using the flags() function. For each parameter we want to tune, we add a corresponding flag_*() function, which can be flag_integer(), flag_boolean(), flag_numeric(), or flag_string() depending on what we need to tune.

Be sure you are using the right type for each of these flags; Keras is quite picky! If Keras is expecting an integer and gets a numeric then you will get an error.

```
FLAGS <- flags(
  flag_integer("kernel_size1", 5),
  flag_integer("strides1", 1)
)
```

Notice how we are giving each flag a name and a possible value. The value itself isn't important, as it is not used once we start running multiple models, but it needs to be the right type for the model we are using.

Next, we specify the Keras model we want to run.

---

[4] https://tensorflow.rstudio.com/tools/tfruns/overview/

[5] https://raw.githubusercontent.com/EmilHvitfeldt/smltar/master/cnn-spec.R

```r
model <- keras_model_sequential() %>%
  layer_embedding(input_dim = max_words + 1, output_dim = 16,
                  input_length = max_length) %>%
  layer_conv_1d(filter = 32,
                kernel_size = FLAGS$kernel_size1,
                strides = FLAGS$strides1,
                activation = "relu") %>%
  layer_global_max_pooling_1d() %>%
  layer_dense(units = 64, activation = "relu") %>%
  layer_dense(units = 1, activation = "sigmoid")

model %>% compile(
  optimizer = "adam",
  loss = "binary_crossentropy",
  metrics = c("accuracy")
)
```

We target the hyperparameters we want to change by marking them as FLAGS$name. So in this model, we are tuning different values of kernel_size and strides, which are denoted by the kernel_size1 and strides1 flag, respectively.

Lastly, we must specify how the model is trained and evaluated.

```r
history <- model %>%
  fit(
    x = kick_analysis,
    y = state_analysis,
    batch_size = 512,
    epochs = 10,
    validation_data = list(kick_assess, state_assess)
  )

plot(history)

score <- model %>% evaluate(
  kick_assess, state_assess
)

cat("Test accuracy:", score["accuracy"], "\n")
```

This is mostly the same as what we have seen before. When we are running these different models, the scripts will be run in the environment they are initialized from, so the models will have access to objects like `prepped_training` and `kickstarter_train`, and we don't have to create them inside the file.

Now that we have the file set up we need to specify the different hyperparameters we want to try. Three different values for the kernel size and two different values for the stride length give us `3 * 2 = 6` different runs.

```
hyperparams <- list(
  kernel_size1 = c(3, 5, 7),
  strides1 = c(1, 2)
)
```

This is a small selection of hyperparameters and ranges. There is much more room for experimentation.

Now we have everything we need for hyperparameter searching. Load up **tfruns** and pass the name of the file we just created along with `hyperparams` to the `tuning_run()` function.

```
library(tfruns)
runs <- tuning_run(
  file = "cnn-spec.R",
  runs_dir = "_tuning",
  flags = hyperparams
)

runs_results <- as_tibble(ls_runs())
```

You don't have to, but we have manually specified the `runs_dir` argument, which is where the results of the tuning will be saved.

A summary of all the runs in the folder can be retrieved with `ls_runs()`; here we use `as_tibble()` to get the results as a tibble.

```
runs_results
```

```
#> # A tibble: 6 x 24
#>   run_dir     eval_ metric_loss metric_accuracy metric_val_loss metric_val_accu~
```

```
#>    <chr>       <dbl>       <dbl>        <dbl>        <dbl>        <dbl>
#> 1 _tuning/20~ 1.00        0.0334       0.993        1.00         0.805
#> 2 _tuning/20~ 0.980       0.0361       0.992        0.980        0.806
#> 3 _tuning/20~ 0.983       0.051        0.987        0.983        0.804
#> 4 _tuning/20~ 0.962       0.0359       0.992        0.962        0.811
#> 5 _tuning/20~ 0.974       0.0315       0.994        0.974        0.811
#> 6 _tuning/20~ 0.965       0.0434       0.989        0.965        0.808
#> # ... with 18 more variables: flag_kernel_size1 <int>, flag_strides1 <int>,
#> #   epochs <int>, epochs_completed <int>, metrics <chr>, model <chr>,
#> #   loss_function <chr>, optimizer <chr>, learning_rate <dbl>, script <chr>,
#> #   start <dttm>, end <dttm>, completed <lgl>, output <chr>, source_code <chr>,
#> #   context <chr>, type <chr>, NA. <dbl>
```

We can condense the results down a little bit by only pulling out the flags we are looking at and arranging them according to their performance.

```
best_runs <- runs_results %>%
  select(metric_val_accuracy, flag_kernel_size1, flag_strides1) %>%
  arrange(desc(metric_val_accuracy))

best_runs
```

```
#> # A tibble: 6 x 3
#>   metric_val_accuracy flag_kernel_size1 flag_strides1
#>                 <dbl>             <int>         <int>
#> 1               0.811                 5             1
#> 2               0.811                 7             1
#> 3               0.808                 3             1
#> 4               0.806                 5             2
#> 5               0.805                 7             2
#> 6               0.804                 3             2
```

There isn't much performance difference between the different choices but using kernel size of 5 and stride length of 1 narrowly came out on top.

10.7   Cross-validation for evaluation

In Section 8.5, we saw how we can use resampling to create cross-validation folds for evaluation. The Kickstarter data set we are using is big enough that we have ample data for a single training set, validation set, and testing set that all contain enough observations in them to give reliable performance metrics. However, it is important to understand how to implement other resampling strategies for situations when your data budget may not be as plentiful or when you need to compute performance metrics that are more precise.

```
set.seed(345)
kick_folds <- vfold_cv(kickstarter_train, v = 5)
kick_folds
```

```
#> #  5-fold cross-validation
#> # A tibble: 5 x 2
#>   splits                id
#>   <list>                <chr>
#> 1 <split [161673/40419]> Fold1
#> 2 <split [161673/40419]> Fold2
#> 3 <split [161674/40418]> Fold3
#> 4 <split [161674/40418]> Fold4
#> 5 <split [161674/40418]> Fold5
```

Each of these folds has an analysis or training set and an assessment or validation set. Instead of training our model one time and getting one measure of performance, we can train our model v times and get v measures (five, in this case), for more reliability.

Last time we saw how to create a custom function to handle preprocessing, fitting, and evaluation. We will use the same approach of creating the function, but this time use the model specification from Section 10.2.

```
fit_split <- function(split, prepped_rec) {
  ## preprocessing
  x_train <- bake(prepped_rec, new_data = analysis(split),
              composition = "matrix")
  x_val   <- bake(prepped_rec, new_data = assessment(split),
              composition = "matrix")
```

```
## create model
y_train <- analysis(split) %>% pull(state)
y_val   <- assessment(split) %>% pull(state)

mod <- keras_model_sequential() %>%
  layer_embedding(input_dim = max_words + 1, output_dim = 16,
                  input_length = max_length) %>%
  layer_conv_1d(filter = 32, kernel_size = 5, activation = "relu") %>%
  layer_global_max_pooling_1d() %>%
  layer_dense(units = 64, activation = "relu") %>%
  layer_dense(units = 1, activation = "sigmoid") %>%
  compile(
    optimizer = "adam",
    loss = "binary_crossentropy",
    metrics = c("accuracy")
  )

## fit model
mod %>%
  fit(
    x_train,
    y_train,
    epochs = 10,
    validation_data = list(x_val, y_val),
    batch_size = 512,
    verbose = FALSE
  )

## evaluate model
keras_predict(mod, x_val, y_val) %>%
  metrics(state, .pred_class, .pred_1)
}
```

We can map() this function across all our cross-validation folds. This takes
longer than our previous models to train, since we are training for 10 epochs
each on 5 folds.

```
cv_fitted <- kick_folds %>%
  mutate(validation = map(splits, fit_split, kick_prep))

cv_fitted
```

```
#> #  5-fold cross-validation
#> # A tibble: 5 x 3
#>   splits                id    validation
#>   <list>                <chr> <list>
#> 1 <split [161673/40419]> Fold1 <tibble [4 x 3]>
#> 2 <split [161673/40419]> Fold2 <tibble [4 x 3]>
#> 3 <split [161674/40418]> Fold3 <tibble [4 x 3]>
#> 4 <split [161674/40418]> Fold4 <tibble [4 x 3]>
#> 5 <split [161674/40418]> Fold5 <tibble [4 x 3]>
```

Now we can use `unnest()` to find the metrics we computed.

```
cv_fitted %>%
  unnest(validation)
```

```
#> # A tibble: 20 x 5
#>    splits                id    .metric     .estimator .estimate
#>    <list>                <chr> <chr>       <chr>          <dbl>
#>  1 <split [161673/40419]> Fold1 accuracy    binary         0.824
#>  2 <split [161673/40419]> Fold1 kap         binary         0.648
#>  3 <split [161673/40419]> Fold1 mn_log_loss binary         0.894
#>  4 <split [161673/40419]> Fold1 roc_auc     binary         0.872
#>  5 <split [161673/40419]> Fold2 accuracy    binary         0.826
#>  6 <split [161673/40419]> Fold2 kap         binary         0.652
#>  7 <split [161673/40419]> Fold2 mn_log_loss binary         0.867
#>  8 <split [161673/40419]> Fold2 roc_auc     binary         0.874
#>  9 <split [161674/40418]> Fold3 accuracy    binary         0.827
#> 10 <split [161674/40418]> Fold3 kap         binary         0.653
#> 11 <split [161674/40418]> Fold3 mn_log_loss binary         0.886
#> 12 <split [161674/40418]> Fold3 roc_auc     binary         0.873
#> 13 <split [161674/40418]> Fold4 accuracy    binary         0.825
#> 14 <split [161674/40418]> Fold4 kap         binary         0.649
#> 15 <split [161674/40418]> Fold4 mn_log_loss binary         0.903
#> 16 <split [161674/40418]> Fold4 roc_auc     binary         0.873
#> 17 <split [161674/40418]> Fold5 accuracy    binary         0.828
#> 18 <split [161674/40418]> Fold5 kap         binary         0.654
#> 19 <split [161674/40418]> Fold5 mn_log_loss binary         0.886
#> 20 <split [161674/40418]> Fold5 roc_auc     binary         0.875
```

We can summarize the unnested results to match what we normally would get
from `collect_metrics()`

```
cv_fitted %>%
  unnest(validation) %>%
  group_by(.metric) %>%
  summarize(
    mean = mean(.estimate),
    n = n(),
    std_err = sd(.estimate) / sqrt(n)
  )
```

```
#> # A tibble: 4 x 4
#>   .metric         mean     n std_err
#>   <chr>          <dbl> <int>   <dbl>
#> 1 accuracy       0.826     5 0.000621
#> 2 kap            0.651     5 0.00118
#> 3 mn_log_loss    0.887     5 0.00589
#> 4 roc_auc        0.873     5 0.000528
```

The metrics have little variance just like they did last time, which is reassuring; our model is robust with respect to the evaluation metrics.

10.8 The full game: CNN

We've come a long way in this chapter, and looked at the many different modifications to the simple CNN model we started with. Most of the alterations didn't add much so this final model is not going to be much different than what we have seen so far.

There are an incredible number of ways to change a deep learning network architecture, but in most realistic situations, the benefit in model performance from such changes is modest.

10.8.1 Preprocess the data

For this final model, we are not going to use our separate validation data again, so we only need to preprocess the training data.

```
max_words <- 2e4
max_length <- 30

kick_rec <- recipe(~ blurb, data = kickstarter_train) %>%
  step_tokenize(blurb) %>%
  step_tokenfilter(blurb, max_tokens = max_words) %>%
  step_sequence_onehot(blurb, sequence_length = max_length)

kick_prep <- prep(kick_rec)
kick_matrix <- bake(kick_prep, new_data = NULL, composition = "matrix")

dim(kick_matrix)
```

```
#> [1] 202092     30
```

10.8.2   Specify the model

Instead of using specific validation data that we can then compute performance metrics for, let's go back to specifying `validation_split = 0.1` and let the Keras model choose the validation set.

```
final_mod <- keras_model_sequential() %>%
  layer_embedding(input_dim = max_words + 1, output_dim = 16,
                  input_length = max_length) %>%
  layer_conv_1d(filter = 32, kernel_size = 7,
                strides = 1, activation = "relu") %>%
  layer_global_max_pooling_1d() %>%
  layer_dense(units = 64, activation = "relu") %>%
  layer_dense(units = 1, activation = "sigmoid")

final_mod %>%
  compile(
    optimizer = "adam",
    loss = "binary_crossentropy",
    metrics = c("accuracy")
  )

final_history <- final_mod %>%
  fit(
    kick_matrix,
    kickstarter_train$state,
```

```
    epochs = 10,
    validation_split = 0.1,
    batch_size = 512,
    verbose = FALSE
  )

final_history
```

```
#>
#> Final epoch (plot to see history):
#>         loss: 0.03273
#>     accuracy: 0.9929
#>     val_loss: 0.7665
#> val_accuracy: 0.8521
```

This looks promising! Let's finally turn to the testing set, for the first time during this chapter, to evaluate this last model on data that has never been touched as part of the fitting process.

```
kick_matrix_test <- bake(kick_prep, new_data = kickstarter_test,
                    composition = "matrix")
final_res <- keras_predict(final_mod, kick_matrix_test, kickstarter_test$state)
final_res %>% metrics(state, .pred_class, .pred_1)
```

```
#> # A tibble: 4 x 3
#>   .metric     .estimator .estimate
#>   <chr>       <chr>          <dbl>
#> 1 accuracy    binary         0.849
#> 2 kap         binary         0.697
#> 3 mn_log_loss binary         0.794
#> 4 roc_auc     binary         0.893
```

This is our best-performing model in this chapter on CNN models, although not by much. We can again create an ROC curve, this time using the test data in Figure 10.11.

```
final_res %>%
  roc_curve(state, .pred_1) %>%
  autoplot()
```

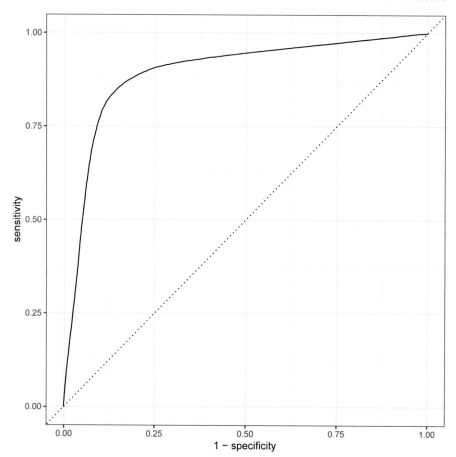

FIGURE 10.11: ROC curve for final CNN model predictions on testing set of Kickstarter campaign success

We have been able to incrementally improve our model by adding to the structure and making good choices about preprocessing. We can visualize this final CNN model's performance using a confusion matrix as well, in Figure 10.12.

```
final_res %>%
  conf_mat(state, .pred_class) %>%
  autoplot(type = "heatmap")
```

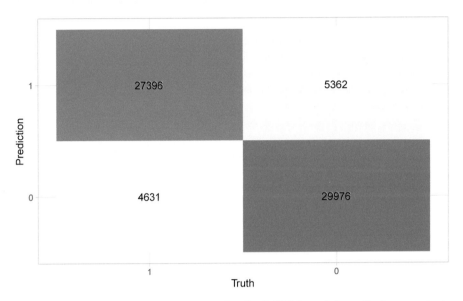

FIGURE 10.12: Confusion matrix for final CNN model predictions on testing set of Kickstarter campaign success

Notice that this final model performs better then any of the models we have tried so far in this chapter, Chapter 8, and Chapter 9.

For this particular data set of short text blurbs, a CNN model able to learn local features performed the best, better than either a densely connected neural network or an LSTM.

10.9 Summary

CNNs are a type of neural network that can learn local spatial patterns. They essentially perform feature extraction, which can then be used efficiently in later layers of a network. Their simplicity and fast running time, compared to models like LSTMs, makes them excellent candidates for supervised models for text.

10.9.1   In this chapter, you learned:

- how to preprocess text data for CNN models

- about CNN network architectures

- how CNN layers can be stacked to extract patterns of varying detail

- how byte pair encoding can be used to tokenize for finer detail

- how to do hyperparameter search in Keras with **tfruns**

- how to evaluate CNN models for text

Part IV

Conclusion

Text models in the real world

Models affect real people in real ways. As the school year of 2020 began with many schools in the United States operating online only because of the novel coronavirus pandemic, a parent of a junior high student reported[6] that her son was deeply upset and filled with doubt because of the way the algorithm of an ed tech company automatically scored his text answers. The parent and child discovered (Chin 2020) how to "game" the ed tech system's scoring.

> Algorithm update. He cracked it: Two full sentences, followed by a word salad of all possibly applicable keywords. 100% on every assignment. Students on @EdgenuityInc, there's your ticket. He went from an F to an A+ without learning a thing.

We can't know the details of the proprietary modeling and/or heuristics that make up the ed tech system's scoring algorithm, but there is enough detail in this student's experience to draw some conclusions. We surmise that this is a count-based method or model, perhaps a linear one but not necessarily so. The success of "word salad" submissions indicates that the model or heuristic being applied has not learned that complex, or even correct, language is important for the score.

What could a team building this kind of score do to avoid these problems? It seems like "word salad" type submissions were not included in the training data as negative examples (i.e., with low scores), indicating that the training data was *biased*; it did not reflect the full spectrum of submissions that the system sees in real life. The system (code and data) is not auditable for teachers or students, and the ed tech company does not directly have a process in place to handle appeals or mistakes in the score itself.

The particular ed tech company in this example does claim that these scores are used only to provide scoring guidance to teachers and that teachers can either accept or overrule such scores, but it is not clear how often teachers

---

[6] https://twitter.com/DanaJSimmons/status/1300639757165191170

overrule scores. This highlights the foundational question about whether such a model or system should even be built to start with; with its current performance, this system is failing at what educators and students understand its goals to be, and is doing harm to its users.

This situation is more urgent and important than only a single example from the pandemic-stressed United States educational system, because:

- these types of harms exacerbate existing inequalities, and

- these systems are becoming more and more widely used.

Ramineni and Williamson (2018) report how GRE essays by African-American students receive lower scores from automatic grading algorithms than from expert human graders, and explore statistical differences in the two grading approaches. This is a stark reminder that machine learning systems learn patterns from training data and amplify those patterns. Feathers (2019) reports that the kind of automatic essay grading described here is used in at least 21 states, and essay grading is not the only kind of predictive text model that has real impact on real individuals' lives[7].

As you finish this book and take away ideas on how to transform language to features for modeling and how to build reliable text models, we want to end by reflecting on how our work as data practitioners plays out when applied. Language data is richly human, and what you and we do with it matters.

---

[7]For more, see this discussion from Rachel Thomas: https://youtu.be/bqCEUQq0z4o

A

Regular expressions

Some people, when confronted with a problem, think: "I know, I'll use regular expressions." Now they have two problems.
— Jamie Zawinski[1]

This section will give a brief overview on how to write and use a regular expression), often abbreviated *regex*. Regular expressions are a way to specify or search for patterns of strings using a sequence of characters. By combining a selection of simple patterns, we can capture quite complicated strings.

Many functions in R take advantage of regular expressions. Some examples from base R include `grep`, `grepl`, `regexpr`, `gregexpr`, `sub`, `gsub`, and `strsplit`, as well as `ls` and `list.files`. The **stringr** package (Wickham 2019) uses regular expressions extensively; the regular expressions are passed as the `pattern =` argument. Regular expressions can be used to detect, locate, or extract parts of a string.

A.1 Literal characters

The most basic regular expression consists of only a single character. Here let's detect if each of the following strings in the character vector `animals` contains the letter "j."

---

[1] https://en.wikiquote.org/wiki/Jamie_Zawinski

```
library(stringr)

animals <- c("jaguar", "jay", "bat")
str_detect(animals, "j")
```

```
#> [1]  TRUE  TRUE FALSE
```

We are also able to *extract* the match with str_extract. This may not seem too useful right now, but it becomes very helpful once we use more advanced regular expressions.

```
str_extract(animals, "j")
```

```
#> [1] "j" "j" NA
```

Lastly we are able to *locate* the position of a match using str_locate.

```
str_locate(animals, "j")
```

```
#>      start end
#> [1,]     1   1
#> [2,]     1   1
#> [3,]    NA  NA
```

> The functions str_detect, str_extract, and str_locate are some of the most simple and powerful main functions in **stringr**, but the **stringr** package includes many more functions. To see the remaining functions, run help(package = "stringr") to open the documentation.

We can also match multiple characters in a row.

```
animals <- c("jaguar", "jay", "bat")
str_detect(animals, "jag")
```

```
#> [1]  TRUE FALSE FALSE
```

Notice how these characters are case sensitive.

```
wows <- c("wow", "WoW", "WOW")
str_detect(wows, "wow")
```

```
#> [1]  TRUE FALSE FALSE
```

A.1.1 Meta characters

There are 14 meta characters that carry special meaning inside regular expressions. We need to "escape" them with a backslash if we want to match the literal character (and backslashes need to be doubled in R). Think of "escaping" as stripping the character of its special meaning.

The plus symbol + is one of the special meta characters for regular expressions.

```
math <- c("1 + 2", "14 + 5", "3 - 5")
str_detect(math, "\\+")
```

```
#> [1]  TRUE  TRUE FALSE
```

If we tried to use the plus sign without escaping it, like "+", we would get an error and this line of code would not run.

The complete list of meta characters is displayed in Table A.1 (Levithan 2012).

A.2 Full stop, the wildcard

Let's start with the full stop/period/dot, which acts as a "wildcard." This means that this character will match anything in place other then a newline character.

TABLE A.1: All meta characters

Description	Character
opening square bracket	[
closing square bracket	]
backslash	\\
caret	^
dollar sign	$
period/dot	.
vertical bar	|
question mark	?
asterisk	*
plus sign	+
opening curly brackets	{
closing curly brackets	}
opening parentheses	(
closing parentheses	)

```
strings <- c("cat", "cut", "cue")
str_extract(strings, "c.")
```

```
#> [1] "ca" "cu" "cu"
```

```
str_extract(strings, "c.t")
```

```
#> [1] "cat" "cut" NA
```

A.3　Character classes

So far we have only been able to match either exact characters or wildcards. **Character classes** (also called character sets) let us do more than that. A character class allows us to match a character specified inside the class. A character class is constructed with square brackets. The character class [ac] will match *either* an "a" or a "c."

```
strings <- c("a", "b", "c")
str_detect(strings, "[ac]")
```

```
#> [1]  TRUE FALSE  TRUE
```

Spaces inside character classes are meaningful as they are interpreted as literal characters. Thus the character class "[ac]" will match the letter "a" and "c", while the character class "[a c]" will match the letters "a" and "c" but also a space.

We can use a hyphen character to define a range of characters. Thus [1-5] is the same as [12345].

```
numbers <- c("1", "2", "3", "4", "5", "6", "7", "8", "9")
str_detect(numbers, "[2-7]")
```

```
#> [1] FALSE  TRUE  TRUE  TRUE  TRUE  TRUE  TRUE FALSE FALSE
```

```
sentence <- "This is a long sentence with 2 numbers with 1 digits."
str_locate_all(sentence, "[1-2a-b]")
```

```
#> [[1]]
#>      start end
#> [1,]     9   9
#> [2,]    30  30
#> [3,]    35  35
#> [4,]    45  45
```

We can also negate characters in a class with a caret ^. Placing a caret immediately inside the opening square bracket will make the regular expression match anything *not* inside the class. Thus the regular expression [^ac] will match anything that isn't the letter "a" or "c."

TABLE A.2: All character classes

Description	Class
Digits; [0-9]	[:digit:] or \\\\d
Alphabetic characters, uppercase and lowercase [A-z]	[:alpha:]
Alphanumeric characters, letters, and digits [A-z0-9]	[:alnum:]
Graphical characters [[:alnum:][:punct:]]	[:graph:]
Printable characters [[:alnum:][:punct:][:space:]]	[:print:]
Lowercase letters [a-z]	[:lower:]
Uppercase letters [A-Z]	[:upper:]
Control characters such as newline, carriage return, etc.	[:cntrl:]
Punctuation characters: !"#$%&' ()*+,-./:;<=>? @[]^_'{|}~	[:punct:]
Space and tab	[:blank:]
Space, tab, vertical tab, newline, form feed, carriage return	[:space:] or \\\\s
Hexadecimal digits [0-9A-Fa-f]	[:xdigit:]
Not space [^[:space:]]	\\\\S
Word characters: letters, digits, and underscores [A-z0-9_]	\\\\w
Non-word characters [^A-z0-9_]	\\\\W
Non-digits [^0-9]	\\\\D

```
strings <- c("a", "b", "c")
str_detect(strings, "[^ac]")
```

```
#> [1] FALSE  TRUE FALSE
```

A.3.1 Shorthand character classes

Certain character classes are so commonly used that they have been predefined with names. A couple of these character classes have even shorter shorthands. The class [:digit:] denotes all the digits 0, 1, 2, 3, 4, 5, 6, 7, 8, and 9 but it can also be described by \\d. Table A.2 presents these useful predefined character classes.

Notice that these shorthands are locale specific. This means that the Danish character ø will be picked up in class [:lower:] but not in the class [a-z] as the character isn't located between a and z.

TABLE A.3: Regular expression quantifiers

Regex	Matches
?	zero or one times
*	zero or more times
+	one or more times
{n}	exactly n times
{n,}	at least n times
{n,m}	between n and m times

A.4 Quantifiers

We can specify how many times we expect something to occur using quantifiers. If we want to find a digit with four numerals, we don't have to write `[:digit:][:digit:][:digit:][:digit:]`. Table A.3 shows how to specify repetitions. Notice that `?` is shorthand for `{0,1}`, `*` is shorthand for `{0,}`, and `+` is shorthand for `{1,}` (Levithan 2012).

We can detect both color and colour by placing a quantifier after the "u" that detects 0 or 1 times used.

```
col <- c("colour", "color", "farver")
str_detect(col, "colou?r")
```

```
#> [1]  TRUE  TRUE FALSE
```

And we can extract four-digit numbers using `{4}`.

```
sentences <- c("The year was 1776.", "Alexander Hamilton died at 47.")
str_extract(sentences, "\\d{4}")
```

```
#> [1] "1776" NA
```

Sometimes we want the repetition to happen over multiple characters. This can be achieved by wrapping what we want repeated in parentheses. In the following example, we want to match all the instances of "NA" in the string. We put `"NA "` inside a set of parentheses and `+` after to make sure we match at least once.

TABLE A.4: Lazy quantifiers

regex	matches
??	zero or one times, prefers 0
*?	zero or more times, match as few times as possible
+?	one or more times, match as few times as possible
{n}?	exactly n times, match as few times as possible
{n,}?	at least n times, match as few times as possible
{n,m}?	between n and m times, match as few times as possible but at least n

```
batman <- "NA NA NA NA NA NA NA NA NA NA NA NA NA NA BATMAN!!!"
str_extract(batman, "(NA )+")
```

```
#> [1] "NA NA NA NA NA NA NA NA NA NA NA NA NA NA "
```

However, notice that this also matches the last space, which we don't want.
We can fix this by matching zero or more "NA" followed by exactly 1 "NA."

```
batman <- "NA NA NA NA NA NA NA NA NA NA NA NA NA NA BATMAN!!!"
str_extract(batman, "(NA )*(NA){1}")
```

```
#> [1] "NA NA NA NA NA NA NA NA NA NA NA NA NA NA"
```

By default these matches are "greedy," meaning that they will try to match
the longest string possible. We can instead make them "lazy" by placing a ?
after, as shown in Table A.4. This will make the regular expressions try to
match the shortest string possible instead of the longest.

Comparing greedy and lazy matches gives us 3 and 7 "NA"'s, respectively.

```
batman <- "NA NA NA NA NA NA NA NA NA NA NA NA NA NA BATMAN!!!"
str_extract(batman, "(NA ){3,7}")
```

```
#> [1] "NA NA NA NA NA NA NA "
```

```
str_extract(batman, "(NA ){3,7}?")
```

```
#> [1] "NA NA NA "
```

A.5   Anchors

The meta characters ^ and $ have special meaning in regular expressions. They force the engine to check the beginning and end of the string, respectively, hence the name **anchor**. A mnemonic device to remember this is "First you get the power(^) and then you get the money(\$)."

```
seasons <- c("The summer is hot this year",
             "The spring is a lovely time",
             "Winter is my favorite time of the year",
             "Fall is a time of peace")
str_detect(seasons, "^The")
```

```
#> [1]   TRUE   TRUE FALSE FALSE
```

```
str_detect(seasons, "year$")
```

```
#> [1]   TRUE FALSE   TRUE FALSE
```

We can also combine the two to match a string completely.

```
folder_names <- c("analysis", "data-raw", "data", "R")
str_detect(folder_names, "^data$")
```

```
#> [1] FALSE FALSE   TRUE FALSE
```

A.6   Additional resources

This appendix covered some of the basics of getting started with (or refreshed about) regular expressions. If you want to learn more:

- RStudio maintains an excellent collection of cheat sheets[2], some of which are related to regular expressions.

- www.rexegg.com has many pages of valuable information, including this "quick start" page with helpful tables[3].

- https://www.regular-expressions.info/ is another great general regular expression site.

- The strings chapter[4] in *R for Data Science* (Wickham and Grolemund 2017) delves into examples written in R.

- Lastly if you want to go down to the metal, check out *Mastering Regular Expressions*[5].

---

[2] https://www.rstudio.com/resources/cheatsheets/
[3] https://www.rexegg.com/regex-quickstart.html
[4] https://r4ds.had.co.nz/strings.html
[5] http://shop.oreilly.com/product/9780596528126.do

B

Data

There are four main text data sets we use throughout this book to demonstrate building features for machine learning and training models. These data sets include texts of different languages, different lengths (short to long), and from very recent time periods to a few hundred years ago.

These text data sets are not overly difficult to read into memory and prepare for analysis; by contrast, in many text modeling projects, the data itself may be in any of a number of formats from an API to literal paper. Practitioners may need to use skills such as web scraping or connecting to databases to even begin their work.

B.1 Hans Christian Andersen fairy tales

The **hcandersenr** (Hvitfeldt 2019a) package includes the text of the 157 known fairy tales by the Danish author Hans Christian Andersen (1805–1875). There are five different languages available, with:

- 156 fairy tales in English,

- 154 in Spanish,

- 150 in German,

- 138 in Danish, and

- 58 in French.

The package contains a data set for each language with the naming convention hcandersen_**, where ** is a country code. Each data set comes as a dataframe with two columns, text and book, where the book variable has the text divided into strings of up to 80 characters.

The package also makes available a data set called EK, which includes information about the publication date, language of origin, and names in the different languages.

This data set is used in Chapters 2, 3, and 4.

B.2 Opinions of the Supreme Court of the United States

The **scotus** (Hvitfeldt 2019b) package contains a sample of the Supreme Court of the United States' opinions. The scotus_sample dataframe includes one opinion per row along with the year, case name, docket number, and a unique ID number.

The text has had minimal preprocessing and includes header information in the text field, such as shown here:

```
#> No. 97-1992
#> VAUGHN L. MURPHY, Petitioner v. UNITED PARCEL SERVICE, INC.
#> ON WRIT OF CERTIORARI TO THE UNITED STATES COURT OF APPEALS FOR THE TENTH
#> CIRCUIT
#> [June 22, 1999]
#> Justice O'Connor delivered the opinion of the Court.
#> Respondent United Parcel Service, Inc. (UPS), dismissed petitioner Vaughn
#> L. Murphy from his job as a UPS mechanic because of his high blood pressure.
#> Petitioner filed suit under Title I of the Americans with Disabilities Act of
#> 1990 (ADA or Act), 104 Stat. 328, 42 U.S.C. § 12101 et seq., in Federal District
#> Court. The District Court granted summary judgment to respondent, and the Court
#> of Appeals for the Tenth Circuit affirmed. We must decide whether the Court
#> of Appeals correctly considered petitioner in his medicated state when it held
#> that petitioner's impairment does not "substantially limi[t]" one or more of
#> his major life activities and whether it correctly determined that petitioner
#> is not "regarded as disabled." See §12102(2). In light of our decision in Sutton
#> v. United Air Lines, Inc., ante, p. ____, we conclude that the Court of Appeals'
#> resolution of both issues was correct.
```

This data set is used in Chapters 4, 6, and 9.

B.3 Consumer Financial Protection Bureau (CFPB) complaints

Consumers can submit complaints to the United States Consumer Financial Protection Bureau (CFPB)[1] about financial products and services; the CFPB sends the complaints to companies for response.

The data set of consumer complaints used in this book has been filtered to 117,214 complaints submitted to the CFPB after January 1, 2019 that include a consumer complaint narrative (i.e., some submitted text). Each observation has a `complaint_id`, various categorical variables, and a text column `consumer_complaint_narrative` containing the written complaints, for a total of 18 columns.

This data set is used in Chapters 5 and 7.

B.4 Kickstarter campaign blurbs

The crowdfunding site Kickstarter[2] provides people a platform to gather pledges to "back" their projects, such as films, music, comics, journalism, and more. When setting up a campaign, project owners submit a description or "blurb" for their campaign to tell potential backers what it is about. The data set of campaign blurbs used in this book was scraped from Kickstarter[3]; the blurbs used here for modeling are from 2009-04-21 to 2016-03-14, with a total of 269,790 campaigns in the sample. For each campaign, we know its `state`, whether it was successful in meeting its crowdfunding goal or not.

This data set is used in Chapters 8, 9, and 10.

---

[1] https://www.consumerfinance.gov/data-research/consumer-complaints/

[2] https://www.kickstarter.com/

[3] https://webrobots.io/kickstarter-datasets/

C

Baseline linear classifier

In Chapters 8, 9, and 10 we demonstrate in detail how to train and evaluate different kinds of deep learning classifiers for the Kickstarter data set of campaign blurbs and whether each campaign was successful or not. This appendix shows a baseline linear classification model for this data set using machine learning techniques like those used in Chapters 6 and 7. It serves the purpose of comparison with the deep learning techniques, and also as a succinct summary of a basic supervised machine learning analysis for text.

This machine learning analysis is presented with only minimal narrative; see Chapters 6 and 7 for more explanation and details.

C.1   Read in the data

```
library(tidyverse)
kickstarter <- read_csv("data/kickstarter.csv.gz") %>%
  mutate(state = as.factor(state))

kickstarter
```

```
#> # A tibble: 269,790 x 3
#>    blurb                                               state created_at
#>    <chr>                                               <fct> <date>
#>  1 Exploring paint and its place in a digital world.       0 2015-03-17
#>  2 Mike Fassio wants a side-by-side photo of me and Hazel eati~ 0 2014-07-11
#>  3 I need your help to get a nice graphics tablet and Photosho~ 0 2014-07-30
#>  4 I want to create a Nature Photograph Series of photos of wi~ 0 2015-05-08
#>  5 I want to bring colour to the world in my own artistic skil~ 0 2015-02-01
#>  6 We start from some lovely pictures made by us and we decide~ 0 2015-11-18
#>  7 Help me raise money to get a drawing tablet              0 2015-04-03
#>  8 I would like to share my art with the world and to do that ~ 0 2014-10-15
```

DOI: 10.1201/9781003093459-C   361

```
#>  9 Post Card don' t set out to simply decorate stories. Our goa~ 0      2015-06-25
#> 10 My name is Siu Lon Liu and I am an illustrator seeking fund~ 0      2014-07-19
#> # ... with 269,780 more rows
```

C.2 Split into test/train and create resampling folds

```
library(tidymodels)
set.seed(1234)
kickstarter_split <- kickstarter %>%
  filter(nchar(blurb) >= 15) %>%
  initial_split()

kickstarter_train <- training(kickstarter_split)
kickstarter_test <- testing(kickstarter_split)

set.seed(123)
kickstarter_folds <- vfold_cv(kickstarter_train)
kickstarter_folds
```

```
#> #  10-fold cross-validation
#> # A tibble: 10 x 2
#>    splits                id
#>    <list>                <chr>
#>  1 <split [181882/20210]> Fold01
#>  2 <split [181882/20210]> Fold02
#>  3 <split [181883/20209]> Fold03
#>  4 <split [181883/20209]> Fold04
#>  5 <split [181883/20209]> Fold05
#>  6 <split [181883/20209]> Fold06
#>  7 <split [181883/20209]> Fold07
#>  8 <split [181883/20209]> Fold08
#>  9 <split [181883/20209]> Fold09
#> 10 <split [181883/20209]> Fold10
```

C.3   Recipe for data preprocessing

```
library(textrecipes)

kickstarter_rec <- recipe(state ~ blurb, data = kickstarter_train) %>%
  step_tokenize(blurb) %>%
  step_tokenfilter(blurb, max_tokens = 5e3) %>%
  step_tfidf(blurb)

kickstarter_rec


#> Data Recipe
#>
#> Inputs:
#>
#>        role #variables
#>     outcome          1
#>   predictor          1
#>
#> Operations:
#>
#> Tokenization for blurb
#> Text filtering for blurb
#> Term frequency-inverse document frequency with blurb
```

C.4   Lasso regularized classification model

```
lasso_spec <- logistic_reg(penalty = tune(), mixture = 1) %>%
  set_mode("classification") %>%
  set_engine("glmnet")

lasso_spec
```

```
#> Logistic Regression Model Specification (classification)
#>
#> Main Arguments:
#>   penalty = tune()
#>   mixture = 1
#>
#> Computational engine: glmnet
```

C.5   A model workflow

We need a few more components before we can tune our workflow. Let's use a sparse data encoding (Section 7.5).

```
library(hardhat)
sparse_bp <- default_recipe_blueprint(composition = "dgCMatrix")
```

Let's create a grid of possible regularization penalties to try.

```
lambda_grid <- grid_regular(penalty(range = c(-5, 0)), levels = 20)
lambda_grid
```

```
#> # A tibble: 20 x 1
#>        penalty
#>          <dbl>
#>   1 0.00001
#>   2 0.0000183
#>   3 0.0000336
#>   4 0.0000616
#>   5 0.000113
#>   6 0.000207
#>   7 0.000379
#>   8 0.000695
#>   9 0.00127
#> 10 0.00234
#> 11 0.00428
#> 12 0.00785
#> 13 0.0144
#> 14 0.0264
```

```
#> 15 0.0483
#> 16 0.0886
#> 17 0.162
#> 18 0.298
#> 19 0.546
#> 20 1
```

Now these can be combined in a tuneable `workflow()`.

```
kickstarter_wf <- workflow() %>%
  add_recipe(kickstarter_rec, blueprint = sparse_bp) %>%
  add_model(lasso_spec)

kickstarter_wf
```

```
#> == Workflow ======================================================
#> Preprocessor: Recipe
#> Model: logistic_reg()
#>
#> -- Preprocessor --------------------------------------------------
#> 3 Recipe Steps
#>
#> * step_tokenize()
#> * step_tokenfilter()
#> * step_tfidf()
#>
#> -- Model ---------------------------------------------------------
#> Logistic Regression Model Specification (classification)
#>
#> Main Arguments:
#>   penalty = tune()
#>   mixture = 1
#>
#> Computational engine: glmnet
```

C.6   Tune the workflow

```
set.seed(2020)
lasso_rs <- tune_grid(
  kickstarter_wf,
  kickstarter_folds,
  grid = lambda_grid
)

lasso_rs
```

```
#> # Tuning results
#> # 10-fold cross-validation
#> # A tibble: 10 x 4
#>    splits                 id     .metrics          .notes
#>    <list>                 <chr>  <list>            <list>
#>  1 <split [181882/20210]> Fold01 <tibble [40 x 5]> <tibble [0 x 1]>
#>  2 <split [181882/20210]> Fold02 <tibble [40 x 5]> <tibble [0 x 1]>
#>  3 <split [181883/20209]> Fold03 <tibble [40 x 5]> <tibble [0 x 1]>
#>  4 <split [181883/20209]> Fold04 <tibble [40 x 5]> <tibble [0 x 1]>
#>  5 <split [181883/20209]> Fold05 <tibble [40 x 5]> <tibble [0 x 1]>
#>  6 <split [181883/20209]> Fold06 <tibble [40 x 5]> <tibble [0 x 1]>
#>  7 <split [181883/20209]> Fold07 <tibble [40 x 5]> <tibble [0 x 1]>
#>  8 <split [181883/20209]> Fold08 <tibble [40 x 5]> <tibble [0 x 1]>
#>  9 <split [181883/20209]> Fold09 <tibble [40 x 5]> <tibble [0 x 1]>
#> 10 <split [181883/20209]> Fold10 <tibble [40 x 5]> <tibble [0 x 1]>
```

What are the best models?

```
show_best(lasso_rs, "roc_auc")
```

```
#> # A tibble: 5 x 7
#>     penalty .metric .estimator  mean     n std_err .config
#>       <dbl> <chr>   <chr>      <dbl> <int>   <dbl> <chr>
#> 1 0.000695  roc_auc binary     0.753    10 0.000824 Preprocessor1_Model08
#> 2 0.000379  roc_auc binary     0.753    10 0.000842 Preprocessor1_Model07
#> 3 0.000207  roc_auc binary     0.752    10 0.000849 Preprocessor1_Model06
#> 4 0.000113  roc_auc binary     0.752    10 0.000858 Preprocessor1_Model05
#> 5 0.0000616 roc_auc binary     0.752    10 0.000865 Preprocessor1_Model04
```

```
show_best(lasso_rs, "accuracy")
```

```
#> # A tibble: 5 x 7
#>     penalty .metric  .estimator  mean     n  std_err .config
#>       <dbl> <chr>    <chr>      <dbl> <int>    <dbl> <chr>
#> 1 0.000379  accuracy binary     0.686    10 0.00111  Preprocessor1_Model07
#> 2 0.000695  accuracy binary     0.686    10 0.00112  Preprocessor1_Model08
#> 3 0.000207  accuracy binary     0.685    10 0.00102  Preprocessor1_Model06
#> 4 0.000113  accuracy binary     0.685    10 0.000926 Preprocessor1_Model05
#> 5 0.0000616 accuracy binary     0.685    10 0.000947 Preprocessor1_Model04
```

```
autoplot(lasso_rs)
```

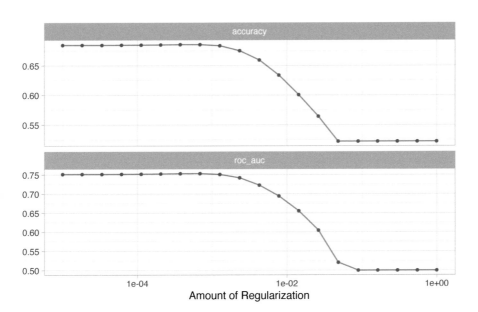

References

Allaire, J., and Chollet, F. 2021. *keras: R Interface to 'Keras'*. R package version 2.4.0. https://CRAN.R-project.org/package=keras.

Appleby, A. 2008. "MurmurHash." https://sites.google.com/site/murmurhash.

Arnold, T. 2017. "A Tidy Data Model for Natural Language Processing using cleanNLP." *The R Journal* 9 (2): 248–267. https://doi.org/10.32614/RJ-2017-035.

Bates, D., and Maechler, M. 2021. *Matrix: Sparse and Dense Matrix Classes and Methods*. R package version 1.3-2. https://CRAN.R-project.org/package=Matrix.

Bender, E. M. 2011. "On Achieving and Evaluating Language-Independence in NLP." *Linguistic Issues in Language Technology* 6 (3): 1–26.

Bender, E. M. 2013. "Linguistic Fundamentals for Natural Language Processing: 100 Essentials from Morphology and Syntax." *Synthesis Lectures on Human Language Technologies* 6 (3). Morgan & Claypool Publishers: 1–184.

Bender, E. M. 2019. "The #BenderRule: On Naming the Languages We Study and Why It Matters." *The Gradient*. https://thegradient.pub/the-benderrule-on-naming-the-languages-we-study-and-why-it-matters/.

Bender, E. M., Gebru, T., McMillan-Major, A., and Shmitchell, S. 2021. "On the Dangers of Stochastic Parrots: Can Language Models Be Too Big?" In *Proceedings of the 2021 ACM Conference on Fairness, Accountability, and Transparency*, 610–623. FAccT '21. New York, NY: Association for Computing Machinery. https://doi.org/10.1145/3442188.3445922.

Benoit, K., and Matsuo, A. 2020. *spacyr: Wrapper to the 'spaCy' 'NLP' Library*. R package version 1.2.1. https://CRAN.R-project.org/package=spacyr.

Benoit, K., Muhr, D., and Watanabe, K. 2021. *stopwords: Multilingual Stopword Lists*. R package version 2.2. https://CRAN.R-project.org/package=stopwords.

Benoit, K., Watanabe, K., Wang, H., Nulty, P., Obeng, A., Müller, S., and Matsuo, A. 2018. "quanteda: An R Package for the Quantitative Analysis of Textual Data." *Journal of Open Source Software* 3 (30): 774. https://doi.org/10.21105/joss.00774.

Boehmke, B., and Greenwell, B. M. 2019. *Hands-on Machine Learning with R*. Boca Raton: CRC Press.

Bojanowski, P., Grave, E., Joulin, A., and Mikolov, T. 2017. "Enriching Word Vectors with Subword Information." *Transactions of the Association for*

Computational Linguistics 5: 135–146. https://www.aclweb.org/anthology/Q17-1010.

Bolukbasi, T., Chang, K.-W., Zou, J. Y., Saligrama, V., and Kalai, A. T. 2016. "Quantifying and Reducing Stereotypes in Word Embeddings." *CoRR* abs/1606.06121. http://arxiv.org/abs/1606.06121.

Boser, B. E., Guyon, I. M., and Vapnik, V. N. 1992. "A Training Algorithm for Optimal Margin Classifiers." In *Proceedings of the Fifth Annual Workshop on Computational Learning Theory*, 144–152. COLT '92. New York, NY: Association for Computing Machinery. https://doi.org/10.1145/130385.130401.

Bouchet-Valat, M. 2020. *SnowballC: Snowball Stemmers Based on the C 'libstemmer' UTF-8 Library*. R package version 0.7.0. https://CRAN.R-project.org/package=SnowballC.

Breiman, L., Friedman, J., Stone, C. J., and Olshen, R. A. 1984. *Classification and Regression Trees*. Boca Raton: CRC Press.

Briscoe, T. 2013. "Introduction to Linguistics for Natural Language Processing." https://www.cl.cam.ac.uk/teaching/1314/L100/introling.pdf.

Caliskan, A., Bryson, J. J., and Narayanan, A. 2017. "Semantics Derived Automatically from Language Corpora Contain Human-Like Biases." *Science* 356 (6334). American Association for the Advancement of Science: 183–186. https://science.sciencemag.org/content/356/6334/183.

Carlini, N., Liu, C., Erlingsson, Ú., Kos, J., and Song, D. 2019. "The Secret Sharer: Evaluating and Testing Unintended Memorization in Neural Networks." In *Proceedings of the 28th USENIX Conference on Security Symposium*, 267–284. SEC'19. USA: USENIX Association.

Caruana, R., Karampatziakis, N., and Yessenalina, A. 2008. "An Empirical Evaluation of Supervised Learning in High Dimensions." In *Proceedings of the 25th International Conference on Machine Learning*, 96–103. ICML '08. New York, NY: Association for Computing Machinery. https://doi.org/10.1145/1390156.1390169.

Chin, M. 2020. "These Students Figured Out Their Tests Were Graded by AI." The Verge. https://www.theverge.com/2020/9/2/21419012/edgenuity-online-class-ai-grading-keyword-mashing-students-school-cheating-algorithm-glitch.

Chollet, F., and Allaire, J. J. 2018. *Deep Learning with R*. Shelter Island, NY: Manning Publications. https://www.manning.com/books/deep-learning-with-r.

Edmondson, M. 2020. *googleLanguageR: Call Google's 'Natural Language' API, 'Cloud Translation' API, 'Cloud Speech' API and 'Cloud Text-to-Speech' API*. R package version 0.3.0. https://CRAN.R-project.org/package=googleLanguageR.

Elman, J. L. 1990. "Finding Structure in Time." *Cognitive Science* 14 (2): 179–211. https://doi.org/10.1207/s15516709cog1402_1.

Ethayarajh, K., Duvenaud, D., and Hirst, G. 2019. "Understanding Undesirable Word Embedding Associations." In *Proceedings of the 57th Annual Meeting of the Association for Computational Linguistics*, 1696–

1705. Florence, Italy: Association for Computational Linguistics. `https://www.aclweb.org/anthology/P19-1166`.

Feathers, T. 2019. "Flawed Algorithms Are Grading Millions of Students' Essays." *Motherboard*. VICE. `https://www.vice.com/en/article/pa7dj9/flawed-algorithms-are-grading-millions-of-students-essays`.

Feldman, R., and Sanger, J. 2007. *The Text Mining Handbook*. Cambridge: Cambridge University Press.

Forman, G., and Kirshenbaum, E. 2008. "Extremely Fast Text Feature Extraction for Classification and Indexing." In *Proceedings of the 17th ACM Conference on Information and Knowledge Management*, 1221–1230. CIKM '08. New York, NY: Association for Computing Machinery. `https://doi.org/10.1145/1458082.1458243`.

Frank, E., and Bouckaert, R. R. 2006. "Naive Bayes for Text Classification with Unbalanced Classes." In *Knowledge Discovery in Databases: PKDD 2006*, edited by Johannes Fürnkranz, Tobias Scheffer, and Myra Spiliopoulou, 503–510. Berlin, Heidelberg: Springer Berlin Heidelberg. `https://doi.org/10.1007/11871637_49`.

Fredrikson, Matt, Jha, S., and Ristenpart, T. 2015. "Model Inversion Attacks That Exploit Confidence Information and Basic Countermeasures." In, 1322–1333. CCS '15. New York, NY: Association for Computing Machinery. `https://doi.org/10.1145/2810103.2813677`.

Fredrikson, Matthew, Lantz, E., Jha, S., Lin, S., Page, D., and Ristenpart, T. 2014. "Privacy in Pharmacogenetics: An End-to-End Case Study of Personalized Warfarin Dosing." In *Proceedings of the 23rd USENIX Conference on Security Symposium*, 17–32. SEC'14. USA: USENIX Association.

Friedman, J. H., Hastie, T., and Tibshirani, R. 2010. "Regularization Paths for Generalized Linear Models via Coordinate Descent." *Journal of Statistical Software, Articles* 33 (1): 1–22. `https://www.jstatsoft.org/v033/i01`.

Gage, P. 1994. "A New Algorithm for Data Compression." *The C Users Journal Archive* 12: 23–38.

Gagolewski, M. 2020. *stringi: Character String Processing Facilities*. R package version 1.6.2. `http://www.gagolewski.com/software/stringi/`.

Garg, N., Schiebinger, L., Jurafsky, D., and Zou, J. 2018. "Word Embeddings Quantify 100 Years of Gender and Ethnic Stereotypes." *Proceedings of the National Academy of Sciences* 115 (16). National Academy of Sciences: E3635–E3644. `https://www.pnas.org/content/115/16/E3635`.

Golub, G. H., and Reinsch, C. 1970. "Singular Value Decomposition and Least Squares Solutions." *Numerische Mathematik* 14 (5). Berlin, Heidelberg: Springer-Verlag: 403–420. `https://doi.org/10.1007/BF02163027`.

Gonen, H., and Goldberg, Y. 2019. "Lipstick on a Pig: Debiasing Methods Cover up Systematic Gender Biases in Word Embeddings but Do Not Remove Them." In *Proceedings of the 2019 Conference of the North American Chapter of the Association for Computational Linguistics: Human Language Technologies, Volume 1 (Long and Short Papers)*, 609–

614. Minneapolis, Minnesota: Association for Computational Linguistics. https://www.aclweb.org/anthology/N19-1061.

Guidotti, R., Monreale, A., Ruggieri, S., Turini, F., Giannotti, F., and Pedreschi, D. 2018. "A Survey of Methods for Explaining Black Box Models." *ACM Computing Surveys* 51 (5). New York, NY: Association for Computing Machinery. https://doi.org/10.1145/3236009.

Harman, D. 1991. "How Effective Is Suffixing?" *Journal of the American Society for Information Science* 42 (1): 7–15. https://doi.org/10.1002/(SICI)1097-4571(199101)42:1%3C7::AID-ASI2%3E3.0.CO;2-P.

Helleputte, T. 2021. *LiblineaR: Linear Predictive Models Based on the LIBLINEAR C/C++ Library.* R package version 2.10-12. https://CRAN.R-project.org/package=LiblineaR.

Hochreiter, S., and Schmidhuber, J. 1997. "Long Short-Term Memory." *Neural Comput.* 9 (8). Cambridge, MA: MIT Press: 1735–1780. https://doi.org/10.1162/neco.1997.9.8.1735.

Honnibal, M., Montani, I., Van Landeghem, S., and Boyd, A. 2020. *spaCy: Industrial-strength Natural Language Processing in Python.* Zenodo. https://doi.org/10.5281/zenodo.1212303.

Howard, J., and Ruder, S. 2018. "Universal Language Model Fine-Tuning for Text Classification." In *Proceedings of the 56th Annual Meeting of the Association for Computational Linguistics (Volume 1: Long Papers)*, 328–339. Melbourne, Australia: Association for Computational Linguistics. https://www.aclweb.org/anthology/P18-1031.

Huang, W., Cheng, X., Chen, K., Wang, T., and Chu, W. 2020. "Towards Fast and Accurate Neural Chinese Word Segmentation with Multi-Criteria Learning." In *Proceedings of the 28th International Conference on Computational Linguistics*, 2062–2072. Barcelona, Spain (Online): International Committee on Computational Linguistics. https://www.aclweb.org/anthology/2020.coling-main.186.

Huston, S., and Croft, W. B. 2010. "Evaluating Verbose Query Processing Techniques." In *Proceedings of the 33rd International ACM SIGIR Conference on Research and Development in Information Retrieval*, 291–298. SIGIR '10. New York, NY: ACM. http://doi.acm.org/10.1145/1835449.1835499.

Hvitfeldt, E. 2019b. *scotus: Collection of Supreme Court of the United States' Opinions.* R package version 1.0.0. https://github.com/EmilHvitfeldt/scotus.

Hvitfeldt, E. 2019a. *hcandersenr: H.C. Andersen's Fairy Tales.* R package version 0.2.0. https://CRAN.R-project.org/package=hcandersenr.

Hvitfeldt, E. 2020b. *textdata: Download and Load Various Text Datasets.* R package version 0.4.1. https://CRAN.R-project.org/package=textdata.

Hvitfeldt, E. 2020a. *textrecipes: Extra 'Recipes' for Text Processing.* R package version 0.4.1. https://CRAN.R-project.org/package=textrecipes.

Hvitfeldt, E. 2020c. *wordsalad: Provide Tools to Extract and Analyze Word Vectors.* R package version 0.2.0. https://CRAN.R-project.org/package=wordsalad.

Hvitfeldt, E. 2020d. *themis: Extra Recipe Steps for Dealing with Unbalanced Data.* R package version 0.1.4. https://CRAN.R-project.org/package=themis.

James, G., Witten, D., Hastie, T., and Tibshirani, R. 2013. *An Introduction to Statistical Learning.* New York: Springer.

Joachims, T. 1998. "Text Categorization with Support Vector Machines: Learning with Many Relevant Features." In *Proceedings of the 10th European Conference on Machine Learning*, 137–142. ECML'98. Berlin, Heidelberg: Springer-Verlag. https://doi.org/10.1007/BFb0026683.

Johnson, S. B. 1999. "A Semantic Lexicon for Medical Language Processing." *Journal of the American Medical Informatics Association* 6 (3). BMJ Group BMA House, Tavistock Square, London, WC1H 9JR: 205–218. https://doi.org/10.1136/jamia.1999.0060205.

Kearney, M. W. 2019. *textfeatures: Extracts Features from Text.* R package version 0.3.3. https://CRAN.R-project.org/package=textfeatures.

Kibriya, A. M., Frank, E., Pfahringer, B., and Holmes, G. 2005. "Multinomial Naive Bayes for Text Categorization Revisited." In *AI 2004: Advances in Artificial Intelligence*, edited by Geoffrey I. Webb and Xinghuo Yu, 488–499. Berlin, Heidelberg: Springer Berlin Heidelberg. https://doi.org/10.100 7/978-3-540-30549-1_43.

Kim, S., Han, K., Rim, H., and Myaeng, S. H. 2006. "Some Effective Techniques for Naive Bayes Text Classification." *IEEE Transactions on Knowledge and Data Engineering* 18 (11): 1457–1466. https://doi.org/10.1109/TK DE.2006.180.

Kim, Y. 2014. "Convolutional Neural Networks for Sentence Classification." In *Proceedings of the 2014 Conference on Empirical Methods in Natural Language Processing (EMNLP)*, 1746–1751. Doha, Qatar: Association for Computational Linguistics. https://www.aclweb.org/anthology/D14-1181.

Kingma, D. P., and Ba, J. 2017. "Adam: A Method for Stochastic Optimization." https://arxiv.org/abs/1412.6980.

Kuhn, M. 2020. *dials: Tools for Creating Tuning Parameter Values.* R package version 0.0.9. https://CRAN.R-project.org/package=dials.

Kuhn, M., and Vaughan, D. 2021b. *parsnip: A Common API to Modeling and Analysis Functions.* R package version 0.1.6. https://CRAN.R-project.org/package=parsnip.

Kuhn, M., and Vaughan, D. 2021a. *yardstick: Tidy Characterizations of Model Performance.* R package version 0.0.8. https://CRAN.R-project.org/package=yardstick.

Kuhn, M., and Wickham, H. 2021a. "Tidymodels: A Collection of Packages for Modeling and Machine Learning Using Tidyverse Principles." RStudio PBC. https://www.tidymodels.org.

Kuhn, M., and Wickham, H. 2021b. *recipes: Preprocessing Tools to Create Design Matrices.* R package version 0.1.16. https://CRAN.R-project.org/package=recipes.

Lampinen, A. K., and McClelland, J. L. 2018. "One-Shot and Few-Shot Learning of Word Embeddings." https://arxiv.org/abs/1710.10280.

Le, Q., and Mikolov, T. 2014. "Distributed Representations of Sentences and Documents." In *Proceedings of the 31st International Conference on Machine Learning*, edited by Eric P. Xing and Tony Jebara, 32:1188–1196. Proceedings of Machine Learning Research 2. Bejing, China: PMLR. http://proceedings.mlr.press/v32/le14.html.

Levithan, J. G. S. 2012. *Regular Expressions Cookbook*. Sebastopol: O'Reilly Media, Inc.

Levy, O., and Goldberg, Y. 2014. "Dependency-Based Word Embeddings." In *Proceedings of the 52nd Annual Meeting of the Association for Computational Linguistics (Volume 2: Short Papers)*, 302–308. Baltimore, Maryland: Association for Computational Linguistics. https://www.aclweb.org/anthology/P14-2050.

Lewis, D. D., Yang, Y., Rose, T. G., and Li, F. 2004. "Rcv1: A New Benchmark Collection for Text Categorization Research." *Journal of Machine Learning Research* 5: 361–397. https://www.jmlr.org/papers/volume5/lewis04a/lewis04a.pdf.

Lex, A., Gehlenborg, N., Strobelt, H., Vuillemot, R., and Pfister, H. 2014. "UpSet: Visualization of Intersecting Sets." *IEEE Transactions on Visualization and Computer Graphics* 20 (12): 1983–1992. https://doi.org/10.1109/TVCG.2014.2346248.

Lovins, J. B. 1968. "Development of a Stemming Algorithm." *Mechanical Translation and Computational Linguistics* 11: 22–31.

Lu, K., Mardziel, P., Wu, F., Amancharla, P., and Datta, A. 2020. "Gender Bias in Neural Natural Language Processing." In *Logic, Language, and Security: Essays Dedicated to Andre Scedrov on the Occasion of His 65th Birthday*, edited by Vivek Nigam, Tajana Ban Kirigin, Carolyn Talcott, Joshua Guttman, Stepan Kuznetsov, Boon Thau Loo, and Mitsuhiro Okada, 189–202. Cham: Springer International Publishing. https://doi.org/10.1007/978-3-030-62077-6_14.

Luhn, H. P. 1960. "Key Word-in-Context Index for Technical Literature (kwic Index)." *American Documentation* 11 (4): 288–295. https://onlinelibrary.wiley.com/doi/abs/10.1002/asi.5090110403.

Ma, J., Ganchev, K., and Weiss, D. 2018. "State-of-the-Art Chinese Word Segmentation with Bi-LSTMs." In *Proceedings of the 2018 Conference on Empirical Methods in Natural Language Processing*, 4902–4908. Brussels, Belgium: Association for Computational Linguistics. https://www.aclweb.org/anthology/D18-1529.

Manning, C. D., Raghavan, P., and Schütze, H. 2008. *Introduction to Information Retrieval*. New York, NY: Cambridge University Press.

McCulloch, G. 2015. "Move over Shakespeare, Teen Girls Are the Real Language Disruptors." *Quartz*. Quartz. https://qz.com/474671/move-over-shakespeare-teen-girls-are-the-real-language-disruptors/.

Mikolov, T., Chen, K., Corrado, G. S., and Dean, J. 2013. "Efficient Estimation of Word Representations in Vector Space." http://arxiv.org/abs/1301.3781.

Miller, G. A. 1995. "WordNet: A Lexical Database for English." *Communications of the ACM* 38 (11). New York, NY: ACM: 39–41. http://doi.acm.or g/10.1145/219717.219748.

Minaee, S., Kalchbrenner, N., Cambria, E., Nikzad, N., Chenaghlu, M., and Gao, J. 2021. "Deep Learning–Based Text Classification: A Comprehensive Review." *ACM Comput. Surv.* 54 (3). New York, NY: Association for Computing Machinery. https://doi.org/10.1145/3439726.

Mohammad, S. M., and Turney, P. D. 2013. "Crowdsourcing a Word–Emotion Association Lexicon." *Computational Intelligence* 29 (3): 436–465. https: //onlinelibrary.wiley.com/doi/abs/10.1111/j.1467-8640.2012.00460.x.

Moody, C. 2017. "Stop Using word2vec." *Multithreaded.* StitchFix. https://mu ltithreaded.stitchfix.com/blog/2017/10/18/stop-using-word2vec/.

Mullen, L. A., Benoit, K., Keyes, O., Selivanov, D., and Arnold, J. 2018. "Fast, Consistent Tokenization of Natural Language Text." *Journal of Open Source Software* 3: 655. https://doi.org/10.21105/joss.00655.

Nothman, J., Qin, H., and Yurchak, R. 2018. "Stop Word Lists in Free Open-Source Software Packages." In *Proceedings of Workshop for NLP Open Source Software (NLP-OSS)*, 7–12. Melbourne, Australia: Association for Computational Linguistics. https://www.aclweb.org/anthology/W18-2502.

Olson, R. S., Cava, W. L., Mustahsan, Z., Varik, A., and Moore, J. H. 2018. "Data-Driven Advice for Applying Machine Learning to Bioinformatics Problems." In *Pacific Symposium on Biocomputing 2018: Proceedings of the Pacific Symposium*, 192–203. World Scientific. https: //doi.org/10.1142/9789813235533_0018.

Ooms, J. 2020a. *pdftools: Text Extraction, Rendering and Converting of PDF Documents.* R package version 2.3.1. https://CRAN.R-project.org/package=pd ftools.

Ooms, J. 2020b. *hunspell: High-Performance Stemmer, Tokenizer, and Spell Checker.* R package version 3.0.1. https://CRAN.R-project.org/package=hunspe ll.

Pedersen, T. L., and Benesty, M. 2021. *lime: Local Interpretable Model-Agnostic Explanations.* R package version 0.5.2. https://CRAN.R-project. org/package=lime.

Pennington, J., Socher, R., and Manning, C. 2014. "GloVe: Global Vectors for Word Representation." In *Proceedings of the 2014 Conference on Empirical Methods in Natural Language Processing (EMNLP)*, 1532–1543. Doha, Qatar: Association for Computational Linguistics. https: //www.aclweb.org/anthology/D14-1162.

Perry, P. O. 2020. *corpus: Text Corpus Analysis.* R package version 0.10.2. https://CRAN.R-project.org/package=corpus.

Peters, M., Neumann, M., Iyyer, M., Gardner, M., Clark, C., Lee, K., and Zettlemoyer, L. 2018. "Deep Contextualized Word Representations." In *Proceedings of the 2018 Conference of the North American Chapter of the Association for Computational Linguistics: Human Language Technologies,*

Volume 1 (Long Papers), 2227–2237. New Orleans, Louisiana: Association for Computational Linguistics. https://www.aclweb.org/anthology/N18-1202.

Porter, M. F. 1980. "An Algorithm for Suffix Stripping." *Program* 14 (3): 130–137. https://doi.org/10.1108/eb046814.

Porter, M. F. 2001. "Snowball: A Language for Stemming Algorithms." https://snowballstem.org.

Ramineni, C., and Williamson, D. 2018. "Understanding Mean Score Differences Between the e-Rater® Automated Scoring Engine and Humans for Demographically Based Groups in the GRE® General Test." *ETS Research Report Series* 2018 (1): 1–31. https://onlinelibrary.wiley.com/doi/abs/10.1002/ets2.12192.

Ribeiro, M. T., Singh, S., and Guestrin, C. 2016. "'Why Should I Trust You?': Explaining the Predictions of Any Classifier." In *Proceedings of the 22nd ACM SIGKDD International Conference on Knowledge Discovery and Data Mining*, 1135–1144. KDD '16. New York, NY: Association for Computing Machinery. https://doi.org/10.1145/2939672.2939778.

Robinson, D. 2020. *widyr: Widen, Process, Then Re-Tidy Data*. R package version 0.1.3. https://CRAN.R-project.org/package=widyr.

Sap, M., Card, D., Gabriel, S., Choi, Y., and Smith, N. A. 2019. "The Risk of Racial Bias in Hate Speech Detection." In *Proceedings of the 57th Annual Meeting of the Association for Computational Linguistics*, 1668–1678. Florence, Italy: Association for Computational Linguistics. https://www.aclweb.org/anthology/P19-1163.

Schofield, A., and Mimno, D. 2016. "Comparing Apples to Apple: The Effects of Stemmers on Topic Models." *Transactions of the Association for Computational Linguistics* 4: 287–300. https://doi.org/10.1162/tacl_a_00099.

Selivanov, D., Bickel, M., and Wang, Q. 2020. *text2vec: Modern Text Mining Framework for R*. R package version 0.6. https://CRAN.R-project.org/package=text2vec.

Sheng, E., Chang, K.-W., Natarajan, P., and Peng, N. 2019. "The Woman Worked as a Babysitter: On Biases in Language Generation." In *Proceedings of the 2019 Conference on Empirical Methods in Natural Language Processing and the 9th International Joint Conference on Natural Language Processing (EMNLP-IJCNLP)*, 3407–3412. Hong Kong: Association for Computational Linguistics. https://www.aclweb.org/anthology/D19-1339.

Shrikumar, A., Greenside, P., and Kundaje, A. 2017. "Learning Important Features Through Propagating Activation Differences." In *Proceedings of the 34th International Conference on Machine Learning - Volume 70*, 3145–3153. ICML'17. Sydney, NSW, Australia: JMLR.org.

Shwartz-Ziv, R., and Tishby, N. 2017. "Opening the Black Box of Deep Neural Networks via Information." https://arxiv.org/abs/1703.00810.

Silge, J., Chow, F., Kuhn, M., and Wickham, H. 2021. *rsample: General Resampling Infrastructure*. R package version 0.1.0. https://CRAN.R-project.org/package=rsample.

Silge, J., and Robinson, D. 2016. "Tidytext: Text Mining and Analysis Using

Tidy Data Principles in R." *JOSS* 1 (3). The Open Journal. http://dx.doi.org/10.21105/joss.00037.

Silge, J., and Robinson, D. 2017. *Text Mining with R: A Tidy Approach.* Sebastopol: O'Reilly Media, Inc.

Speer, R. 2017. "How to Make a Racist AI Without Really Trying." *Concept-Net Blog.* http://blog.conceptnet.io/posts/2017/how-to-make-a-racist-ai-without-really-trying/.

Srivastava, N., Hinton, G., Krizhevsky, A., Sutskever, I., and Salakhutdinov, R. 2014. "Dropout: A Simple Way to Prevent Neural Networks from Overfitting." *Journal of Machine Learning Research* 15 (56): 1929–1958. http://jmlr.org/papers/v15/srivastava14a.html.

Sugisaki, K., and Tuggener, D. 2018. "German Compound Splitting Using the Compound Productivity of Morphemes." Verlag der Österreichischen Akademie der Wissenschaften.

Sweeney, L. 2000. *Simple Demographics Often Identify People Uniquely.* Data Privacy Working Paper 3. Carnegie Mellon University. https://dataprivacylab.org/projects/identifiability/.

Tang, C., Garreau, D., and Luxburg, U. von. 2018. "When Do Random Forests Fail?" In, 2987–2997. NIPS'18. Red Hook, NY: Curran Associates Inc.

Tibshirani, R. 1996. "Regression Shrinkage and Selection via the Lasso." *Journal of the Royal Statistical Society. Series B (Methodological)* 58 (1). [Royal Statistical Society, Wiley]: 267–288. http://www.jstor.org/stable/2346178.

Ushey, K., Allaire, J., and Tang, Y. 2021. *reticulate: Interface to 'Python'.* R package version 1.20. https://CRAN.R-project.org/package=reticulate.

Van-Tu, N., and Anh-Cuong, L. 2016. "Improving Question Classification by Feature Extraction and Selection." *Indian Journal of Science and Technology* 9 (17): 1–8. https://doi.org/10.17485/ijst/2016/v9i17/93160.

Vaughan, D. 2021a. *slider: Sliding Window Functions.* R package version 0.2.1. https://CRAN.R-project.org/package=slider.

Vaughan, D. 2021b. *workflows: Modeling Workflows.* R package version 0.2.2. https://CRAN.R-project.org/package=workflows.

Vaughan, D., and Dancho, M. 2021. *furrr: Apply Mapping Functions in Parallel Using Futures.* R package version 0.2.2. https://CRAN.R-project.org/package=furrr.

Vaughan, D., and Kuhn, M. 2020. *hardhat: Construct Modeling Packages.* R package version 0.1.5. https://CRAN.R-project.org/package=hardhat.

Vosoughi, S., Vijayaraghavan, P., and Roy, D. 2016. "Tweet2Vec: Learning Tweet Embeddings Using Character-Level CNN-LSTM Encoder-Decoder." In *Proceedings of the 39th International ACM SIGIR Conference on Research and Development in Information Retrieval,* 1041–1044. SIGIR '16. New York, NY: Association for Computing Machinery. https://doi.org/10.1145/2911451.2914762.

Wagner, C., Graells-Garrido, E., Garcia, D., and Menczer, F. 2016. "Women Through the Glass Ceiling: Gender Asymmetries in Wikipedia." *EPJ Data*

Science 5 (1). SpringerOpen: 5. https://doi.org/10.1140/epjds/s13688-016-0066-4.

Weinberger, K., Dasgupta, A., Langford, J., Smola, A., and Attenberg, J. 2009. "Feature Hashing for Large Scale Multitask Learning." In *Proceedings of the 26th Annual International Conference on Machine Learning*, 1113–1120. ICML '09. New York, NY: Association for Computing Machinery. https://doi.org/10.1145/1553374.1553516.

Wenfeng, Q., and Yanyi, W. 2019. *jiebaR: Chinese Text Segmentation*. R package version 0.11. https://CRAN.R-project.org/package=jiebaR.

Wickham, H. 2019. *stringr: Simple, Consistent Wrappers for Common String Operations*. R package version 1.4.0. https://CRAN.R-project.org/package=stringr.

Wickham, H. 2020. *httr: Tools for Working with URLs and HTTP*. R package version 1.4.2. https://CRAN.R-project.org/package=httr.

Wickham, H., Averick, M., Bryan, J., Chang, W., McGowan, L. D., François, R., Grolemund, G., et al. 2019. "Welcome to the Tidyverse." *Journal of Open Source Software* 4 (43). The Open Journal: 1686. https://doi.org/10.21105/joss.01686.

Wickham, H., and Grolemund, G. 2017. *R for Data Science: Import, Tidy, Transform, Visualize, and Model Data*. Sebastopol: O'Reilly Media, Inc.

Wickham, H., and Hester, J. 2020. *readr: Read Rectangular Text Data*. R package version 1.4.0. https://CRAN.R-project.org/package=readr.

Willett, P. 2006. "The Porter Stemming Algorithm: Then and Now." *Program: Electronic Library and Information Systems* 40 (3). Emerald: 219–223. http://eprints.whiterose.ac.uk/1434/.

Zhang, X., Zhao, J., and LeCun, Y. 2015. "Character-Level Convolutional Networks for Text Classification." In *Proceedings of the 28th International Conference on Neural Information Processing Systems - Volume 1*, 649–657. NIPS'15. Cambridge, MA: MIT Press.

Zou, F., Wang, F. L., Deng, X., and Han, S. 2006. "Evaluation of Stop Word Lists in Chinese Language." In *Proceedings of the Fifth International Conference on Language Resources and Evaluation (LREC'06)*. Genoa, Italy: European Language Resources Association (ELRA). http://www.lrec-conf.org/proceedings/lrec2006/pdf/273_pdf.pdf.

Zou, F., Wang, F. L., Deng, X., Han, S., and Wang, L. S. 2006. "Automatic Construction of Chinese Stop Word List." In *Proceedings of the 5th WSEAS International Conference on Applied Computer Science*, 1009–1014. ACOS'06. Stevens Point, Wisconsin: World Scientific; Engineering Academy; Society (WSEAS). http://dl.acm.org/citation.cfm?id=1973598.1973793.

Index

accuracy, 164, 246

area under the receiver operator
characteristic curve, *see*
ROC AUC

automated grading, 345, 346

bias, 45, 93–96, 102–104, 150, 237,
271, 345

binary cross-entropy, 246

black box, 271, 324

censoring, 158, 195, 197, 200, 204

classification, xiii
challenges, 184

coefficient of determination, 115

computational speed, 126, 129, 132,
135, 174, 182, 266, 300

context
importance of, 49

corpus, 43, 75, 77, 93, 94, 227
definition, 44

CRAN, xv

data leakage, 227, 238

data type
character, 9

deep learning, 81
comparing, 226

dialects
African American Vernacular
English, 7

downsampling, 185

embeddings, 85, 225
FastText, 87, 90, 93
GloVe, 87–93, 95, 257, 261
pre-trained, 88, 90, 91, 95, 257,
261, 268

word2vec, 87, 90, 93, 95

embeddings, pre-trained, 94

feature engineering, 108, 201, 206,
209, 227, 228, 239, 272, 341

functions, 32

hashing function, 133, 134, 136, 137,
139
challenges, 136

integer index, 240

inverse document frequency, 45, 47,
74, 227

language
naming, 6
Non-English, 6, 10, 28, 50, 52,
55, 56, 68, 137, 138
Non-Latin, 33
obscene, 48
signed, 4
structure, 303
structures, 286

lemma, 129, 130, 132

lemmas, 68–70, 142, 153

lemmatization, *see* lemmas

linguistics, 3, 4

machine learning
comparing, 226
unsupervised, xvi, 60

matrix
confusion, 164–166, 170, 189,
190, 208, 215, 252, 300, 308,
322, 340
sparse, 59, 73–75, 77, 87, 135,
179, 182

matrix factorization, 80
misspellings, 38, 49
models
    analysis, 228
    challenges, 120, 220, 266, 271, 337
    comparing, 113
    explainability, 324, 327–329
    in production, 168
    interpretability, *see* models, explainability
    pre-trained, 268
    sensitivity, 7
    training, 6
    tuning, 144, 170, 330
morphology, 3, 5, 50, 54, 318

network architecture, 225, 226, 231, 255, 273, 303, 306, 309
neural network
    convolutional, 303, 305
    densely connected, 231
    feed forward, 231
    long short-term memory, 273, 275
    recurrent, 3, 276, 283

optimization algorithm, 245, 246, 307
overfitting, 237, 278, 281, 282, 285

part of speech, 68, 133
personally identifiable information, *see* PII
phonetics, 3
phonology, 3
PII, 158, 195, 200, 201
PMI, 79
point-wise mutual information, *see* PMI
postprocessing, 96
pragmatics, 3
precision, 70
preprocess, 337
preprocessing, 22, 25, 41, 58, 73, 108, 118, 122, 126, 129, 130, 138, 153, 158, 159, 179, 182, 185, 191, 200, 227, 237, 239, 253, 255, 272, 274, 295, 297, 300, 301, 305, 310, 340
    challenges, 10, 26, 40, 43, 45, 48, 49, 56, 60, 63, 67, 92, 94–96, 137, 242
    impact, 289, 290
Python, 69, 231

regex, 11, 29–31, 33, 103, 158, 200, 202–205
regression, xiii
regular expressions, *see* regex
RMSE, 115
ROC AUC, 164
root mean squared error, *see* RMSE

semantics, 3, 87, 92, 261
sentiment classifier, 23
singular value decomposition, *see* SVD
singular versus plural, 53, 65, 85
skipgram windows, 78–80
speech, xvi, 4
stemming algorithm
    Hunspell, 56, 58
    Lovins, 63
    Porter, 54–56, 61, 65, 66, 71
    Snowball, 63
stop word lists
    SMART, 38–40
    Snowball, 38, 39, 41, 55, 122, 125, 255
    Stopwords ISO, 38, 39
stop words
    document, 38
    global, 37
    subject, 37
SVD, 80, 85
syntax, 3

term frequency, 74, 227
term frequency-inverse document frequency, *see* tf-idf
text generation, xvi
tf-idf, 74, 95, 108, 133, 160, 182, 227

tokenization
    character, 16
    definition, 10
    ligatures, 17
    n-gram, 19, 126, 128, 129, 142,
        153
    package, 34
    punctuation, 25
    specialty, 26
    subword, 317, 323
translation, xvi, 276

Unicode, 12

variables
    dummy, 192
vector, 77
    character, 9

word segmentation, 33